FORMULA ONE

THE BUSINESS OF WINNING

Russell Hotten

TEXERE

NEW YORK · LONDON

Copyright © 2000 Russell Hotten

Photographs copyright © 2000 Action Plus except
Murray Walker and Brooklands photographs which
are reproduced courtesy of *Mail on Sunday*.

First published in Great Britain in 1998 by Orion Business

This edition published by

TEXERE LLC
55 East 52nd Street
New York, NY 10055
Tel: +1 (212) 317 5106
Fax: +1 (212) 317 5178
www.etexere.com

UK subsidiary office

TEXERE Publishing Limited
71–77 Leadenhall Street
London EC3A 3DE
Tel: +44 (0)20 7204 3644
Fax: +44 (0)20 7208 6701

Library of Congress Cataloging in Publication Data

ISBN 1-58799-011-3

Printed and bound in Great Britain

10 9 8 7 6 5 4 3 2 1

For Helen and Freya
Neither got the attention they deserved

Contents

Acknowledgements

FOR EITHER ADVICE, encouragement, door-opening, suggestions or corrections, I am grateful to Nicky Samengo-Turner, Guy Edwards, Norman Howell, Ron Dennis, the Motor Industry Research Association, John Lovesey, Frank Williams and his team's sponsor Andersen Consulting, Stewart Grand Prix, and Andrew Chowns. I also received help from people who prefer to remain nameless. They know who they are, and I thank them.

Thanks also to *Autosport* magazine for access to their library, and for keeping me up to speed on an eventful past couple of years in the life of Formula One. That goes for *F1 Racing*, too. I must also record my appreciation to those race fans from around the world who responded to my queries via the Internet, effectively acting as unpaid researchers.

Finally, Formula One is blessed with some excellent writers, and I have drawn information and inspiration from a number of books, including: *Colin Chapman: The Man and His Car*, by Gerard Crombac (Haynes); *Schumacher*, by Timothy Collings (Bloomsbury); *Williams Grand Prix Engineering*, by Alan Henry (Patrick Stephens); *The Death of Ayrton Senna*, by Richard Williams (Viking); *Racers*, by Richard Williams (Penguin); *Inside Formula 1*, by Nigel Roebuck (Patrick Stephens); *Cosworth: The Search for Power*, by Graham Robson (Patrick Stephens); *Sponsorship and the World of Motor Racing*, by Guy Edwards (Hazleton); *Racing Stewart: The Birth of a Grand Prix Team*, by Maurice Hamilton (Macmillan); *Playing to Win*, by Beverly Aston and Mark Williams (Institute for Public Policy Research); *Formula One Racing*, by Norman Howell (Weidenfeld & Nicolson); *Nigel Mansell: My Autobiography* (James Allen); *The Power and the Glory: A Century of Motor Racing*, by Ivan Rendall (BBC Publications); *Bruce McLaren: The Man and His Racing Team*, by Eoin Young (Haynes).

Introduction

FORMULA ONE IS where sport meets technology for the business of entertainment. The *sport* takes place between March and October twice a month, for two hours on a Sunday. Everything else is *business* and *technology* – and it never stops. Even the *entertainment* is an all-year affair, with what happens off the track often more fun than what happens on it. Formula One has changed dramatically in the 1990s, transformed by the power of money. Racing is driven by a relentless search for fractional improvements in lap times. To that end, tens of millions of pounds are needed each year in order to research ways to shave 0.1 seconds off the time it takes to drive around a racetrack. With the exception of yacht racing, no other sport exists where the basic tool of competition – the racecar – is so expensive. Money oils the wheels of Formula One, and the teams with the biggest budgets are the ones that cross the finishing line first. A middle-ranking Formula One constructor needs to raise between £25 million and £35 million each year in sponsorship to compete. Ferrari or McLaren will spend twice that. Increasingly, only blue-chip companies can afford to sponsor Formula One these days. And they do so because, according to Formula One's governing body, every race is seen by an average audience of 350 million potential customers on TV screens in 202 countries. Only the Olympics and football's World Cup surpass these viewing figures, but they only take place every four years.

With so much power and money involved, with so many vested interests, Formula One has ceased to be a sport for the people who own and control it. Grand Prix racing is now an entrepreneurial business that exists to satisfy the marketing strategies of international companies. And it works too, turning every team owner, nearly all the racing drivers, and plenty of other Formula One insiders, into millionaires. The richest of them all is Bernie Ecclestone, variously called the Czar, the Ringmaster or the Mr Big of Formula One. He exercises almost total control over Formula One. As a vice-president of the rule-making body, the Fédération Internationale de l'Automobile (FIA), Ecclestone has considerable political clout. As the owner of Formula One's commercial interests, including television broadcast rights, he has considerable economic power. Indeed, Ecclestone's control is such that the European Commission is investigating whether there is an abuse of monopoly position. Until the EC makes up its mind, Ecclestone's plan to float his Formula One Holdings on the stock market is on hold. With a price tag of between £1.5 billion and £3 billion, a flotation would make Ecclestone one of the richest people in Britain. Or rather, his wife will be, thanks to an offshore family trust. In a sport where the bizarre is taken for granted, few eyebrows were raised when it was learned that the main beneficiary of Ecclestone's rolling international circus was a former Armani model from Croatia, called Slavica.

Formula One has its fair share of critics who like to talk about the good old days, before commercialism and the demands of television infiltrated every layer of the sport. Television broadcasters world-wide really caught the Formula One bug in the 1990s. Commercialism has been part of motorsport since the first competitions were held in France in the 1890s. For much of the twentieth century racing was dominated by large companies, mostly based on the Continent like Renault and Mercedes-Benz, for whom grand prix racing was an extension of their production car operations. Their racing teams were backed by tyre and oil companies, and other allied trades. The resources these teams were able to muster made them invincible. Competing was done in the name of marketing and technological research or, during the years of Fascism in Germany and Italy, for ideological purposes. It was not until the 1950s and '60s that Britain began to gain the upper hand. A convergence of factors – economic, engineering and luck – led to Britain becoming the centre of racing. After the Second World War the abandoned airfields were perfect meeting places for Britain's amateur racers. A small network of motoring clubs emerged, serviced by former aerospace engineers who had maintained aircraft during the war. It was not long before a cottage industry of specialists emerged. Known as Grand Prix Valley, this collection of some 500 small motorsport engineering firms is now the economic heart of the world's motorsport industry. From rally teams to America's IndyCar racing teams, they all came to 'the

Valley', where anything from a V12 engine to the smallest widget is available. Seven of the 11 teams competing in Formula One are based in Britain.

The emerging British teams of the 1970s and '80s were a disparate collection of enterprises. Part of the problem was that the organisation of Formula One was a shambles. There was no real calendar of races, and often teams would not even show up. Bernie Ecclestone changed all that. He made teams agree to compete in all the races, and he sorted out a proper prize money structure. Ecclestone began arranging the teams' travel and accommodation and negotiated with the circuit owners. Basically, Ecclestone sorted out the politics and the planning, and left the team owners to get on with what they did best: racing. His masterstroke was to see the potential attraction of Formula One as televisual entertainment. An explosion in television coverage of Formula One is what has driven the sport's growth in the 1990s. Ecclestone packaged Formula One into a television sport, and then sold the rights to broadcast it to the highest bidders. In the 1990s the value of these broadcast rights has soared. As audience figures went up, so did the desire to advertise in, and sponsor, Formula One. Money has poured in as a result, and Ecclestone, the team bosses and the drivers have grown very rich on the proceeds.

Modern Formula One is often accused of having more style than substance. However, the sport must have something to recommend it, otherwise so many people would not find it so entertaining. What is more, Formula One's popularity is growing fast, especially in Asian countries. British television audiences have grown by 43 per cent in five years, and the number of women viewers has also risen since 1994, by 10 per cent in Europe, according to market researchers. The reasons for grand prix racing's popularity are many and complex. Some fans are still attached to racing's long and distinguished history. Stories of pre-Second World War aristocratic drivers setting sail from Britain to do battle with the likes of Mercedes-Benz or Auto Union are part of racing folklore. The great races, the great cars, and the great drivers have inspired some of the best sports writing. Stirling Moss: it is a name that could have been coined by a Hollywood scriptwriter. Along with stars like Juan Manuel Fangio or Ayrton Senna, the legendary British driver strikes a romantic chord in the hearts of race fans.

For other fans, Formula One is the ultimate sport for the late twentieth century: fast, furious, colourful, technology-driven. The Roman Games and Formula One have something in common. Their origins are in the transport of the day: the chariot and the car; men with a 'machine' doing battle, sometimes until death. Attending a Formula One race is a shock to the senses. The sound, the sight and the unmistakable smell are never forgotten. After experiencing a race live, watching on television is like living life in black-and-white, with the sound down. But even non-fans who have never been to a grand prix are, at the very least, intrigued by the sport. There is something aspirational about Formula One. Fast cars, wealth, glamour, sex, danger. They are a potent mixture. Other sports contain elements of these, but none contains them all. This is why the personalities and events of Formula One now find a place in news reports and in style magazines, not just on the sports pages. Marketing surveys show that non-fans believe that Formula One has crossed over into current-affairs news, and so is something to keep a watch on. Controversies surrounding Formula One's biggest financial backers, tobacco companies, are largely responsible for this.

There was one other important event that boosted grand prix racing. The shocking death of the great Brazilian driver Ayrton Senna in 1994 proved the rule that all news is good news for Formula One. Television footage of Senna, motionless in the wreckage of his crashed Williams car, were beamed around the world. It was a tragic and very public death, but it seems to have marked a watershed in interest in Formula One. It heightened publicity in the sport for several years afterwards. The manslaughter charges in Italy faced by the Williams directors following the accident were only dismissed at the end of 1997. For two years after the death, Formula One went through a period of soul-searching over safety, allegations of cheating, and its future. Yet, it came out the other side more popular and vastly richer.

Those fans brought into the sport by the tragedy have remained supporters. And suggestions that sponsors would be turned off by such a spectacle proved groundless. Rothmans, the main sponsor of the Williams team, survived the bad publicity, and continued to invest some $32 million a year in the team. The car makers, allied trades and tobacco manufacturers that traditionally sponsored Formula One have been joined by fashion houses, finance companies, airlines and jewellers. The secrecy surrounding Formula One's finances means no one knows how much money today's sponsors really put into the teams. However, based on the turnover of the constructors, much of which is made up of sponsorship and prize money, it is possible to make a back-of-the-envelope calculation. About $650 million would be a conservative figure. This excludes personal sponsorship of the drivers, hospitality expenses, and trackside and support marketing.

The racing teams themselves are mere tools in this multi-million-dollar grab for public attention. Even Ferrari, the most prestigious team on the grid and the one constructor that for years repelled the onward march of sponsorship, has succumbed. The distinctive blood-red racecars have gone a shade more orange, to match the colour of a Marlboro cigarette packet. Team bosses like McLaren's Ron Dennis have learned the language of business, the better to exploit the growing commercial importance of Formula One. His business interests now stretch beyond motorsport, into engineering and aerospace consultancy. The factory facilities at Williams Grand Prix Engineering are a microcosm of an efficient motor manufacturer, containing the sort of best practice expected of a hi-tech company.

On the engineering side, the British teams cannot be beaten. McLaren and Williams took Formula One into a new era of electronics and computer wizardry. It was why Bernie Ecclestone once described racing drivers of the 1990s as lightbulbs: you just plug one in and let the car do the rest. But, as we will see, for sheer marketing brilliance, no one could beat Benetton Formula, owned by the publicity-conscious Italian clothing group. The team's former head, Flavio Briatore, cared nothing for the technology. He liked the showbusiness. There was always a film star or top footballer walking around the Benetton pits, or doing a photo shoot at the factory. Style, glamour, colour: these were what interested Briatore. It brought millions of new fans to racing, people who realised you did not need to understand the principles of fluid dynamics or active suspension to enjoy Formula One. And it brought millions of dollars into Benetton's bank account. The team's racecars always had far more decals pasted on to the light-blue chassis than any other vehicle.

McLaren and Williams have dominated the constructors' championship since the mid-1980s, but they could not have done it without the engines of Honda and Renault. The two teams were the beneficiaries of Honda's and Renault's technological and global marketing strategies. Honda used Formula One to hot-house its engineers and catch up on its Western car-manufacturing rivals. Renault's plan was to shed its lumbering state-owned image and inject a little flashiness into its products. Today, the marketing is more important to engine suppliers than technology transfer. But, as we will see in Chapter Seven, a motorist browsing in the car showroom still has reasons to be grateful to motor racing. The spin-offs from Formula One technology for production cars may be a little harder to spot these days, but they are definitely there.

In all this talk about machinery, it is easy to lose sight of the fact that motor racing is still a people sport. Racing drivers remain the focus of public adulation and are the reason hundreds of millions of fans watch Formula One each season. But the drivers have not been immune to the creeping commercialism. Men like Michael Schumacher, the fourth richest sportsman in the world according to *Forbes* magazine, are one-man enterprises whose main commodity is driving racecars. Schumacher earns a minimum of $35 million a year from salary and endorsements. Around $10,000 will buy a sponsor its name on a baseball cap or the lapel of a fire-proof racing suit. No wonder Formula One dispensed with laurel wreaths at podium award ceremonies. They just got in the way of the brand names. For a team owner, there is much more to consider when choosing a driver than ability and salary. The choice will also depend on nationality and the interests of the engine suppliers. Several drivers, backed by personal sponsors, pay teams for the privilege of a place behind the wheel. Today's Formula One driver needs to be sponsor-friendly and schooled in the art of public relations. They spend far more time touring the world at the behest of their sponsors than practising at the racetrack.

The growth of Formula One must be regarded as one of the business success stories of recent years. And there is no sign of that expansion being checked. In Asia, for example, interest is growing fast, yet the market for sponsors and television broadcasters remains largely untapped. Even the Middle East may become ripe for Formula One. Lebanon hopes to host a leg of the racing series, turning the event in Beirut into the Monaco Grand Prix of the Middle East. There are hurdles ahead, however. Formula One must face the challenge of losing its tobacco sponsors, though this 'problem' has been much exaggerated. And the financial crisis in Asia could delay the planned staging of grand prix races in Malaysia, South Korea and China. 'Delay' is the operative word. It is governments themselves that are bringing Formula One to these countries, because they see it as more than just a sport. Staging a race is viewed as a symbol of technological advance, like building the world's tallest skyscraper. Another challenge is the expansion of CART, the American single-seater racing series, which is increasingly popular in Asia and winning television audiences in Europe. Yet, given the market for motor racing, there is every sign that the world is big enough for two global series. Perhaps Formula One's biggest hurdle is itself. The organisational structure of Formula One is in desperate need of reform. The sport is just too big for one man – Bernie Ecclestone – to control. The flotation of Formula One Holdings is designed to address this and several other issues about the sport's future. But with the flotation delayed, there remains a lot of in-fighting and confusion over where the sport is heading. One of the most damaging things that can happen to a sport is for it to split, as boxing discovered. It has happened before in Formula One – and Ecclestone was part of it, so he should know the dangers.

Chapter One: MILESTONES

Birth of a Business

'THE CURSE OF commercialism is the ruin of every sport.' It is a charge all too frequently levelled against Formula One in the modern era. In fact, these words were written in 1906 by Charles Jarrott, one of Britain's most successful early racing drivers. In his book *Ten Years of Motors and Motor Racing*, Jarrott deplored the decline of the amateur driver and the power of rich car manufacturers to buy success. 'The result,' Jarrott wrote, 'is that only men who make it their business to drive these cars can hope to be successful.' As Jarrott knew all too well, motor racing and commerce have been exploiting each other since cars first competed in anger. Sponsorship is not a new phenomenon in grand prix racing. This chapter looks at the emergence of *the business* of European racing, and goes on to explore the important changes in Britain which led to it becoming the centre of the motorsport industry. The story, however, must start in France. The first recorded motor race, over 78 miles between Paris and Rouen in 1894, was sponsored by the Parisian newspaper *Le Petit Journal*. The owner, Pierre Giffard, was a big fan of the new horseless carriages and was intent on showing they could be reliable and safe. Officially it was not a race, and some of the entries were no more than tractors. The winner would not necessarily be the vehicle crossing the line first, but the one that covered the course 'without danger, and was easy to handle and in addition was cheap to run'. The first prize went jointly to a Peugeot and a Panhard. The unofficial winner, however – for the thousands of people lining the streets to watch – was the driver who completed the course fastest, Count Jules de Dion. For the public, competitive racing had begun. They swarmed to races in large numbers – and where there are crowds, business is not far behind.

In 1895 de Dion and other vehicle makers arranged a 1,200km race

covering a round trip between Paris and Bordeaux. The event was
heavily sponsored, by newspaper owner James Gordon Bennett and
millionaire American industrialist William K. Vanderbilt, among
others. This time, it was a 'real' race, where prize money went to the
car first past the post, not to those who turned in the best performance
under Pierre Giffard's rules. Later, when British-born Gordon Bennett,
owner of the *New York Herald*, wanted to set up a French edition of
his paper in 1900, motor racing was used as a promotional tool. He put
up an international trophy for a series of races between national teams.
Bennett had one eye on increased sales from a public fascinated by this
new sport, and another on higher advertising revenues from the motor
manufacturers. Car makers such as Peugeot, Mercedes and Renault
quickly spotted the potential of these races to show off their new
inventions. The vehicles were stripped of mudguards, seat cushions
and all other non-essentials – the first sign that racing cars were diverg-
ing from standard models. But essentially, manufacturers competed
with the same 'win on Sunday, sell on Monday' philosophy that drove
their involvement throughout the twentieth century.

Organised racing began to spread elsewhere in Europe, and it was
increasingly popular in America. On 10 October 1901, Henry Ford
drove his own racing car to victory at Grosse Pointe, Detroit. It launched
his career as a car maker. However, France was to remain the centre of
the racing world for many more years to come. Why France? A simple
explanation is sheer convenience. France had many straight roads criss-
crossing the country, making it eminently suitable for racing. But there
were other, more important economic reasons. Britain may have led the
industrial revolution, and Germany invented the internal combustion
engine, but the governments of both countries banned racing on public
roads because of fears over safety. Until 1896 a car travelling on British
roads had to be preceded by a man on foot waving a red flag. The law
was later abolished, but the early hostility of the British and German
authorities to the motor car gave the French just enough time to build
a supremacy. Not that concerns over safety were absent in France. By
the early 1900s, several people in France had died during races, both
drivers and spectators. The Paris police chief, and then the government
itself, considered banning racing on several occasions. But the powerful
motor industry had already established a link between car sales and
racing, and fought off all attempts to stop them. Cars had captured the
public's imagination and it was not long before France had established
the world's largest motor industry.

The death of Marcel Renault in the 1903 Paris–Madrid race – in which an estimated three million spectators lined the route – finally forced the authorities to clamp down on racing on unpoliced roads. So, in 1906 the first 'Grand Prix' was held at Le Mans on closed roads, though the era of permanent circuits was still nearly two decades away. This 1906 grand prix was won by the Renault car company. There was a great outpouring of national pride. Other countries, though, were quick to challenge French supremacy. The following year, the French grand prix was won by Italy's Fiat, and in 1908 by Mercedes of Germany. Motor racing was becoming truly international.

As motor racing gained in popularity, the organisation and support network became more professional. Engineers would travel along with the racing drivers, tending to mechanical faults that were often caused by the harsh road conditions. A network of allied trades grew up around motor racing and, importantly, it spurred development of engines. The 1908 Targa Florio race in Sicily, which was to become one of racing's legendary events, saw the appearance of 'pits', shallow dug-outs by the side of the track where mechanics changed the detachable rims that had been developed to replace permanently attached wheels. Even so, the tyre companies still had a lot of research to do. Most of the cars were still too heavy and too fast for the rubber. Michelin and Pirelli invested heavily in improving their tyres, and began advertising the fact on the perimeter fences of the closed circuits. Across the Atlantic, meanwhile, advertising and sponsorship were beginning to take off in a much bigger way. In 1910 American Barney Oldfield's Christie-built racecar carried emblazoned across its side: 'My Only Life Insurance: Firestone Tyres'. That was tame compared with what was to follow. While European racing was carried out under the banner of the manu-facturer, America was later to have its Cocktail Hour Cigarette Special racing car and even a Frostie Root Beer & Pennsylvania Bicentennial Special.

Back in Europe, racing was interrupted by the First World War, and many drivers went to the USA to race at Indianapolis, a location that is now as synonymous with racing as Le Mans. Although the first purpose-built racing track was opened in Europe in 1907, at Brooklands, in Surrey, it was America that showed the way in circuit development. The trouble with road racing – at least for the sponsors and entre-preneurs who organised races – was that spectators watched for free. America's one- and two-mile oval tracks were loved by the promoters, who could charge entrance fees and create a captive audience for advertisers. Spectators didn't complain. They could, after all, see more of the action. US oval tracks, however, could in no way simulate road conditions. Consequently, a gulf emerged between America and Europe over racecar technology. Whereas ovals put the emphasis on the brute power of the engine, the European tracks that were developed after the First World War were winding and had sharper corners, which meant that manoeuvrability, better brakes and tyres, and more all-round flexibility were important in European racecars.

In sponsorship, as in racecar engineering, the continents were divided. In America showmanship and the chequebook called the shots. In Europe, commercialism was confined to technical sponsorship, and the sport remained largely an activity for gentlemen racers. However, Europe was to see more sinister forms of exploitation of grand prix racing. National pride is boosted by sporting success, and Italy and Germany both used racing for ideological and economic purposes. In 1927, Italy's Fascist leader Benito Mussolini backed the establishment of the Mille Miglia – a 1,000-mile race on some of the toughest public roads in the country. Black-shirted Fascist officials controlled the crowds as the cars set off from Brescia. Mussolini's aim was twofold: to pull the Italian motor industry out of decline, and restore national honour after Le Mans superseded the Targa Florio as Europe's premier racing event. He succeeded in both objectives – and put Italian car manufacturers at the forefront of motor racing.

From 1934, however, the balance of power in racing began shifting from Italy to Nazi Germany. Auto Union, later to become Audi, and Mercedes-Benz thrived on huge financial support from the state. Adolf Hitler was a fast-car enthusiast and saw the propaganda potential of racing, as of athletics. The authorities whipped up interest in the sport, and in 1934 more than 300,000 spectators turned up for a race at the Nürburgring. When Bernd Rosemeyer, one of the greatest drivers of his generation, was killed in a race in 1938, he was given a military funeral in Berlin. Hitler had told the Ministry of Transport to give every support to the development of motor racing. With the largesse of the German state behind them, manufacturers made great technological strides. Lighter alloys were used in car construction, new fuels were developed, and independent suspension on all four wheels introduced. German engineers were particularly skilled in introducing the principles of aerodynamics into racecar design. 'The Titans', as the mighty 600bhp Mercedes and Auto Unions were named, were the product of a state's desire to demonstrate its superiority in racing.

After the Second World War a new racing formula, originally called Formula A – later Formula One – was established for cars of 1,500cc supercharged, and 4,500cc unsupercharged. The minimum race distance was cut from 500km to 300km, allowing the Monaco Grand Prix to be re-introduced after a two-year interval, in 1950. That year the Fédération Internationale de l'Automobile (FIA) unveiled plans for a Formula One world drivers' championship. Some much-needed shape was being given to the rather shambolic structure of top-level racing, though it was to be two decades before Bernie Ecclestone made a serious attempt to organise Formula One. Much to the frustration of team owners and drivers, the new Formula One rules did not allow commercial sponsorship, while across the Atlantic tens of millions of dollars were flowing into professional racing. The sport in Britain was dependent on men like industrialist Sir Alfred Owen, head of the Owen Organisation, who were prepared to finance a racing team out of their own pockets. On the Continent, the major car companies continued to run their own teams. In Italy, Fiat began subsidising Ferrari, and in Germany the mighty Mercedes-Benz made its return to grand prix in 1952. The smaller British teams were outgunned by the financial muscle and bigger research departments of the Germans, and especially of the Italian teams of Alfa Romeo, Maserati, Lancia and Ferrari.

A study of the motorsport industry published by the Institute of Public Policy Research, *Playing to Win*, highlights an important difference between the British and Continental attitudes to motor racing. What gave the mainland European manufacturers an advantage, particularly the Italians, was that they had long since established a link between selling road cars and competing in motorsport. About 120 miles south of Milan is the village of Maranello, home to this day of the Ferrari factory. In 1954, Ferrari's racing factory was staffed by 220 mechanics and the factory contained more than 100 advanced machine tools. Enzo Ferrari invested heavily in facilities in order to supplement his racing by selling ultra-modern sports cars for the road. The factory turned out about 150 road cars each year. Maserati, based near Ferrari, did the same, achieving road-car sales of about 85 vehicles a year. Both used prestige from racing success to sell high-priced sports cars. Other Italian companies, including Lancia, joined the bandwagon. There was a bias in these companies' marketing programmes towards racing, a bias that was alien to British car manufacturers. Britain had engineers just as good as those of Italy, but there was no history of a link between racing and selling road cars. As the report explained: 'Italy did not dominate motor racing because it was better than Britain; rather it was better than Britain because it dominated racing and Italian personnel had built up skills and experience through years of racing success.'

When British racecar talent did finally shine through, it did so not because of the support of the large car manufacturers, but because of a series of dreadful accidents, lucky breaks, and economic changes. At the Le Mans 24 Hour race in 1955, a Mercedes crashed through a barrier into the crowd, killing 85 people and injuring scores of others. Mercedes pulled out of racing after 1955, and the political pressure on other manufacturers to do the same was intense. Switzerland even outlawed motor racing. Suddenly, car manufacturers and other sponsors from allied trades saw how motor racing could turn into a public relations disaster. Two years later, ten spectators were killed at the Mille Miglia in Italy. The Vatican attacked Enzo Ferrari, and although he did not withdraw from racing, the climate of opinion was turning heavily against motorsport. The death at the age of 35 of Alberto Ascari, one of motor racing's legendary drivers, at Monza in 1955, cast another cloud over Italian racing. Within another two years Lancia and Maserati were out of competitive racing because of financial problems. Ferrari was left to carry the Italian flag, but was to struggle against a new generation of constructors emerging in Britain.

All this had two important consequences for the development of Formula One in Britain. Firstly, it left the field open for specialist manufacturers who were not dependent upon selling road cars to finance their racing. Secondly, it ensured that racing only had a future if it was conducted on smooth, closed circuits where spectators could be protected. Britain had plenty of these permanent circuits – defunct Second World War airfields, which had become home to a number of racing clubs. Britain had produced plenty of talented drivers, but they achieved their success at the wheel of foreign-made cars. Now, more investment was going into developing home-grown racecars. In 1956 Tony Vandervell, a rich industrialist, ardent patriot and owner of the Vanwall racing team, commissioned Colin Chapman of Lotus to develop a new lightweight chassis. Stirling Moss drove the Vanwall VW5 to second place in the 1958 drivers' world championship, behind Mike Hawthorn in a Ferrari. A world championship for constructors was introduced for the first time, and won by Vanwall. That year was a watershed for British constructors, with racecars from Lotus, Cooper, and BRM also making their mark. Elsewhere in motor racing, Jaguar was triumphing in the Le Mans 24 Hour race, dominating races between

1954 and 1958, while Aston Martin was succeeding in world sports-car racing.

Vanwall's success was short-lived. With owner Tony Vandervell suffering ill-health and the tragic death of the team's driver, Stuart Lewis-Evans, Vanwall withdrew from Formula One at the end of 1958. But Lotus and Cooper, and later BRM and Brabham went on to even greater things and assert the superiority of British racecar construction. Cooper and Lotus cars had crushed the overseas opposition in Formula Junior racing – for unsupercharged cars up to 1,100cc – and were destined to do the same in the higher formula. Cooper captured the 1959 and 1960 world championships with a revolutionary rear-engine design (though Auto Union also used a rear engine) powered by an all-conquering British-built Coventry Climax engine, also used by Lotus. The weight distribution and handling created by the new Cooper design changed Formula One chassis development for ever. It was Colin Chapman, owner of Team Lotus, who made the second great post-war contribution to Formula One design. His monocoque (or one-piece) chassis was introduced with the Lotus 25 in 1962. It was the first modern racecar, dispensing with a heavy internal frame. These constructors' success on the racetrack did more than bring national sporting glory. Importantly, they supported and, in turn, fed off a growing number of small British component suppliers which remain crucial to this day. Britain's collection of top drivers now had the cars to match their skill. Between 1962 and 1973, British Formula One teams won 12 world championships, with drivers such as Jim Clark, Jackie Stewart and Graham Hill at the wheel.

One of the features of Formula One today is that innovations transfer easily between teams. No sooner had a designer stolen a march on a rival, than the other teams catch up. Even in the 1960s technical innovation in motorsport moved easily across borders. So it is curious that Britain's domination with the Cooper rear-engine design held up for so long. The reason lies in the size of the British teams vis-a-vis their larger Continental rivals. The smaller the team, the more it is able to adopt to changing circumstances. Ferrari or Alfa Romeo, on the other hand, simply could not adapt quickly. As the IPPR report explained: 'Ferrari and Porsche were vertically integrated operators who built racing cars to be run by their own teams, but who typically declined to sell them to "privateers" or independent teams. The British specialist manufacturers, by contrast, typically sold new and second-hand racing cars to anyone who wished to buy one. As a consequence, therefore, Britain still dominated the Formula One grid numerically.'

British racecar engineers and the teams prospered because they could purchase engines off-the-shelf. The availability of the superb Coventry Climax engine left club constructors the freedom to concentrate on chassis design, aerodynamics and innovation. Academics Beverly Aston and Mark Williams, in their pamphlet *Playing to Win*, explained the importance of this. 'When a reliable engine was found, a racing formula tended to develop around it. With the output of the engine fixed, the bulk of the engineering effort focused exclusively on squeezing competitive advantage from adjusting the weight and size of every other parameter (chassis, position of the engine, suspension, transmission, wheels and so on). Winning races with an underpowered engine, offset by an ultra-light car with independent rear suspension, was viable in the UK because racing took place on smooth surfaces. But such an environment did not exist in the rest of Europe, where racing was conducted on bumpy roads. With their smaller air forces, France, Italy and Germany had fewer concrete, heavy-bomber airfields to race on, so their cars had to be ruggedly built to withstand the stresses of such indifferent surfaces.'

In 1965, however, Coventry Climax, unable to cope with the increasing cost of development, announced that it was withdrawing from Formula One engine production from the end of that year. The decision was a shock, not least to Lotus founder Colin Chapman, who had built a strong relationship with engineers at Coventry. None of the constructors – neither Lotus, Cooper nor Brabham – had the money to fund a new engine programme. That year Chapman asked renowned racing engineer Keith Duckworth whether he could build an engine if money could be raised to fund development. His answer was yes. It was American car maker Ford that agreed to put up the money. It was arguably the best £100,000 that Ford ever spent. The company still uses derivatives from this first engine to this day. The now legendary, Ford Cosworth DFV F1, a three-litre eight-cylinder engine, made its first appearance in 1967 in the Lotus 49 at the Dutch Grand Prix. Lotus had had exclusive use of the DFV, an engine so powerful that no other team could catch them. That in itself was a problem. Chapman and Walter Hayes, the Ford vice-president who agreed to fund the development programme, agreed that the engine would have to be made available to other teams. Otherwise, Lotus would sweep the board and competition on the track would be dead. The DFV probably single-handedly saved the British motorsport industry. In 1968 McLaren and

Matra used the DFV, followed by Brabham in 1969 and March and de Tomaso in 1970. The DFV became the standard Formula One engine, powering cars that won every world championship between 1968 and 1974.

The British teams were small, aggressive, ambitious companies. But they felt constrained by lack of finance. They could not call on the resources of Mercedes, Ferrari or Renault. The British owner-entrepreneurs had to rely on limited sponsorship from their technical suppliers or the benevolence of wealthy supporters. This new generation of young men emerging on the Formula One scene grew tired of antiquated rules that seemed to favour the larger teams and constrain their own aspirations. For 70 years, racing had been an elitist sport, where royalty did not just attend races but, in the case of Prince Bira of Thailand, participated. The new team owners wanted to shake up Formula One, and create a sport where anyone with talent and determination could have a chance to succeed. What this meant in practice was the removal of restrictions on commercial sponsorship. In 1968 the sport's governing body bowed to the pressure, and allowed general advertising to be carried on racecars. A landmark sponsorship deal was signed between Gold Leaf, part of Players Tobacco, and Lotus in 1968. Lotus's founder, Colin Chapman, had been involved in a lot of racing in America and seen the extent of sponsorship. Chapman's racing green Lotus became the red, white and gold 'Gold Leaf Team Lotus'. In 1970 cosmetics group Yardley became a sponsor of BRM. And in 1972 Marlboro too began sponsoring BRM, switching to McLaren in 1974 in a partnership that survived until the tobacco company moved to Ferrari in 1997. Since then every kind of corporation has used Formula One cars as a billboard, from condom manufacturers to airlines to building societies.

The growth of commercial sponsorship went hand-in-hand with improved organisation of the sport under the auspices of the Formula One Constructors' Association (FOCA). Bernie Ecclestone and Max Mosley, the two most powerful men in Formula One, brought with them a new professionalism. UK constructors needed sponsors to survive, but sponsors would not spend millions of pounds on a two-bit sport with an amateur approach. Ecclestone and Mosley set about improving contracts with circuit owners and television broadcasters. They also encouraged and cajoled the teams into becoming more professional. Remarkably, before FOCA imposed order on the way Formula One was run, constructors were under no obligation to turn up for every grand prix race. As for the drivers, they have Jackie Stewart to thank for improving their conditions. He formed the Grand Prix Drivers' Association to improve safety and ensure that some money from sponsorship found its way into higher salaries. He also opened the way for personal sponsorship, which turned racing drivers into some of the highest paid sports stars in the world. Formula One had broken free from being the preserve of Continental car manufacturers and allied trades. It had entered a new era of commercialism. Formula One was turned into a highly successful business – rich and influential; a British success story at a time when so much of British business was in decline. In the next section we look in more detail at the roots of that success: how a bunch of engineers and designers working out of garages brought the mighty Mercedes-Benz and Ferrari racing teams to their knees.

The British are Coming

THE SECOND WORLD WAR military planners who dotted Britain with huge concrete airfields did motor racing a great service. With the war over and the fleets of Allied bombers grounded, these redundant airfields became ideal racing circuits for motorsport enthusiasts. Silverstone, the Northamptonshire track that is the epicentre of the motor racing industry, started life as home to B52 bombers. Goodwood, in Sussex, and Thruxton, in Hampshire, were among other defunct sites turned into thriving centres for club racing and the associated engineering firms that kept the cars in working order. The importance these airfields played in enabling Britain to become the heart of the motorsport industry cannot be underestimated. The circuits became a melting pot of drivers, technicians and businessmen, all with ideas about how to improve the cars and expand the sport. This cross-fertilisation gave motorsport in Britain the start it needed to challenge the dominant racing teams on the Continent.

Although prior to the Second World War Britain remained on the fringes of motor racing, its cars being no match for the Continentals; it was not as if Britain had no motoring heritage. The first Lanchester cars went into production in 1900. A Scottish vet, John Boyd Dunlop, had patented the pneumatic tyre 15 years earlier. And in 1907 Hugh Locke King spent £150,000 of his own money building the Brooklands circuit in Surrey, the world's first dedicated racetrack. But the government's early suspicion of racing on public roads had held back British racecar invention while developments in the rest of Europe continued apace. Even Walter Owen Bentley, founder of the legendary Bentley cars, preferred to import French DFPs and fine tune them for racing. Eventually, of course, he manufactured his own vehicles. The Bentleys, driven by a group of gentlemen racers dubbed the Bentley Boys, achieved success at Le Mans throughout the 1920s, and could have gone on to greater things. But it all ended in grief with the 1929 Wall Street crash. Bentley financed the team out of the profits of road-car sales, but the crash turned his rich customers into paupers and in 1931 the company had to be rescued by Rolls-Royce. A further attempt to build a British racecar company was made in 1933, by Raymond Mays. He was a good driver, disheartened that all the best cars were foreign-made. Mays established English Racing Automobiles, near his home in Lincolnshire, to build racecars with modified Riley engines for the *Voiturette* Formula Two class. Mays was the first major racecar builder to bring commercial backing to an English constructor. The company prospered, even though the British privateers racing the ERAs achieved only moderate success on the track. However, everything was put on hold when war broke out in 1939. It put an end to serious racing in Europe and any attempt by British teams to challenge their Continental rivals until it was over.

Instead of ruining British chances on the racetracks, however, the war gave British racing a stimulus. A by-product of the war was to sow the seeds of technical developments that would to be adopted and adapted by the racing industry. Wartime research into aircraft production resulted in breakthroughs in disc brakes, radial tyres, fuel injection, turbochargers and a host of other advances that found their way into motoring. Thousands of British engineers had refined their skills in the war effort, either working in aerospace factories or as maintenance engineers at the airfields. After demobilisation a lot of this expertise found its way into motor racing as a civilian army of technically brilliant men took up racing as a hobby or used their expertise to set up small automotive engineering businesses. In the subsequent years, other people were to refine their skills in the growing British road-car industry. Together they laid the foundations for a cottage industry of specialists that still thrives today. Called Grand Prix Valley, and situated in a triangle bordered by the M1, M4 and M42 motorways, this sector consists of hundreds of motorsport companies surviving off Formula One, IndyCar and other types of racing. Though small, Grand Prix Valley is a vibrant, successful and profitable part of the UK. But it was born out of impoverished times.

The early post-war years were a time of raw material shortages, so innovation and adaptation were the watchwords of the new racing enthusiasts. Petrol was rationed and hire purchase restricted. The Labour government urged industry to put its efforts into boosting the balance of payments by exporting more. Companies making cars with better export potential received bigger rations of steel. Cars for the domestic market were purged of all their luxury fittings, unlike those destined for overseas. In 1947 only 142,000 new cars were registered in Britain, 50 per cent of domestic production. The rest went for export. For the bulk of the British motoring public, cheap and cheerful cars were all they could afford. With Purchase Tax at 33.3 per cent even for cars under £1,000, the Austin Seven, which cost around £300 in 1945, was one of the few vehicles within most people's reach. (It was also popular among racing enthusiasts because it was easy to strip down and modify for racing.) A Ford Anglia cost about £126 in 1940, but in 1945 it cost £293. With average earnings around this time at about £280, owning even a modest car took a sizeable chunk out of the annual wage. Under the strict economic regime luxury vehicles faced a hefty 66.6 per cent duty. Many of the wealthy car enthusiasts who traditionally kept such niche car manufacturers afloat simply could no longer afford to. Lea Francis and Armstrong Siddeley were among the famous names to go bust.

These economic circumstances impelled like-minded racing enthusiasts to organise a club network in order to utilise each other's skills, and barter and borrow car components. Groups of constructors, designers, component suppliers and engine specialists grew up around the old airfields. Arguably the most influential of these was the 750 Motor Club. It promoted heavily the idea of the DIY racing car by disseminating technical information in the club magazine, which became the shop window for buying and selling components. The list of pioneers who cut their teeth at the 750 Motor Club reads like a Who's Who of racecar engineering: Colin Chapman, founder of Lotus, and Eric Broadley, founder of Lola; Adrian Reynard, whose Reynard Racing supplies cars for Indy racing; Mike Costin, co-founder of engine supplier Cosworth Engineering, and Brian Hart, of Hart Engines. In turn, these companies became a hot-bed of talent who went on to form their own engineering firms and join racing teams. The founders of Ilmor Engineering, which supplies the Mercedes engine to McLaren, had been at Cosworth. And much-admired engineers John Barnard, of Ferrari and McLaren, and Patrick Head, of Williams, were trained at Lola.

Britain's circuit club network was unique in European racing. On the Continent, racing teams were still part of larger companies: Renault, Ferrari, Alfa Romeo, Maserati, Mercedes-Benz. These manufacturers could subsidise their research and development in racing with the sale of road cars, and their large in-house engineering departments gave them economies of scale. Although Britain had Vanwall and BRM, they were in the shadows of their Continental rivals. Enzo Ferrari famously dismissed the club culture of the UK industry as 'garagistes'. Yet, when the Continental companies succumbed to financial problems, the unique organisation of the British teams survived. Simply put, by force of economic circumstances, the British teams had learned how to design and construct single-seater cars more cheaply and with fewer staff.

For the Continental racecar teams, the starting-point was to build an engine to out-perform the rest of the grid. Their thinking centred around producing a car that had brute power. The Continentals had a target brake horsepower of about 300. This emphasis limited thinking about design. The gearbox and transmission were fixed, resulting in the classic layout of the front-engined car. The seminal contribution to racing was to think more deeply about other factors affecting a car's performance, notably aerodynamics. One of the first UK constructors to fully develop and exploit the effects of design, size and weight in racing cars was the Cooper Car Company, which emerged out of the 500cc Club. From a small factory in the Surrey suburb of Surbiton, Charles Cooper built a motorbike-powered single-seater car for his son, John, using the layout pioneered by the pre-war German Auto Union grand prix cars. Here, the engine and transmission were positioned between the driver and the back wheels. A consistent race winner in the late 1940s, the Coopers really took off after 1950, when the 500cc formula was given international Formula Three status. Even when the car was scaled up to the new formula, the innovative new Coopers were demonstrating a formidable challenge to the dominant Ferraris and Maseratis. The car's entry into Formula One came when an experimental Cooper was raced by Jack Brabham in the 1955 British Grand Prix, using a two-litre six-cylinder Bristol engine. The performance was disappointing, as Brabham was unplaced. However, in 1958 Rob Walker, heir to the Johnny Walker whisky company, put a new Coventry Climax in a Cooper car and recruited Stirling Moss to drive it. The combination was devastating, bestowing glory on both the men and their machinery. Moss demolished the opposition at that year's Argentinian Grand Prix.

The Coopers were essentially simple cars, designed around a plan that Charles and John used to mark out in chalk on the floor of their garage. Compared to the mid-engined Auto Unions designed by

Ferdinand Porsche in the 1930s, the technology used was not much of an advance. Yet, because the two men understood weight distribution, the Coopers became the first cars born out of the UK club network to achieve major success on the international stage. The superiority of the mid-engine design proved overwhelming in race after race, and other constructors were forced to follow suit. Even Italian manufacturers, who initially resisted the change, gave in. The Cooper design had created a revolution in the understanding of the power-to-weight ratio in a racing car. While the cars lacked the raw power of the Ferraris and Vanwalls, the disadvantage was cancelled out by the lightness of the chassis. It meant the Coopers had better acceleration and better braking, and because the car was lower there was less wind resistance. The UK club constructors built on this knowledge, and in the 1960s were increasingly to dominate top-level racing. Only Ferrari was presenting a serious challenge.

In a BBC radio interview John Cooper explained his method: 'When we started after the war we were very short of materials, and you had to improvise on a lot of things. We had a drawing office, but if we were thinking of ideas we used to sketch it on the floor. Design was really common sense in those days. I remember saying to Enzo Ferrari at lunch at Monza in 1957 or 1958, when are you going to put the engine behind the driver? And he said, "Never. Have you ever seen a horse pushing a cart?" Within two years he was starting to put them in the back. I was a little surprised when Enzo built his rear-engine car; I was surprised when Colin Chapman did. Colin was one of the greatest racing car designers of all time and he realised the capabilities of a mid-engine car. If somebody copied us, we used to think, well, we must be right. It did not worry us in those days.'

While the race club structure was crucial in laying the foundations of Britain's grand prix success, it by no means tells the whole story. Britain's growing domination took place against a background of changes in Formula One regulations. In an attempt to limit Continental teams' emphasis on ever greater power and muscle in their cars, racing's governing body progressively reduced engine sizes during the immediate post-war years. These essentially biased the construction of Grand Prix cars towards the lighter and more efficient designs being researched by British teams. Perhaps the most important change, at least for UK constructors, was made in 1958. The use of special fuel mixtures were outlawed and ordinary commercial petrol made mandatory. Furthermore, race distances were reduced from 500 to 300 kilometres. As

Aston and Williams point out: 'Shorter race distances meant that refuelling and tyre changes became unnecessary. Fuel consumption with aviation fuel was better than with alcohol fuels, thus smaller tanks could be used. Lighter loads permitted smaller wheels and tyres, and thus lighter chassis components and down-sized brakes. By scaling-up light cars the UK club constructors were competitive in Formula One, despite an underpowered engine, because minimal size and weight had been central to the design.'

Colin Chapman grasped the principles of racecar weight and design like no other constructor of his time. His understanding of roadholding was to reverberate around the world of grand prix. What mattered to Chapman was not engine power, it was how to keep the racecar 'glued' to the road at speed. The kernel of Chapman's idea was disarmingly simple: if the racecar is based around increasingly more powerful engines, it would mean producing a heavier vehicle. This, of course meant it was more difficult to control driving around corners, or setting off from the grid, or when slowing down from high speed. In Chapman's monocoque the driver had to lie flat, thus lowering the centre of gravity. Also, the wheels carried wider tyres to enable better grip. And independent suspension on all four wheels helped distribute the weight of the car equally. But Chapman's most dramatic innovation was in developing what came to be known as 'ground effects'. At its simplest, Chapman put tubes along the sides of his car, creating a vacuum which sucked the vehicle to the track with forces up to three times that of gravity. Chapman, another designer who came up through the 750 Motor Club, founded Lotus Engineering in London in 1952 with money borrowed from his wife. Ten years later the path-breaking Lotus 25 racecar made its debut, at the Dutch Grand Prix. It was the first of several revolutionary cars made by Chapman. This one was the first modern racecar to be built with a monocoque chassis, something used in the aerospace industry for many years. It gave lightness and strength. Colin Chapman's cars went on to a total of 70 grand prix wins, with drivers like Jim Clark, Graham Hill and Ayrton Senna. He changed racecar design for ever, though his inventiveness was not always appreciated by the racing authorities. From now on the officials would be fighting a constant battle to get innovations under control, in an attempt to create a level playing field for the competitors. Chapman, and those designers who followed him, saw it as their job to get around the rules. The two sides – the inventors and the regulators – have engaged in many long and bitter disputes ever since.

By the time Chapman died of a heart attack in 1982 (he was under great pressure over his links with the failed de Lorean sports car venture which cost the UK taxpayer tens of millions of pounds), Britain was the centre of the motor racing world. A conjunction of forces – changes in both the economic environment and the racing rulebook, brilliant engines and innovative engineers, lucky breaks and visionary thinking – were working in Britain's favour. The legacy of all this is that, today, no Formula One team competes without some input from either British designers, drivers or component suppliers. Britain also plays one further important role in Formula One – it is the seat of power. At the same time as the Formula One industry was gravitating away from the Continent, so was political control. Using the UK constructors as a bridgehead, Bernie Ecclestone wrested power from the European 'old guard' who ran motorsport. British domination was complete. Once in control, Ecclestone set about refashioning Formula One into a sport for the age of global television. It is to his remarkable role as the Czar of Formula One that we now turn.

Chapter Two: THE PROFESSIONALS

The Ringmaster

CONTROL OF FORMULA ONE lies ostensibly inside a grand building
on the Place de la Concorde in Paris. It is somehow fitting that the
headquarters of the Fédération Internationale de l'Automobile should
be located in such imperious splendour. The FIA is an historic organisation, arguably carrying more political and economic clout than any
other sporting federation. The FIA is the governing body of world
motorsport, setting technical and procedural rules for a variety of
competitions, not just Formula One. Representatives of 145 motoring
organisations from 113 countries have a seat at the FIA, including the
Royal Automobile Club for the United Kingdom. The FIA's jurisdiction
extends from karting, to electro solar racing, to rallying. And it also
lobbies on behalf of road and motoring interests all over the globe. For
instance, it represents 40 million motorists in the European Union
through affiliated organisations. In reality, however, Formula One is not
run from Paris, but from a large glass-fronted office block overlooking
London's Hyde Park. These are the offices of Bernard Charles Ecclestone, the semi-autocratic emperor who cracks the whip in Formula
One's international circus. It was Ecclestone who took grand prix away
for the amateurs, forced the teams and circuit owners to become more
professional, and put Formula One on countless television screens
throughout the world. In the process he turned himself, and many
others beside, into millionaires.

Ecclestone did not achieve such power single-handed. Max Mosley,
a friend and now president of the FIA, shared Ecclestone's vision,
and worked the political channels tirelessly to ensure changes were
enforced. Nor could Ecclestone have succeeded without the acqui-
escence of some teams, in particular Ferrari, probably the only constructor which could alone challenge Ecclestone's authority if it so

wished (but never has). Nevertheless, Ecclestone is far more than *primus inter pares*. Only the eminent and unparalleled become universally known by a singular name. And throughout Formula One, Ecclestone is known simply as Bernie. In 1997 he almost became Sir Bernie. John Major, the former British prime minister, put forward Ecclestone's name for a knighthood. It is unclear why he did not receive his honour. However, it did coincide with some embarrassing revelations about Ecclestone's donations to the Conservative and Labour parties, and government plans to exempt Formula One from a ban on tobacco sponsorship.

Ecclestone is a short man, not much over five feet. He has, however, developed an identity that transcends his size. Over twenty years Ecclestone has taken on some of the biggest egos in sport and won. He has manoeuvred himself into a position whereby there is no aspect of Formula One that is outside his jurisdiction; no area on which he is not consulted. It is Ecclestone who decides which countries and circuits stage races, and who broadcasts them; who wanted to introduce refuelling during races; who steered Michael Schumacher to Benetton in 1991 and brought Jacques Villeneuve from IndyCars to Williams in 1996; who cleared the takeover of Tyrrell by British American Tobacco. When journalists want pit-passes, they go to Ecclestone. When Gianni Agnelli, head of Ferrari's owner Fiat, turned up at the 1997 British Grand Prix without his pit-pass, a functionary refused him entry until he located it. That is because Ecclestone demands that everything is rigidly controlled. If he wants the removal of a hot-dog stand from the Interlagos circuit in Brazil, he can have it done. If there is a dispute between teams, it can normally be resolved when Ecclestone holds court in the silver-grey motorhome – known as The Kremlin – that he takes to the racetracks. When movie star Sylvester Stallone signed a contract in 1997 to make a film about Formula One, he had to first negotiate with Ecclestone.

Running a global sport (although Formula One does not currently race in the United States, so is not strictly global) confers huge power on an individual, be it Juan Antonio Samaranch through the Olympics or Joao Havelange through international football. Such men threaten, cajole, form and break alliances, divide and rule, make many enemies and few friends. What they do is try to unify their sports, keeping the disparate elements and egos together. And they succeed through close personal involvement and attention to detail. There are few things more damaging to a sport than a split in the ranks. Boxing has never recovered from its divisions, and other sports have failed to capitalise and grow on their popularity because of their inability to unite. Ecclestone, who in fact built his power base after threatening to split the sport in 1980, has successfully kept Formula One together ever since. But Ecclestone is much more than a Samaranch or a Havelange. Why? Because Ecclestone not only rules Formula One, he also owns a large slice of the sport's commercial interests. Ecclestone is a natural entrepreneur; a deal maker. However, this would mean little had he not had one thing: 25-year licences granted by the FIA World Council to exploit Formula One's popularity.

Ecclestone's power and money emanate from four sources: firstly, he holds an FIA licence to negotiate the sale of worldwide television rights to broadcast Formula One; secondly, as head of the Formula One Constructors' Association he handles the interests of the teams, organising their travel arrangements to the races and negotiating with the circuit owners (all for a fee); thirdly, he is vice-president of the FIA, which puts him at the heart of the rule-making body; finally, he has built a collection of other business interests, not just in Formula One, but in other forms of motorsport and motorcycling. Ecclestone's most lucrative operation is the one which handles television rights, Formula One Promotion and Administration.[1] This is the core of the company he hopes to float on the London stock exchange, Formula One Holdings, following a corporate restructuring of his empire.

Ecclestone never talks about his wealth, usually deflecting questions on the topic with a retort such as: 'Only me and the taxman know what is in my bank account.' In everything he does, Ecclestone is short on words and long on action. His refusal to explain himself, though, makes trying to understand the motives and rewards that drive him more difficult. Putting a precise figure on Ecclestone's financial worth is difficult, though a trawl through the accounts that his businesses must file with the UK authorities gives some indication. His main companies earned him about £1.7 million in salary and dividends in 1992, rising dramatically to about £29.7 million in 1993 and £29.3 million in 1994, then dropping to around £12 million in 1995. The figures are erratic, partly because not all the accounts are available at

---

[1] As of mid-1997 Ecclestone's other interests included being a director of: International Sportsworld Communications; Formula One Racing Promotions; FOCA Enterprises; FOCA Administration; FOCA Communications; Mid-Week Auctions; Pentbridge Properties; Parmalat UK; Formula One Race Car Engineering; Rapid Freight; Motor Racing Developments; Special Events Productions.

the same time, but mostly because Ecclestone is reinvesting heavily in his operations. He is putting an estimated £50 million of his own money into developing a mobile digital broadcasting studio. Ecclestone has all the trappings of wealth: a Lear jet, a collection of cars, and homes in Corsica and Gstaad, Switzerland, as well as an ex-model for a wife, called Slavica, whom he married at Chelsea Registry office in 1985. The *Sunday Times* newspaper, which each year publishes a list of Britain's top 500 richest people, put Ecclestone's wealth at £275 million in 1997. This ranked him joint 58th in the list, alongside the Forte hotels family and the shipping magnate, John Goulandris. If the flotation of Formula One Holdings goes ahead, it may earn up to £750 million for Ecclestone and his family trusts. That would take him into the top ten richest people in Britain. Such wealth has brought jealousy and enmity, even from some who were themselves enriched by what Ecclestone did for Formula One. They call him 'Bernie' to his face and 'Ecclestein' behind his back. The blazered snobs who used to run motorsport thought a seat at Formula One's top table was no place for a working-class son of a trawlerman. Constant references are made in newspapers to his tinted glasses, as if they signify someone with something to hide, rather than a man with failing eyesight. He is dismissed as a former back-street secondhand car salesman made good. In fact, his successful Weekend Car Auctions business was sold to British Car Auctions, while his motorbike business was built into Britain's second largest chain of dealerships. Their sale made him a rich man, able to afford a serious challenge at becoming a racing driver. Listening to his detractors you would suspect that Ecclestone has a closet overflowing with skeletons (one story tried to link him with the Great Train Robbery). He can be disarmingly blunt, and ruthless in negotiation. The way he ditched the BBC and sold the British broad-casting rights to Formula One to ITV – giving the BBC one hour's notice – was brutal. His close associates, however, say he can be enormously charming, and is not immune to a little self-deprecation: he once told Flavio Briatore, the former Benetton boss, that his dream as a young boy was 'to be much taller. I always wanted to be taller. I am the only horse rider who has carried a ladder around with him.' These would be somewhat anodyne comments if made by most people. But for Ecclestone they are rather candid.

One remark often made about Ecclestone is that he is always prepared to do a favour and never breaks a promise. Another comment is that he can be a good friend, but a very bad enemy. There certainly seems to be an air of caution when Ecclestone's name is mentioned. Ask Formula One insiders to talk about him and there is always a pause for breath while they consider the consequences. Those who agree want cast-iron guarantees that they will remain anonymous. One man who is aware of the problem is Karel van Miert, the European Commissioner probing the complex relationship between Ecclestone's companies and the FIA. His office is investigating a number of leads from people who declined to make formal complaints because they did not want to get on the wrong side of Ecclestone. Van Miert's office said informal complaints were not uncommon, but in this case the numbers involved were unusually high. With so many people dependent on Ecclestone for their livelihoods, one can understand the reticence. Ecclestone rarely gives full interviews, preferring to confine himself to the odd pithy comment. The biggest clue to what makes him tick was a remark he made in 1996: 'Basically I am a dealer. I deal constantly. Whatever there is for sale, I'll buy it and I'll sell it. I like doing deals, I always have. I don't run or jump or drive motor cars – I just do deals.' Apart from considering a bid to buy *The Times* newspaper group, which eventually went to Rupert Murdoch, his business deals have been largely confined to Formula One. The sport is his hobby, his life, his reputation.

His entrepreneurial flare has been nurtured since the age of 15, when he began trading in motorbikes even before he was legally allowed to ride them. Ecclestone was born at St Peter's, Suffolk, in 1930, but moved to Bexleyheath, Kent, after his father, a trawler captain, and became an engineer. Ecclestone took a BSc in chemical engineering and looked to be heading for a mundane career in industry. In the 1940s, however, he gave up working in a laboratory and began trading in motorbikes full time. Ecclestone worked briefly for a dealer before going into partnership and running his own garage in Bexleyheath. He then bought out his partner, and expanded the business rapidly, acquiring premises and dealerships on the back of a booming British motorcycle industry. He raced motorbikes for a while, and then cars, competing in small 500cc single-seaters alongside celebrated names like Stirling Moss and Peter Collins, who went on to run Lotus.

It was during his early years as a racer that Ecclestone became friends with one Stuart Lewis-Evans, whose father ran a garage in Bexleyheath. The two young men raced together, until Ecclestone had an accident at Brands Hatch and decided, aged 26, that a driving career might not be the way forward. He did, though, travel extensively to the races to watch his friend, who grew into a middle-ranking grand prix driver, first with Connaught and then Vanwall. The racing roadshow appealed to Ecclestone, and he became the youngest owner of a grand prix outfit when he bought the ailing Connaught team. However, he was unable to reverse the team's slow decline. In 1958 Lewis-Evans died from severe burns suffered in a crash at the Moroccan Grand Prix, robbing the motor racing world of a talented driver who never got to show his full potential. Ecclestone was stunned by the death of his friend, and although for a while he remained on the fringes of racing, he then turned his attention to commerce and property. Ecclestone's passion for racing was re-ignited in the mid-1960s when he met and befriended Jochen Rindt, later becoming the Austrian driver's manager. However, yet another friendship ended in tragedy. Rindt, whom Ecclestone still regards as the best driver ever to compete in Formula One, died in 1970 during practice for the Italian Grand Prix. This time Ecclestone did not withdraw from Formula One, but plunged deeper into it. In 1971 he went back into team ownership, buying the entire assets of Motor Racing Developments, owner of the Brabham team, for around £31,000.

These were years of triumph for the British kit-car manufacturers over the traditional Continental teams. Between 1966 and 1973 the home-grown talent made up the bulk of the grid. But they lacked political muscle compared with the 'grandee' teams abroad such as Ferrari and Renault. In the mid-1960s Colin Chapman, Ken Tyrrell and Jack Brabham put their names to a loose coalition to represent the interests of UK teams, the Formula 1 Constructors' Association (F1CA). It is a common myth that F1CA (later to become FOCA) was the brainchild of Ecclestone. F1CA was, in fact, the idea of Andrew Ferguson, team manager of Lotus. But it is certainly true that once Ecclestone secured control he used his position and power effectively, melding the UK teams into a powerful negotiating force. Ecclestone did not even attend his first meeting until 1972. According to author Gerard Crombac, who was at that meeting, Ecclestone served the tea and said little. Soon, however, Ecclestone's confidence and influence grew, though it was not until 1978 that he became president of the association. Most of his fellow team owners cared little for the administration and politics of Formula One. They were engineers and former drivers who just wanted to race, and they were only too happy to hand over the reigns of FOCA and let Ecclestone get on with it. The first thing he did was tackle the costs of competing. As Formula One grew, so did the logistics of moving the racing teams around the world every two weeks. Ecclestone chartered Boeing aircraft to transport the 90 tons of Formula One freight, and he arranged travel plans and hotel bookings for the race-team staff. He was paid a fee for the job, but he also saved the teams time and money.

Next, Ecclestone began negotiating with the circuit owners on the behalf of the FOCA teams. The importance of this for the development of Formula One cannot be overstated. Originally, all grand prix events were separate and independently financed. Competitors would turn up at the track and independently negotiate an appearance fee. Some of the deals might include a bit of trackside advertising thrown it. But it was all rather hit or miss. Circuit owners could never be certain that all the teams would turn up, even for the top races. Sometimes, when the British Grand Prix was being staged, newspaper editors would send sports reporters to the shipping ports to see which teams got off the boats. Competition was totally disorganised. If ever Formula One was to expand, it had to become more professional. Ecclestone's masterstroke was to promise circuit owners a full grid of teams: teams had to commit themselves to a full season of racing. This pleased the crowds, it pleased the sponsors, and it pleased the television stations.

In the late 1970s and early 1980s the circuits were charged a fee of about £500,000 to stage a race. What FOCA gets from the circuits today is shrouded in secrecy. Confidentiality and get-out clauses govern the contracts with the circuits, putting FOCA in an extremely powerful position. But occasionally slips are made and details leak. In 1993, following a row over financial irregularities, it was revealed that South Africa paid $6 million to host a race. The fee for the Hungarian Grand Prix is about $7m. And Silverstone, which hosts the British Grand Prix, is believed to pay $10 million a year. Today, the average fee for staging a grand prix is thought to be $10 million, adding up to $160 million a year. Ecclestone used these circuit fees to pay start-money to the teams, and to introduce a prize-fund structure based on a team's performance the previous year. It ensured that all the teams, not just those at the front of the grid, would receive money from turning up to compete. In return for being guaranteed a full grid, the circuits were required to relinquish exclusive rights to trackside advertising and hospitality. As Formula One grew into a popular television sport, these rights became a huge money-making enterprise. Advertisers were offered better facilities to install their billboards at circuits, and the standards of corporate

hospitality improved immeasurably. This business, along with mer-
chandising rights, was put in the hands of Ecclestone's friend Paddy
McNally, a former reporter on *Autosport* magazine, who had moved to
Switzerland to set up sponsorship for Marlboro cigarettes.

In 1984 McNally created the Geneva-based Allsport Management,
which pays Ecclestone a fee to do its hospitality and advertising work.
The other directors are a lawyer, Luc Argand, and Anne Richard, though
the business is wholly owned by McNally. It was McNally who set up
the exclusive Paddock Club, enabling sponsors to entertain their VIP
guests at all grand prix events at about £1,000 each, twice the cost of
the best hospitality at most other blue-riband sporting events in the
UK. Circuit advertising is about to undergo a revolution. Ecclestone's
own television company is looking at 'virtual advertising' so he can
superimpose different adverts simultaneously on the same hoardings
for different TV markets. With around 40 main trackside hoardings per
race, costing roughly $100,000 a time, the money-making potential
is increased substantially. Merchandising, too, is woefully underdeveloped compared with, say, CART racing in America, or a sport
like football. The Paddock Club, trackside advertising and merchandising are estimated to earn revenues of around $40 million. The
potential, though, as Formula One takes advantage of new technology
and growing interest in the sport, is a lot more.

Behind all these changes lies Ecclestone's belief that Formula One
had to become more efficient. Already the costs of competing were
soaring. Research and development by the constructors was soaking up
tens of millions of pounds, and more sponsors were needed to finance
it. But sponsors were not going to allocate more funds unless they got
something more in return. And that meant getting television broadcasters to take Formula One more seriously. Ecclestone's problem was
that the broadcasting rights for Formula One belonged to the FIA. The
FIA, of course, owned the championship, but did not realise that it was
sitting on a goldmine. Ecclestone did. In the late 1970s and early 1980s
there were a series of skirmishes as Ecclestone and FOCA sought
to wrest control from the establishment running the sport. In 1978
Ecclestone made a tactical error when he supported the appointment
of Jean-Marie Balestre as president of the Fédération Internationale
du Sport Automobile (FISA, the sports arm of the FIA). Balestre, a
quarrelsome, bullying personality, had his own plans for dominating
Formula One. Balestre drew support from the grandee teams and powerful allied trades like the oil company Elf, all of whom represented

the traditional motor industry. After his election Balestre walked the corridors of the motoring clubs and track owners drumming up support for his plan to regain the right to negotiate with circuit owners and control the distribution of prize income to the racing teams.

The moves brought him into head-on confrontation with Ecclestone and the British constructors that made up FOCA. Two quotations sum up the hostility between the men. In 1979 Ballastre rounded on the British: 'Let me tell you something, those people don't know what they're in for, they don't understand power, they're just little men playing with toys, making cars in garages: who do they think they are? They don't own motorsport.' A few months later Ecclestone launched his own attack: 'Who the hell is FISA? They are a bunch of nobodies, they appointed themselves and they think they own racing, when all they really have is a bunch of clubs around the world and self-important people living off the back of the sport.' Ecclestone's outburst was prompted by Balestre's announcement that he intended to rewrite the technical regulations. 'Sliding skirts' (developed by Colin Chapman and used to increase downforce and, therefore, speed) were to be banned from 1981. Also, the minimum weight limit for Formula One racecars was being raised to 585 kilograms. For the British, who specialised in lighter cars based around the latest aerodynamic design, this move appeared to be a deliberate attempt to favour the heavier turbocharged cars of France and Italy.

The in-fighting came to a head when FISA introduced compulsory briefings for drivers before races. It was a small matter, but the last straw for the British teams. At the 1980 Spanish Grand Prix, FISA tried to impose fines on those drivers who failed to turn up for the briefing. When the FOCA drivers refused to pay, Balestre abandoned the grand prix, and Renault, Ferrari and Alfa Romeo pulled out in support. The FOCA teams went ahead as planned. In November 1980, FOCA announced a breakaway World Federation of Motor Sport to run a new $10 million championship with a $1 million guaranteed purse for the winning driver. This new World Professional Drivers' Championship was to have 18 races. Balestre responded by announcing a 14-race series, some on identical dates and circuits. Squabbles continued over which of the teams would side with which camp. There were legal threats about restraint of trade and interference with contracts. Ligier, under pressure from sponsors, defected to Balestre, who also added the British Toleman team to his camp. Fed up with the bickering, the Goodyear tyre company, one of the major sponsors at that time, temporarily withdraw from the sport. The tobacco company Marlboro stood on the sidelines, embarrassed by the whole affair.

The FOCA championship was the first off the grid, running the 1981 South African Grand Prix under its own aegis, with full television coverage that attracted an audience of several millions. The move gave Ecclestone a clear advantage, and signalled the first cracks among the Balestre camp. Renault, whose executives were aghast at such a large event taking place without their name appearing on the television screen, were the first to break ranks. It was clear that the British teams had the upper hand. On 19 January 1981 a summit was held at Maranello, home of Ferrari. A truce was called and, in March, Ecclestone and Balestre emerged with the so-called Concorde Agreement, a deal negotiated by FOCA's in-house lawyer, Max Mosley. FOCA agreed to recognise FISA's role as supreme rule maker, but in reality it was a victory for Ecclestone, who emerged with almost everything he wanted, including a licence to negotiate worldwide television rights. FOCA also kept its right to negotiate contracts with circuit owners and distribute the proceeds. Income from television was divided, with about 50 per cent going to the teams, and the remainder distributed between Ecclestone and FISA. Soon afterwards, Ecclestone was invited to become vice-president of the FIA.

Throughout the 1980s Ecclestone, always with Max Mosley at his side, progressively shaped Formula One. The key was to maintain uniformity and stability, so that television broadcasters and sponsors always knew what they were getting. Ecclestone set out his aim in 1988: 'At the moment all the FIA championships are a bit fragmented, with everyone in their own country doing what they think is best. It is a bit like any big company. I mean, McDonalds couldn't have one of their franchises sticking more beef in their burgers or using a different logo. It's the same principle for the FIA. The only obstacle to getting it right is people. Lots of people are frightened that they will lose power they think they have, but probably don't have anyway.' In order to consolidate Formula One into a single definable entity, Ecclestone had to ensure that every aspect of the sport received his attention. His obsessiveness over presentation is legendary. (It was not unknown for him to use a helicopter to ensure that the teams' motorhomes were always in a straight line.) He once said: 'I like to see that things are going on in the right way; like a guy who owns a restaurant would want to walk through and see that the restaurant is being run properly. I always feel that in large companies, where the managers or owners are not more or less semi hands-on, if not completely hands-on, then you find it is not that successful.'

For Ecclestone it is of paramount importance that Formula One retains a positive image. Everyone must be left with the impression that the sport is clinically efficient and ultra-professional. He likes the drivers to be well turned out, the motorhomes to be spotless, and even the wheels of the trucks to be positioned so that sponsors' names are the right way up. If a production company wants to produce a motorsport video game, it cannot use the Formula One names without a licence from Ecclestone. On the surface, it looks like another attempt by Ecclestone to squeeze every penny out of Formula One. In fact, it has more to do with Ecclestone's desire to keep a grip on Formula One's image. The cost of a licence is tiny compared with the revenues coming from elsewhere. What concerns Ecclestone is that Formula One receives positive marketing. A video-games licence states that Formula One must not be depicted unfavourably in the videos. With motor racing attracting hundreds of millions of pounds because of its glamorous, clean-cut image, his concern is that the Formula One brand name is not derided.

In a sport where the personal touch – a handshake or a promise – is as important as a legal contract, it is wise to have allies throughout Formula One. Probably all the team bosses owe Ecclestone a favour or two, and his associates have found positions throughout the organisational structure of Formula One. His pals from his old days at Brabham have certainly not been forgotten. These include Charlie Whiting, a former chief mechanic at Brabham who became the FIA's technical delegate – to spot the cheats and rule-benders – and then race director. He works alongside Herbie Blash, former Brabham team manager. And Eddie Baker, a former mechanic, runs 'Bakersville', FOCA's huge broadcasting unit, along with Nigel de Strayter, another ex-Brabham mechanic. There are others, too. And then there is Max Mosley, former boss of the March racing team, and now president of the FIA. Ecclestone and Mosley have been indivisable for years, sharing the same aspirations for Formula One, working towards the same ends. One carries the money, the other the contracts, so the saying goes (another says: one carries the gun, the other fires it). When Mosley defeated Balestre for the FISA presidency in 1991, the Ecclestone revolution was almost complete. Two years later, when FISA was dissolved into the FIA, and Mosley became president of the restructured organisation, the takeover was finished.

Max's New Deal

BY 1994, FORMULA ONE was heading for a crisis. Outrage over the deaths of drivers, serious questions raised about cheating, criticism that racecars were just computers on wheels: none of the teams seemed concerned about trying to disperse the gathering stormclouds. Bernie Ecclestone's plan to expand his global empire looked under threat. Step forward Max Mosley, president of Formula One's rule-making body, the Fédération Internationale de l'Automobile. A quiet, unassuming man, Mosley nevertheless carries a big stick. He demanded change. The teams didn't like it one bit. Tough luck. Mosley and Ecclestone are a formidable, if unlikely double-act – an educated gentleman and a grafter who clawed his way to the top. Perhaps what unites them is that they are both outsiders now working at the centre of what is a very establishment activity. Mosley is the son of Sir Oswald Mosley, leader of the British Union of Fascists in the 1930s, and Diana Mitford, both of whom were detained during the Second World War. Mosley junior studied physics at Christ Church, Oxford, where he was secretary of the Union. He then read for the bar, and practised as a barrister between 1964 and 1969, specialising in patent and copyright law. Ecclestone, as we have seen, was schooled at the university of hard knocks. Yet, they shared the same vision for Formula One. While Ecclestone concentrated on organising the racing teams, circuit owners and television stations, Mosley pursued a political path through motorsport's governing authority.

Although Mosley was destined for a legal career, his heart was with motor racing. He tried to make it as a driver, but like many racers he had the determination but not the talent. Unlike other racers, though, he spotted this early, and after crashing at the Nürburgring decided to give up any ambition for a life at the wheel. In 1969 Mosley was one of a foursome who co-founded the March team. This quartet included Robin Herd, a highly accomplished racing designer. The team failed to live up to its early promise, and in 1977 Mosley sold his stake in March to become FOCA's legal counsellor. Ecclestone was already the Formula One constructors' representative on what was then the key governing body FISA (Fédération Internationale du Sport Automobile), and Mosley joined him as deputy member of the executive committee between 1978 and 1983. From 1986 to 1991 Mosley sat on the FIA's Manufacturers' Commission. Mosley's stand against Jean-Marie Balestre for the presidency in 1991 was the first time the Frenchman's power had been challenged since ten years earlier, when another Englishman, Basil Tye, suffered a heavy defeat. The arrogant Balestre claimed to have forgotten that an election was pending, and only began campaigning a few weeks before the vote. Mosley, however, had been preparing for months. He plotted much of his campaign from the Tuscan villa of former Conservative government minister Lord Lambton during the summer of 1991. He worked tirelessly to win the support of motor-sport representatives in most of Asia, southern Africa, Central America, Scandinavia, the Middle East and the US. The traditional European clubs, meanwhile, mostly backed Balestre. This did not matter. Mosley deposed Balestre by 43 votes to 29. The clear-out of the old guard was not completed until the 1993 election for seats on the motor sports council. Five established representatives lost their places. At the same general assembly Mosley ran for president of the FIA, facing Jeffrey Rose, then chairman of the RAC and part of the old order. Mosley won, comfortably.

The presidency of the FIA is an unpaid job. Mosley survives – very well – on earnings from the family estate. But the position is an excellent launch pad to other things, in Mosley's case to a possible career in European politics. He has not been idle at the FIA. It took him a year to get his feet under the table, but after that he moved fast. His aims have been to improve safety, and to put some of the entertainment back into the sport that was lost with the proliferation of in-car computer aids. Public and political concern about racing's safety erupted in 1994, a traumatic year for the sport in which two drivers died – the first deaths for 12 years. Mosley's response was to plan a series of controversial rule changes. He maintained they were to preserve the integrity of the sport. His critics saw a hidden agenda: to preserve the sport as an acceptable medium for sponsors and ensure that Formula One remained attractive to television broadcasters. It was not long before the teams and some drivers rose up in opposition. Mosley had beaten Balestre on a platform promising consensus, not confrontation, yet he had little time for the warring egos and was uncompromising with those he thought were damaging Formula One.

Mosley nailed his colours to the mast in 1993, when he questioned the return to Formula One of the outspoken French driver, Alain Prost. Mosley asked Frank Williams to withdraw Prost's nomination for a super-licence to race. Mosley had been angered by Prost's criticisms, reported in the media, of his stewardship. The FIA president felt that criticism from one of Formula One's leading figures would damage the image of the sport. In a letter to Williams, Mosley wrote: 'I do not believe you or your sponsors can control him [Prost]. Indeed, I am sure you have clauses in your contract which cover this situation but have had no effect. And even if he cannot be quoted directly, he will probably find a way to poison the atmosphere just at the time we most need to improve it. He clearly thinks he should be running everything. He pontificates about things he does not understand and he describes the entire governing body in contemptuous and offensive terms. He even attacks Formula One for being too concerned with money when he has probably taken a bigger share than anyone. Can you think of anything more calculated to persuade the head of a major corporation not to take his company into Formula One than constant attacks and abuse from a triple world champion whom the public respect and admire? Don't forget sponsors and heads of companies, indeed all the decision-makers on whom we depend, read this stuff. And because he is a three-times world champion, they think he knows what he is talking about.'

Mosley had been worried by the growing use of computer gadgetry in Formula One. They had turned the sport into a race between machines rather than men. This was not good for television entertainment, and a turn-off for the sponsors. In 1993 the FIA took measures to eliminate the use of active suspension (a computer-controlled system to provide the optimum ride), traction control (to help grid starts) and other electronic devices. It was not just that these systems take a lot of the driver skill away, they also favoured the richer teams who alone had the money to spend on researching such devices. Mosley feared that Formula One, quite simply, was becoming predictable and boring. Even Walter Thoma, president of Philip Morris Europe, the company that has put more money into Formula One than any other, observed wryly: 'The message about world recession seems to have taken a great deal of time to penetrate the world of Formula One.'

A war of words between Mosley and the teams raged through 1993. Constructors had spent millions of pounds and hired the best engineers to come up with technological improvements, and now the FIA just wanted to ban them. Williams estimated that it had invested £13 million in the active suspension system that took Alain Prost to his fourth drivers' title in 1993. At McLaren, around £10 million was invested in active suspension. Mosley swept aside all the arguments, and added for good measure a ban on anti-lock brakes. Also refuelling during races was reintroduced, a determined – and ultimately successful – attempt to increase the spectacle in Formula One.

However, these controversies were nothing compared with what was to come. The public relations adage has it that 'all publicity is good publicity'. Certainly, some disturbing events in 1994 have had a lasting impact in heightening interest in Formula One around the world. But for many politicians, some sponsors, and for critics who detest Formula One's symbolic role in the car culture,[2] 1994 was a year of grave concern. The most serious incidents were the deaths of two drivers, Ayrton Senna and Roland Ratzenburger (Senna's fatal crash was a worldwide news story and the accident still resonates around Formula One), and a near fatal injury of a third, Karl Wendlinger. There were allegations of cheating by teams, and of compromising safety; a wheel flew off into the crowd; a mechanic was run over in the pit-lane; a Benetton car was engulfed in a ball of flames while being refuelled. It appeared as though the drive for success – which in Formula One means the drive to raise the sponsorship needed to fund research – had pushed teams to cut corners.

Politicians in several European countries began questioning whether Formula One should be banned. Officials wondered whether the FIA was really in control of its sport. After Senna's death at Imola in May 1994 even the Vatican, not for the first time, intervened. A papal statement said the race should have been stopped and cancelled. 'It went on despite everything, and death itself was made into a brutal spectacle, the spark of the sponsors prevailed over death silencing man.' In Italy, home of the historic Ferrari marque, 80 MPs signed a parliamentary motion that Formula One should be outlawed. With so much concern being voiced, it was not long before sponsors, the

---

[2] In a bizarre attempt to deflect the growing anti-F1 lobby, the FIA in 1997 launched a pilot scheme (costing £33,000) to offset the 440 tonnes of carbon each year caused by the sport. About 25,000 trees were planted in Chiapas, Mexico, which the FIA believes will neutralise this carbon.

companies that oil the wheels of Formula One, began to ask themselves whether they were using the correct marketing vehicle. Mosley recalled that the controversy was spinning out of control. 'Then the panic spread to the big car manufacturers, because they were coming under pressure from factions on their boards who were hostile to motorsport, which all the big manufacturers have. You had pictures of Karl Wendlinger sitting half-dead in his car, with Mercedes-Benz all over it. You knew that in Stuttgart there would be problems. And that was just one example.'

Ecclestone and Mosley's strategy to coalesce Formula One into a global television event was in deep trouble. The very legitimacy of the sport was being questioned. There was an urgent need to re-examine the rules. The task was to address the deep concern about safety, while keeping hold of the tens of millions of new fans who were tuning into the sport. It was no good trying to explain that all the incidents were unrelated; that they were just a series of deeply unfortunate coincidences. There was a perception that there was something rotten at the core of Formula One. Mosley ordered some immediate changes in safety procedures, and set in train a consultation process to tackle the escalating speeds being reached by racing cars. Some teams and drivers, cocooned in their world of racing, would subsequently accuse Mosley of over-reacting. But he understood the bigger picture. Politicians, especially in Brussels, wanted action. As Mosley put it, the task was to put out the fire in the house immediately, and then refine and adjust the remaining problems over time. A whole raft of measures was introduced. Engine capacity was reduced, and there were new rules on stronger chassis structures and more stringent mandatory crash tests. Circuits were altered to make some corners less dangerous. So-called 'black boxes', designed to record pre-crash data, were to be introduced, and there were to be limitations on brake technology. The two most controversial measures, drawn up for introduction in 1998, were the narrowing of cars by 10 per cent, and the introduction of grooved tyres.

Formula One will never be safe. However, it is possible, as Jackie Stewart often says, to manage risk. And that management is becoming all the more important now that the sensitivities of blue-chip companies and their shareholders are involved in Formula One in large number. And what about the planned flotation of Formula One? Just as the share price of a football club falls when it gets knocked out of a major competition, so the more accidents in Formula One, the more damaging to the share price. If sponsors and television broadcasters turn away from Formula One because it becomes too hot to handle,

Formula One Holdings will flop. Dead drivers are bad for business. It was not until Jackie Stewart began campaigning for improved safety when he was a driver in the late 1960s and '70s that the subject was taken at all seriously. There used to be no safety-belts, gravel traps, fire protection suits, or decent medical facilities. Stewart remembers that after one accident he was taken to the medical tent, where the only doctor was a gynaecologist. Circuit owners were reluctant to invest in better facilities because of the costs, and there was little pressure from the governing body to improve things. As for the cars, there was little crush protection built into them. There used to be a blasé attitude in the sport to grand prix deaths, probably because memories of the carnage of the Second World War were still fresh in peoples' minds. After all, were not racing drivers fighter pilots of the track? Now attitudes have completely changed. Society in the late twentieth century demands ever greater standards of safety in all walks of life. Given that sponsors, politicians and the public at large could not ignore Formula One's safety problems, how could Max Mosley?

Several of the racing teams, notably Williams and McLaren, regarded Mosley's rule changes as a knee-jerk reaction. The race bosses objected strongly to the introduction of treaded tyres and narrower racecars, both measures designed to slow vehicles and increase overtaking (though, on the evidence of the 1998 season, it has not worked). What concerned the teams was the wasted effort that had gone into developing technology that would now be redundant. For instance, a lot of aerodynamic data that the top constructors had built up over the years would become irrelevant under the new conditions. Drivers, too, complained bitterly that the changes would make driving less challenging. Jacques Villeneuve became the most vocal critic. His opinions carried significant weight, and not just because he was the favourite to win the world championship. Villeneuve's father, Gilles, died during practice for the 1982 Belgian Grand Prix at Zolder; he was the last driver to die in a Formula One race before the fateful weekend that killed Ratzenburger and Senna. Jacques knew about tragedy on the track. Nevertheless, his views on the changes were uncompromising. 'I think Formula One has gone a little overboard on safety,' he said. 'We are already twenty times safer than we were. If someone other than Ayrton had died, they wouldn't care so much.' He added: 'Because Ayrton Senna died, and it got a lot of people on the FIA's backs, it's not right to hurt yourself on TV any more.' These were blunt comments, but his views were shared by others too politically correct to say so in public.

As Mosley saw the changes as simply non-negotiable, it was only a matter of time before there was a showdown with Villeneuve. That came after Villeneuve was quoted – misquoted, according to the driver – in the German magazine *Der Spiegel* as calling the new rules 'ridiculous' and 'shit'. Villeneuve was hauled before the FIA's World Council just days before the 1997 Canadian Grand Prix to explain himself. He escaped with a reprimand, though the fact that the driver was called to Paris for the hearing when he should have been preparing for his home grand prix was seen by many as a very deliberate part of the punishment. Villeneuve had a miserable race, spinning off the track on his home turf. Mosley remains unrepentant. He told *F1 Racing* magazine: 'It's right and proper that he [Jacques] should say what he says, but it's equally right and proper that I should see that he goes out of the sport just as healthy as he came into it.' This effectively put paid to any further dissent over rewriting the safety rules. There was no point in further protest, because the FIA had no intention of changing its mind. Like it or lump it, it was the only deal on offer.

Mosley and Ecclestone win all the arguments because they hold all the aces. The teams and drivers, if left to their own devices, would squabble among themselves, resulting in the undoing of every attempt to consolidate and give uniformity to the Formula One series. But what if a rival promoter – say, for argument's sake, boxing's Don King, Virgin boss Richard Branson, or Mark McCormack's International Management Group – decided to establish a rival series? Mosley and Ecclestone sought to head off a split by locking teams into long-term agreements. The Concorde Agreement was up for renegotiation, and this was Mosley's first real chance for a root-and-branch revision of the rules governing Formula One. Under the new terms, to cover Formula One from 1997 to 2001, all the teams had to sign a five-year agreement to take part in every race. It guaranteed the television companies a full grid of 20 or more cars, including the big names, regardless of whether the teams changed hands. Teams would be unable to take part in other single-seater series (IndyCars, for example) without permission. Only by signing the agreement would the constructors be able to share a slice of Formula One's income. Three teams, Williams, McLaren and Tyrrell, refused to sign the new agreement, instantly depriving themselves of millions of pounds in television revenues. Tyrrell's refusal indicated the seriousness of the issue, as the team is one of the sport's also-rans and could ill afford to lose the money.

The Concorde Agreement gives teams 47 per cent of the TV revenues collected by Ecclestone. These earnings have been around $160 million, giving the seven teams that signed Concorde an annual income of $22 million. With TV income set to rise over the next few years, analysts predict the teams could be earning as much as $70 million a year. So what was it that so upset the dissenting teams that they effectively threw away the chance of earning some easy money? Linked to the new Concorde Agreement were plans to give Ecclestone greater control over exploiting the commercial rights to Formula One. In particular, the FIA extended broadcasting rights to 25 years, arguing that it gave the FIA stability with a long-term commercial partner, Bernie Ecclestone. For Ecclestone, it meant he got the stability he needed to invest heavily in the digital television technology that he thinks will generate huge revenues from pay-per-view. The Concorde Agreement is a somewhat archaic document, and there is no doubt that it needed updating for the new commercial era. But the dissenting teams feared an increasing erosion of their power. According to one of the negotiators, the teams felt Mosley's deal with Ecclestone was done behind their backs. The team bosses wanted more say, not less, in who the FIA struck commercial deals with in the future. And they wanted more say, not less, in the way they exploited their own businesses. McLaren's Ron Dennis felt particularly strongly that the teams should be more involved in the management and ownership of Formula One. For years, the teams had seemed unaware of the money to be made from exploiting their brand names. Now they could see how much money Formula One was generating, they resisted any attempt to hand over more power to Ecclestone.

Even those teams that had endorsed the revised Concorde Agreement began to wonder if they might have mistakenly short-changed themselves. The clash of egos, the gnashing of teeth, could be heard at every grand prix during 1997. And all this was happening, as we will see in more detail in the next section, at the time Bernie Ecclestone was trying to get the flotation of Formula One off the ground. 'The teams can go to hell,' said Ecclestone. 'Some of them think they have me by the balls, but their hands aren't big enough.' There was claim and counter-claim. Had one of the signatories only signed a single page of the document, rather than all of it? Had all the relevant pages outlining the increased power for Ecclestone been shown to everyone? Despite months of talks, had Ron Dennis really sent a letter to the FIA asking for 100 points of clarification about the Concorde? The answers are either yes or no depending who you talk to. What everyone agrees on, however, is that it was frustrating and time-consuming. Mosley considered tearing up the whole Concorde Agreement and starting a new book of rules setting out technical and financial controls.

At the heart of the dispute were two issues: who was responsible for Formula One's success, and could anyone actually own the sport. Mosley believes the dissident teams are guilty of a fundamental misconception – that Ecclestone's business interests somehow belonged to them. For Mosley and Ecclestone, the teams are performers, and that is what they get paid for. The commercial side is the responsibility of the rule-makers; the performers are just there to play by the rules, like tennis players or cricketers. In a letter to Ken Tyrrell, Mosley explained: 'One does not come to own a restaurant by eating in it each day or a theatre by appearing in it nightly. One does not even acquire shares. The same is true of the FIA F1 World Championship. Such rights can change hands, whether permanently or temporarily, only by the agreement of the parties who own them.'

Ecclestone once described Formula One before commercialism set in as 'a group of people having fun, with a bit of commercial side to it'. He admits that money matters have taken a lot of fun out of the sport. But it is now safer, more popular, richer and can look forward to the sort of future that no team owner ever dreamed of just a few years ago. Through a mixture of ruthlessness and charm, Ecclestone and Mosley have transformed Formula One. But the changes are not over. The plans for a flotation will continue their revolution.

Formula One Goes Public

FORMULA ONE'S WORST-KEPT secret went public in March 1997. Bernie Ecclestone was planning to float the sport's commercial interests on the stock market. It unleashed a feeding frenzy of activity by financial journalists normally fed on a diet of much drier stories. What became one of the hottest new stories of the year was well known in Formula One circles. Major sponsors were already aware of the plans, and in 1996 Max Mosley had said a flotation was a 'probability'. Formula One's rulebook – the Concorde Agreement – was being revised with a public share offering in mind. Still, when the plans were made official there was an outburst of publicity unheard-of for such a financial story. Why? Because Formula One is a unique operation, able to grab the attention of fan and non-fan alike. The combination of speed, power, sex and danger is an intoxicating mixture. To this quartet Ecclestone was now adding a fifth element: money. Everyone had known, of course, that Formula One was a rich man's sport. What they did not know, however, was just how rich. In order to turn his private businesses into a listed company, Ecclestone would have to do something he had not done before – reveal something of the enormous wealth generated by the sport. Going public, though, opened a Pandora's box of problems, and it was not long before the plans were mired in controversy.

Ecclestone's intention was to package his disparate Formula One interests into a new company, Formula One Holdings (FOH) and float it on the London (and possibly Frankfurt or New York) stock exchange. He hired the Wall Street investment bank Salomon Brothers as his financial adviser and co-ordinator of the float. FOH's main asset is a contract with the FIA to handle the commercial affairs of the Formula One world championship. The company negotiates with the circuit owners, supplies pay-per-view television broadcasts and takes a cut of profits from merchandising. It also exploits the Formula One brand name, through projects such as Sylvester Stallone's forthcoming grand prix film, or potentially via diversifications, such as themed restaurants. However, FOH's most lucrative business is the sale of Formula One broadcasting rights to the world's television stations. It is a big money-spinner. In 1997, FOH earned about £200 million, and made operating profits of £85 million. Of this, 47 per cent is divided between the racing teams, whilst the FIA is paid a large, though undisclosed, flat fee.

It was the fact that Ecclestone would have to come out of the shadows and shine some light on Formula One's finances that made the flotation so appetising. Part of the man's strength came from the secrecy surrounding his affairs. Yet, the more that details of the flotation were brought out into the open, the more people with vested interests stood back to ponder the consequences. Occasionally, fascinating titbits leaked, enabling outsiders to build up a picture of Ecclestone's operation. For instance, the bulk of Formula One's commercial interests were tied up in offshore family trusts, owned by a Jersey-based company of which Mr Ecclestone's wife, Slavica, owned 80 per cent. (Not that there is anything sinister about this. Presumably, it was simply a normal estate planning exercise to distance Ecclestone from inheritance taxes. Even so, it was still something of a revelation to learn that the bulk of the racing business was ultimately owned by a 6ft 2in former Armani model from Croatia.) Ecclestone had spent years positioning Formula One where he wanted it. He had almost total control, and had quietly turned himself into a multi-millionaire while avoiding the public gaze. Now he was planning to subject himself and Formula One to the scrutiny of financial journalists, analysts, shareholders, and stock exchange regulators. Nicky Samengo-Turner, a City of London investment banker and a Formula One corporate financier, believes the culture shock will weigh heavily on Ecclestone. 'His way of doing business does not sit comfortably with the demands of a stock market listing,' said Samengo-Turner. 'For Ecclestone, a handshake and a promise are as important as a lengthy contract drawn up by lawyers. A short fax message, or a quiet word in the paddock, is preferable to the endless rounds of meetings required when running a public company with shareholders to look after.'

Ecclestone is a natural entrepreneur, and life in the Square Mile is often too restrictive for such men. Other entrepreneurs have tried the stock market route, and found the culture stultifying. Richard Branson floated his travel and music group Virgin, but bought it back because the City cramped his style. It is the job of merchant bankers, stockbrokers and lawyers to be overly concerned with process. This is anathema to Ecclestone. So, why did he want to take his company public? A simple human reason is that at the age of 66, Ecclestone had to start thinking about his retirement or death. He has one daughter from a first marriage, and two from his second. A flotation would realise some of the inherent value of the company in the form of shares, which would then go into trusts and secure the family's financial future. In one of Ecclestone's typically straight-to-the-point remarks, he explained how to be a success in Formula One: 'First get in, then get rich, then get respectable.' He has quite obviously achieved the first two. A flotation could bestow the third – putting the organisation on a more conventional footing and tying up the loose ends before he dies.

Another reason to float was the timing. The value of television rights to sporting events was soaring, as shown by ITV's willingness to pay £65 million for Formula One – ten times what the BBC had been paying. Broadcasters such as BSkyB and Kirch Group have made the acquisition to sports rights the key to building their media empires. Ownership of rights to screen football, boxing or cricket events has become the battleground between terrestrial and satellite companies. For Ecclestone, it made sense to float before the bubble burst. The final reason for floating was that Formula One had grown too big for one man to control. Business history is littered with cases where companies have lost their way because an autocratic leader failed to resolve the issue of succession. Everyone, Ecclestone included, thought it was time to impose a more professional management structure on the company. The demands of being a public company with outside shareholders would, in any case, require a more formal system of control. Ecclestone planned to stay as chief executive, but surround himself with an impressive team of executives. These included bringing in Helmut Werner, the former Mercedes boss, as non-executive chairman. Werner had quit the Mercedes car group in January 1997 after losing an internal fight to prevent the company being demerged from its parent, Daimler-Benz. The big tobacco battalions were given a say on the board with the appointment of Walter Thoma, former head of European business at Philip Morris, as a director. No Formula One board would be complete without some link with Ferrari. This went to Marco Piccinini, Ferrari's former team manager, who became the deputy chief executive. The board line-up was completed by David Wilson, a former senior executive at the Ladbroke group, and Robert Rowley, from Reuters.

Salomon Brothers and this management team first had to decide how much FOH was worth. That done, they could then decide how many millions of shares to issue and at what price they would be sold. Set the share price too high, and no one would buy them, and the flotation would be an embarrassing flop. Set it too low, and Ecclestone would not get as much for his company as it was worth. A problem was that there was no equivalent company on any stock market to compare with FOH. The nearest examples were media companies, because FOH's value would be based largely on revenues from broadcasting contracts. Analysts in the City of London were at first steered towards a potential value of between £2.5 billion and £3 billion, but this figure was quickly scaled down. A series of rows that swirled around Formula One did little to inspire investor confidence, and by the end of 1997 forecasts put the value of FOH at no more than about £1.5 billion.

Even so, this was still a tidy sum for those sharing in the flotation. Under the original plan, the basic deal worked on by Salomon was as follows: FOH's contract with the FIA to exploit the sport's commercial interests would be extended. The contract currently runs until 2010, but as part of the flotation it would be extended by another ten years. In return for the extension, the FIA, a non-profit-making organisation, would get 10 per cent of the shares in a floated company. It had still to be resolved whether the teams would be offered about 10 per cent, and whether these shares would be free. Ecclestone would retain a 30 per cent stake, and the remaining 50 per cent would be sold to members of the public and financial institutions, such as pension funds and insurance companies. The flotation was pencilled in for July 1997, to coincide with the British Grand Prix at Silverstone. This date turned out to be hopelessly optimistic. The flotation blew up in Salomon's face, and the whole timetable had to be revised. Salomon's handling of the project was subject to a sneering whispering campaign. The ability of the firm to handle such a big project was being questioned. After the initial rush of positive publicity about the flotation, deep scepticism began to destabilise the plans. Previously the financial community's confidence and enthusiasm had been high, but now Ecclestone had lost that early momentum.

Crucial to the valuation was how much FOH would earn from pay-per-view receipts from fans buying into Ecclestone's digital broadcasts. Digital television offers viewers the chance to switch between several channels showing different parts of the action. Depending on whom you believed, digital was either the future of Formula One broadcasting, or a minority interest for die-hard anoraks. The more conservative analysts put PPV revenues at around £60 million by the year 2004, rising to £125 million-plus in 2005, by which time total television revenues were forecast to exceed £400m a year. Because the television market is so competitive, the rights to top sporting events are likely to hold their value whatever the success of PPV. But with so many variables to consider, the City of London's initial enthusiasm began to wane. A view emerged that an organisation like Formula One did not really have a place on a stock market in the first place. After all, FOH owned no factories, no racetracks, no cars. There would be products from merchandising and from exploiting the brand name, but FOH owned no tangible assets to speak of – just broadcasting signals beamed from racetracks around the world.

What made these broadcasting signals so valuable, however, was that they gave television companies access to a valuable asset – the millions of (mostly) young and middle-aged men who watch Formula One. Advertisers are willing to pay highly to get their products screened to this high-spending sector of the population. What is more, Formula One is in a unique position when it comes to advertising. In today's digital age, broadcasters can offer a multitude of channels. The problem for advertisers is that these channels segregate and divide the viewing audience. The number of events that attract mass audiences are declining. Formula One, however, offers companies the chance to cut through the barrage of channels, and hit a global customer market in one sitting.

Dismissing FOH's flotation just because it does not manufacture a product is, then, invalidated by the fact that Formula One has the potential to be a highly lucrative and growing company for its shareholders. The economist Hamish McRae suggests that investors should not worry about buying shares in 'weightless' businesses like Formula One. These are the successful businesses of the future. And Formula One, he argues, 'is the ultimate global weightless business, a business where the product can be reduced to a string of digital computer signals, flashed around the world. This is the future – in the sense that international trade will increasingly be in intangibles. The idea that firms whose main value is in royalties or rights should be traded on the stock market is not at all new. Much of value of pharmaceutical companies lies in their patents, and once key patents expire the companies have to hope they have other winners in the pipeline. Much of the value of publishers is in their backlist rather than in new titles. But

Formula One is perhaps the most extreme example of value lying just in an idea.' The nature of economic competition in the late twentieth century makes it difficult for countries to gain an advantage, because technology crosses boundaries so fast. (Take the example of Formula One: a constructor's innovation quickly spreads to rival teams.) In the future, McRae believes, economic advantage will come not so much from a country's ability to make things, as from the ability to generate ideas that can then be sold to the world. 'It means that originality, flair and entrepreneurship will be increasingly prized,' he says. Ecclestone has proved that he has these qualities in abundance.

The theory is sound, but in practice the flotation of Formula One became a minefield. Salomon was dogged by difficulties from the moment it started work on the project. The first hurdle concerned the amount of information to be disclosed in the Formula One prospectus. This is the document that goes out to potential investors when the shares are first marketed. It contains forecasts about a company's profits and performance, helping investors to judge whether buying shares in it represents value for money. Regulators at the London Stock Exchange required a fair degree of transparency in the FOH prospectus, especially as Formula One was a unique flotation. But the draft prospectus prepared by Salomon immediately ran into problems over just how much detail should be included about the commercially sensitive TV contracts. Several stockbroking analysts, whose research advises clients about the investment potential of companies, complained about the shortage of financial and contractual information. 'How the hell can we express an opinion when there is so little to go on?' was a remark that summed up the view of most media analysts. The acrimony burst into the open after Salomon invited a select group of institutional investors to attend Formula One events to see Ecclestone's television broadcasting unit and 'experience' the atmosphere of a grand prix. The problem was that it only heightened the intense envy felt by financiers kept out of the group and encouraged 'outsiders' to talk down and speculate about the flotation's likely success.

Then, the size of revenues earned from Ecclestone's much-vaunted digital broadcasting was called into question. The reason was that, in Germany, an experiment in pay-per-view Formula One shown on the DF1 station, owned by the media tycoon Leo Kirch, ran into problems. Only 30,000 viewers had subscribed to the service, and fewer than 10,000 were watching grand prix racing. Launched in late 1996, the station was reported to be losing £7 million a week. And in France, by the autumn of 1997, only 30,000 of Canal Plus's 500,000 digital satellite subscribers had signed up for Formula One. As a foretaste of the digital future on which FOH's revenues were based, it did not bode well. David Wilson, FOH's finance director, dismissed all this as mere teething troubles. 'There isn't anybody who thinks pay-TV won't happen,' he said confidently in May 1997. But this was not the point. That pay-per-view would happen was never in doubt. What concerned potential investors, trying to gauge whether FOH was a good bet, was how many people would pay for the service.

The following month, in June 1997, a more serious challenge emerged. Wolfgang Eisele, whose television company had screened FIA-sanctioned European truck racing, took the FIA to court when he lost the contract. He claimed the FIA's monopoly of television rights was an abuse of competition law under the Treaty of Rome, and a Frankfurt district court ruled that he had a case. Eisele's interim injunction against the FIA was eventually thrown out by a higher court, but the issue had serious knock-on effects for Formula One. The European Commission launched an investigation into the FIA–Ecclestone deal over broadcasting Formula One in Europe. Karel van Miert, the EC Competition Commissioner, did not like what he found. As a rule-of-thumb, competition lawyers regard exclusive contracts of more than five years, as long. Therefore, a contract lasting until 2010 (and possibly to be extended further) could be regarded as excessively so. Any suggestion that Ecclestone's licence to sell broadcasting rights might be illegal was clearly going to be damaging to a company whose profits come mainly from television. Van Miert did not mince his words. He believed the way Formula One is run to be an abuse of its 'dominant and monopoly position'. The flotation plan looked like sinking into a sea of red tape. The list of concerns van Miert wanted to look at was long, including: the ban on owners of circuits organising contests not approved by the FIA; forcing circuit owners to hand over broadcasting rights; obliging broadcasters who want to screen IndyCar racing to pay more for screening Formula One. 'At the moment,' said van Miert, 'the whole set-up is layer upon layer of exclusive deals amounting to cartel behaviour added to abuse of dominant position for the benefit of one company.' Tough stuff, and an indication that the issue was not going to be resolved by a quick chat and a handshake in Ecclestone's motorhome.

Meanwhile, back in London, problems for Salomon Brothers were mounting. Rivalry to become the global financial co-ordinator of the flotation had been intense. Each of the contenders spent millions of pounds preparing to impress Ecclestone with their beauty parades. Having won the contract, Salomon would recoup the money several times over, and be guaranteed huge media coverage. However the global marketing of a flotation is not handled by only one firm, and as is normal practice Salomon brought in a syndicate of other banks to help. It is a complicated business. The syndicate allows the world to be divided up geographically, with certain investment banks given areas to cover that suit their own nationality and therefore 'placing power' strengths. Also, global co-ordinators and lead managers bring in other finance houses on a back-scratching basis, in the hope of being invited into future syndicates. The banking syndicate for Formula One included: Morgan Stanley, Deutsche Morgan Grenfell, SBC Warburg, Merrill Lynch, NatWest Markets, BZW and Nikko. All could expect to earn between $1 and $5 million in fees. Being left off the syndicate, therefore, was bad news. Among the firms that were excluded from Salomon's banking syndicate was an arch rival, the Wall Street giant Goldman Sachs. This snub to Goldman Sachs, real or perceived, dogged the flotation plans throughout the summer.

In July 1997 it emerged that BZW, one of the syndicate banks, together with Goldman Sachs, were secretly advising on a rival deal involving Formula One Holdings. BSkyB, 40 per cent owned by Rupert Murdoch, was considering taking a major stake in FOH. Sam Chisholm, chief executive of BSkyB, is a friend of both Ecclestone and John Thornton, one of Goldman's most senior executives and a main board director of the Ford Motor Company. On the agenda was whether BSkyB should buy a tranche of FOH in return for the right to show pay-per-view Formula One races on its satellite digital station to be launched in 1998. News of this other deal was a major embarrassment for Salomon's Christian Purslow, the man who was responsible for getting the flotation under way. Not only was one of the syndicate banks, BZW, going behind his back; the firm was working alongside one of Salomon's adversaries, Goldman Sachs, who had a vested interest in undermining the float.

Purslow's temper began to fray. He accused BZW of 'very un-blue-chip behaviour', a rather pompous way of saying that one of London's established investment banks was breaching confidences. The Cambridge University and Harvard-educated Purslow told BZW to stop advising on the rival plan or leave the syndicate. His fear was that a lot of privileged information accessible to BZW could be passed to a third party, notably Goldman Sachs. At a tense meeting on 15 July, Peter

Middleton, chief executive of European Operations at Salomon, and his namesake Sir Peter Middleton, BZW chairman, met to thrash out their differences. Salomon demanded assurances that no confidential details had been passed on. According to one of Purslow's office colleagues: 'Christian wanted blood on the carpet. But in the end it was settled in a very British way, with a handshake. The assurances about not passing information to third parties were given by BZW, but a sour taste remained.'

Amazingly, there was yet another advisory deal going on being put together behind Purslow's back. What he did not know was that at the same time as the BZW affair, another bank in his syndicate, SBC Warburg, was carrying out advisory work for Ecclestone. Salomon was supposed to be Ecclestone's exclusive financial adviser. Yet, Warburg was working on an unspecified 'exercise' for Ecclestone and the FIA. In fact, this was a specific look at the true value of the television rights and the position of the FIA as legal title holder to the Formula One name. Salomon's credibility appeared irreparably damaged as far as the flotation was concerned. The message seemed to be that all bets were off; that Ecclestone was considering a range of other options. Suddenly everyone seemed to want a piece of Formula One. There was talk that Joe Lewis, the secretive billionaire owner of Glasgow Rangers and Vicenza football clubs, was set to do a private deal with FOH through his English National Investment Company. In Italy it was reported that Fiat, owner of Ferrari, was to take a major stake, a story which owner Gianni Agnelli, Fiat's controlling father figure, described as 'bullshit'. Investors in America and the Far East were touted as potential partners for Ecclestone. Executives from Bankers Trust met with Ecclestone at the British Grand Prix in 1997 in the hope of doing a deal. The whirlwind of negotiation and speculation – some of which was simply malicious gossip – was severely detrimental to City confidence in the flotation. Ecclestone admitted that he seriously considered calling it off. His frustration with the City exploded in anger: 'All these people want to do is have bloody meetings with everybody. Most of the ethics of a car dealer are probably a lot higher than the way these people operate.' As a former car dealer, Ecclestone should know.

It was obvious for weeks that the flotation would not meet its July timetable. Alternative dates in the autumn or in early 1998 were pencilled in, though these looked equally optimistic (and turned out to be so). Bernie Ecclestone had made few public comments on the flotation but on 23 July the lawyer acting for his family trusts was forced to clarify the situation: 'My client has asked me to make it clear that Salomon Brothers are the shareholders' exclusive financial adviser and any proposals put forward will be put forward by Salomon Brothers. An initial public offering is my client's preferred course of action and progress is being made on preparing the company for flotation. No decision has ever been made with respect to timing.' If Ecclestone hoped this would put a lid on speculation about the float, however, he was wrong. There were still formidable obstacles ahead.

One of the biggest hurdles was one that received least public attention. Ecclestone and three Formula One teams were head-to-head in opposition over the future direction of the sport. As we saw in the last section of this chapter, two of the most important teams on the grid, Williams and McLaren, and one of the oldest, Tyrrell, refused to sign the Concorde Agreement. The finishing touches to the Concorde Agreement should have been agreed at a FOCA meeting on 6 June 1997. They were there to decide whether the teams would share in a floated company, and in any increase in revenues from television and the prize fund. Ecclestone stormed out of this meeting after just five minutes. 'It was a bear pit,' recalls one of the participants. 'We were never going to agree on anything.' Until an agreement was reached, the flotation was never going to go ahead, whatever Ecclestone might have said in public. Journalist Alan Henry, one of the sharpest observers of Formula One politics, hit the nail on the head: 'I fear all this will make the FOCA/FISA wars of the early eighties look like a prayer meeting. So fasten your seat-belts and hang on tight.'

It was not that the teams were against turning Formula One into a public company. As Frank Williams, one of the dissidents, said: 'It would be good for our business, and for all the teams. The sport is growing and, as times move on, things need to change.' But the constructors did not want to accept a deal at any price – and certainly not at the price Ecclestone was offering. At the heart of the division were differences over who really owned Formula One. Ecclestone regards the teams as actors in a show that he controls. The teams view their position slightly differently. 'The show cannot go on without the actors,' said Williams. 'We are partners.' Until this point, the teams had represented themselves, negotiating individually to secure a better deal out of the flotation. Notoriously difficult to unite, the constructors had always looked to Ecclestone to settle their differences. But eventually the three dissenters, in league with their lawyers, brought in their own financial advisers. The appointment of the heavyweight Anglo-

German bank Dresdner Kleinwort Benson to advise on the issues and implications relating to the Concorde Agreement was bad news for Ecclestone and Salomon. The constructors meant business. They were intent on fighting for better terms.

McLaren's Ron Dennis believes that, for the first time, the teams realised the importance and power of unity. He would not name names, but it was clear he had Ecclestone and Mosley in mind when he said: 'The current management tends to successfully divide and rule. The competitiveness that is inherent in the teams for racing, very much works against them when they are pitched against each other in other matters. A flotation may help the teams come together in a more constructive way that allows them to understand and feel secure about their future.' In other words: don't let competition on the track divide us off it. Unity is strength. The teams wanted a free stake in Formula One – of up to 20 per cent – and a larger slice of television revenues. Formula One's supremo was having none of it. As he was taking all the risks, Ecclestone argued, he did not owe the teams anything more. More power for the teams, with their warring egos, would destroy all he had built over 30 years, Ecclestone said. 'They [the teams] can't agree on anything, not even on how to share their money out. They think they can run the business – I know they can't.' Rumours circulated that Formula One would divide into rival championships, as American racing had done. The likelihood of a split was grossly exaggerated, but for potential City investors, unclear about the finer points of Formula One, the damage to the flotation was done.

By the autumn of 1997 Ecclestone and Salomon were fighting a rearguard action to keep the flotation plans on an even keel. The bickering and legal battles were destroying the value of the company. Even some sponsors began to voice concern. Shell, the oil company and one of Formula One's biggest backers, was concerned about not being consulted. An executive, referring to Ecclestone's 'theatre' and 'actors' metaphor, said: 'The actors in the show are going to get a piece of the action. But the sponsors, who pay the salaries of the actors, seem to have been excluded from any dialogue. Given that the financial projections are critical to the evaluation of Formula One, it is interesting that Salomon Brothers have nothing to say to the sponsors and the impact it is going to have on them. We could, after all, change our minds as to whether this was still the right event to be sponsoring.' For Henderson, an investment company that sponsors the Williams team, all the talk about flotation was a distraction from the sport.

Lyndsay Firth-McGuckin, the firms marketing head, said: 'The sponsors were more interested in where Formula One was going as a sport than Bernie Ecclestone was in us as sponsors. Our concern is to make sure the sport retains its kudos, and that the viewing figures remain high.'

There were times when it seemed difficult to imagine things getting any worse. For years, the internal affairs of Formula One had been kept under wraps. Ecclestone took his cut, so did the FIA and the teams, and all the hangers-on. Now Formula One was public property. The plans for the flotation had made it so. What Ecclestone needed was a few months' peace in which investor confidence could be rebuilt. But the genie was not going back in the bottle. In November 1997, the biggest furore of Ecclestone's life erupted. It started when prime minister Tony Blair, personally intervened to exempt Formula One from a proposed ban on tobacco sponsorship. This was just a few months after his health secretary, Frank Dobson, had promised there would be no exemptions. And the Labour Party's own general election manifesto had been categorical: 'Smoking is the greatest single cause of preventable illness and premature death in the UK. We will, therefore, ban tobacco advertising.' Although there is a difference between advertising and sponsorship, such subtleties were not the issue here. So, Labour's U-turn looked suspicious, and the further one looks into this, the easier it is to see why.

Tessa Jowell, a junior health minister in Dobson's department, was given the job of explaining away the change of heart. She had played a central role in drawing up the government's proposals on tobacco sponsorship. Jowell just happens to be married to David Mills, a former non-executive director of the Benetton team and a millionaire solicitor whose clients included Silvio Berlusconi, one of Italy's richest businessmen. There is no evidence that Jowell was acting on behalf of vested interests; she was given official clearance by her civil service chief to continue her work; and Mills resigned from Benetton on 20 May 1997, shortly after Labour won the general election, because he wanted to avoid a potential conflict of interest. There were, however, some very alarmist claims made about the consequences for Formula One if a cigarette advertising ban was imposed. Benetton's Flavio Briatore, Eddie Jordan and Ecclestone spoke of thousands of UK job losses and the shift of Formula One to Asia, where interest in the sport was booming. These claims, dealt with in more detail later in this book, seemed to have been swallowed wholesale by the government. There was an outpouring of anger from the representatives of other sports, who felt Blair had been got at by people closer to the centre of power than they.

Ecclestone and the FIA were certainly accorded some high-level access to lobby their case. Tony Blair, who with his family was an official guest at the 1996 British Grand Prix, had become a fan of the sport. Mosley and Ecclestone were able to have a more private meeting with the prime minister at 10 Downing Street on 10 October 1997. It was at this meeting that Blair appears to have been persuaded that Formula One should not be bound by the tobacco ban. The introductions were made by a man called David Ward, director-general of the FIA but one-time chief researcher for the former Labour Party leader John Smith. He also set up meetings with other ministers. Other sporting bodies dependent on tobacco, such as the British Darts Organisation, say they were only given access to government officials, not ministers.

However, what really concerned the conspiracy theorists was that Ecclestone had given £1 million to the Labour Party in January 1997. He had also, in the past given the Conservative Party up to £8 million over several years. Both Blair and Ecclestone tried to fight off claims that this had been an attempt to buy influence. As the row intensified, the Labour Party actually returned the £1 million to Ecclestone, who then tried to persuade the head of the public standards watchdog, Lord Neill, to let the party take it back. For a man who had just paid an annual personal tax bill of £27 million, another £1 million did not matter to Ecclestone. But he insisted that it was his right to make the donation. 'Anything less implies that I have done something wrong and is a gross, insulting and irrational restriction of my freedom,' Ecclestone told him.

Unluckily for Ecclestone, it was a time when British politics was going through one of its periodic bouts of moral panic. The word 'sleaze' had entered the political vocabulary, becoming a byword for politicians on the make or with their noses in the trough. Lord Neill had set up an inquiry into party political funding, and asked Ecclestone to give evidence to better understand the reasons why businessmen make large donations to parties. Not surprisingly, the publicity-shy Ecclestone declined the invitation and Lord Neill had no powers to force him to give evidence. However, it has emerged that Ecclestone did send a three-page letter to Lord Neill, which revealed that the £1 million pledged to the Labour Party was because Tony Blair had promised not to raise top rate of taxation. In the letter, Ecclestone's most comprehensive response to the row that engulfed him, he denies he ever sought to buy influence, and said the affair was damaging his reputation. He also dismisses ideas that he personally would have been harmed by a ban on tobacco sponsorship. A ban, Ecclestone said, would increase his revenues from television income. 'Perhaps the greatest irony of this affair is that I stood to gain substantially from an outright ban on tobacco sponsorship,' wrote the Formula One boss. 'Since I share the TV income with teams and my costs would have increased only modestly even with a huge take-up in demand, I personally would have gained substantially from an immediate ban on tobacco sponsorship. If I was concerned with my own self-interest, I should have encouraged the British government to ban tobacco sponsorship on the shortest possible timescale.' He goes on: 'I would like to emphasise that prior to my donation, Tony Blair, then Leader of the Opposition, was encountering some opposition from within the Labour movement for his decision to retain a top rate of personal income tax at 40 per cent. Others apparently supported increasing it to 50 per cent or perhaps to the 60 per cent level that existed before 1988. I strongly welcomed Mr Blair's stand on this issue which was clearly unpopular with some of his party. As a substantial contributor to the Inland Revenue, I clearly have benefited from his decision. However, my contribution was made after the policy was decided by Mr Blair. I made my donation because I was impressed with Mr Blair's leadership of the Labour Party, and I wanted to reinforce his independence in a party substantially dependent on finance from trade unions.' Ecclestone clearly resents Lord Neill telling the Labour Party to return the 'entirely lawful' £1 million donation because it suggested there was something wrong in giving money. 'This is a problem as far as UK public opinion is concerned but it is a far more serious matter for my reputation overseas, where I conduct 90 per cent of my business. News coverage abroad is frequently reduced to the assertion that I attempted to bribe the British government not to ban tobacco advertising in Formula One.'

The flotation of Formula One is not dependent upon tobacco money continuing to flow into the sport. Cigarette sponsorship is most important to the teams, which will eventually find alternative sources of funds to keep the wheels turning. But the damage done by this tobacco row should not be underestimated. It destroyed a lot of favourable sentiment towards Formula One. In the financial community, largely ignorant of Formula One, any criticism or whiff of scandal, no matter how unjustified, will cause investors to panic. Nicky Samengo-Turner watched the flotation saga unfold with a mixture of amusement, amazement and frustration. 'I've never known a flotation to be handled so badly. There were problems at every turn. It was like trying to plug holes springing up in a bucket of water: once you stop one leak, another spurts out elsewhere. It was ludicrous to think that you could take an operation like Formula One, which had for years been run by word-of-mouth and a few arcane contracts, and turn it into a listed company within months. Each time there was a bit of bad publicity, Salomon Brothers had to do another round of meetings with potential investors to win back the hearts and minds.' For the moment, the flotation is dead. Ecclestone's best bet may now be to go for a trade sale. Samengo-Turner has his own idea: that the teams incorporate into a new company, and raise enough funds in the City to buy out Ecclestone. Easier said than done, though surely not beyond the wit of a team of corporate financiers and lawyers. The one sticking-point, of course, is Ecclestone himself. He has made clear his belief that the constructors could not run a bath, let alone Formula One. As we are about to see, the teams are a disparate bunch.

Chapter Three: ITALIAN STYLE

Introduction

IN THE NEXT two chapters we look at the constructors, their transformation from sports organisations into profitable businesses, and their role in raising Formula One's popularity. Modern grand prix racing is dominated by the Italians and the British. The former, especially, have always brought a special quality to Formula One. Motorsport's origins owe much to France, important advances in engineering were made in Germany, and Britain is the economic home of Formula One. But the Italian connection is of critical importance for the sport's image as rich and provocative. The essence of grand prix – those qualities that generate interest and therefore money – are glamour and excitement, and Italian racing has these in abundance. The circuit at Monza, host to the Italian Grand Prix since 1950 (except in 1980 when it was held at Imola), is the spiritual home of motor racing. Always a place of dramatic atmosphere, with its long straights and fast corners Monza has been the scene of some of the most memorable races. Hero-worship in Formula One normally revolves around an individual, but in Italy it is the car. Alfa Romeo and Maserati may have gone by the wayside as Formula One contenders, but Ferrari remains king of the track for tens of millions of fans. More recently Ferrari has been joined by another Italian outfit, Benetton. Formerly run by the buccaneering Flavio Briatore, Benetton sensationalised and scandalised motor racing. The adage 'all publicity is good publicity' could have been coined for Briatore. His antics received massive media coverage, thus generating greater and valuable public interest in the sport. Maybe it is traditional British reserve, or the fact that the racing heritage is not as ingrained, but even all-conquering English teams such as McLaren and Williams have never sparked the same sort of passion. As we will see later, during the 1980s and '90s the British team owners injected a new professionalism into Formula One. Essential though this was, they also brought a certain 'greyness' to the sport. Ferrari, and then Benetton, ensured that the colour remained. Another feature which distinguishes these two from the UK teams is that they do not just promote their sponsors, they also promote their parent companies. Ferrari's racing division is a marketing arm for the road cars; Benetton advertises its owner, the international clothing company, Benetton Group. Most other teams exist very much as a medium for sponsorship only, although this will change as teams like McLaren and Williams diversify and establish their brand names in other activities.

Ferrari: F1's Elder Statesman

FERRARI IS A symbol, an aspiration and a business. It is the interplay between these three that makes the team so important to Formula One. Sponsors trade off the image of Formula One, and Formula One trades off the image of Ferrari: speed, risk, sex, money. New York's Museum of Modern Art exhibits the Ferrari 641 driven by Alain Prost in the 1990 world championship, evidence surely that Formula One has crossed into popular culture. No other team's racing car could possibly evoke the spirit of Formula One. There is a mystique about Ferrari that radiates throughout the rest of motorsport. Without a red Ferrari on the grid, grand prix racing would be diminished. Other teams come and go; sixteen have tried and failed to succeed in Formula One since 1991 alone. Ferrari, however, has been a constant feature in the ever-changing world of Formula One. The team has competed in every championship since the formula was established in 1950, though Ferrari's pedigree goes back still further. The company's legendary founder, Enzo Ferrari, was a racing driver in the 1920s, and acts as an historic link with motorsport's early years. However, Ferrari is not just a racing team. Uniquely among Formula One constructors, Ferrari manufactures its own engines and road cars (about 75% of components are made in-house). The same processes that go into building a racing car go into building the road cars. This bridges the gap between Formula One and the aspirations of millions of fans. No other team can make this connection. In Enzo's days, road cars were produced to finance the racing. Today, the racing team is a promotional tool for the road car division, with a budget linked to the success of that division. This is central to understanding Ferrari in the 1990s. The marque might be a national icon, but it is run by hard-headed businessmen with their eyes on the profit and loss account. When Fiat, the Italian car giant, bought

Ferrari, the Formula One operation was in bad shape. The racing division had lost its lead in technology, and rivals were employing new materials and making advances in aerodynamics. There was a cabal within Fiat that would have happily got rid of the racing team so they could just concentrate on producing road cars. Instead, the whole operation was given new management and a second chance. The company has been turned upside-down. The road car division is now profitable, and the signs are that the racing team is back to its winning ways at last. This is good for the business of Formula One. The sport needs a successful Ferrari. It is estimated that one-third of spectators attending grands prix outside Italy are there to watch, and hear the distinctive growl of, the Ferraris. The team's popularity and size give it immense influence within Formula One's corridors of power. Marco Piccinini, Ferrari's former team manager, is a director of the company Bernie Ecclestone wants to float on the stock market. It is perhaps no surprise that Ecclestone recruited somebody who knows Ferrari from the inside.

Enzo Ferrari, an irascible but charismatic figure, founded his Scuderia Ferrari workshop at Modena in November 1929. Most of his work came through Alfa Romeo, another famous Italian car maker. Enzo's company would look after the Alfa's racing drivers, most notably the legendary Antonio Ascari, service the vehicles and deliver them to the races. When Alfa Romeo's own racing operation folded in 1932, Enzo persuaded the company to let him form a semi-independent works team. The team would be no match for the grand prix entrants from Germany's Mercedes-Benz and Auto Union. But no matter – it was Enzo's first taste of running his own team, and he liked it. In 1938, however, Milan-based Alfa Romeo took Alfa Racing back in-house. Enzo was made *Direttore Sportivo*, but he found working in this new environment too restricting. Rows with his Alfa superiors were commonplace. Enzo craved the independence and freedom to run a team his way, and within a year he had walked out. He set up a venture manufacturing machine tools, floating it as Auto Avio Costruzioni S.p.A in September 1938. Enzo's severance deal with Alfa Romeo stipulated that he should not build or race cars under his own name for four years, though he continued to design vehicles and study the principles of motor manufacturing. The Second World War put an end to serious racing in Europe. But by 1945 Enzo, having moved his factory to Maranello, was already preparing to build racing and road cars under his own name. In 1947 the first car branded Ferrari began competitive racing, and in May that year Franco Cortese drove a red

1500cc 125 Sport to victory at the Rome Grand Prix. A legend was born.

Ferrari celebrated its 50th anniversary in 1997 with a year-long series of events honouring the racing and road cars. The marketing experts at Maranello worked overtime, generating acres of news coverage in journals throughout the world. Already the most talked-about team in Formula One, Ferrari became the most talked-about production car company that year as well. However, it was not all good news. Despite its new management, new drivers, improved racecar, and an annual budget of some £100 million (the biggest in Formula One), success continued to elude the racing team. Certainly, performances had been improving thanks to Michael Schumacher in the driving seat, but not fast enough for the passionate Italian *tifosi*. Given the luxury of Ferrari's huge resources, how could it fail to win, they asked. So, Ferrari's birthday party was a chance to celebrate, but also a chance to dwell on where it all went wrong. The team last won a driver's world championship in 1979, with Jody Scheckter, and last took the constructors' title in 1983 thanks to René Arnoux and Patrick Tambay. Alain Prost might have won the drivers' title for Ferrari in 1990 had it not been for a cynical shunt off the track by Ayrton Senna, which handed the title to the Brazilian. That year seemed to symbolise Ferrari's failure: fortune was against the Italian team.

Michael Schumacher came within a whisker of winning the world drivers' championship in 1997, but even that season ended in despair for Ferrari. The German's attempt to ram Jacques Villeneuve out of the final race of the season (if both drivers had retired, Schumacher would have won the championship by one point) left his reputation in tatters. The universal condemnation might not have been so great had it not been for the fact that Schumacher had tried a similar manoeuvre against Damon Hill in 1994. It was difficult to know what made Formula One race fans more angry: Schumacher's action against Villeneuve, or the subsequent mild slap on the wrist from the FIA. While the chorus calling for a racing ban grew louder, Schumacher was simply stripped of his second place in the championship – hardly much of a sanction. Why the leniency? One possible explanation lies in Ferrari's importance for Formula One. The world's favourite racing team desperately needs the world's best driver at the wheel. Formula One, sponsors and television broadcasters, even Bernie Ecclestone's planned flotation, would all benefit if the glory days returned to Ferrari. Schumacher is Ferrari's best hope for nearly twenty years. And what is good for Ferrari is good for grand prix racing.

The roots of Ferrari's decline are to be found in the wider economic changes that have affected the European motor racing industry over the past four decades. Motor racing has, of course, always been a close relation of the car industry, particularly the motor manufacturers in mainland Europe. Engine development was the central focus of these companies; engineering research went into building bigger and more powerful units. However, in Britain alternative theories about the best way to get speed out of a vehicle were being explored. As we saw in Chapter One, in the 1960s aerodynamics, design and the principles of roadholding became as important as engine power. Britain, with its large aircraft industry, provided a pool of skilled engineers who were able to apply their knowledge to the design of racing cars. Italy's aircraft industry was comparatively small, and specialist car makers like Ferrari remained rooted in a mechanical culture that lacked the innovation of British entrepreneurs such as John Cooper and, later, Colin Chapman.

Ferrari, indeed all the Continental teams, were slow to adapt and utilise the subtle design changes that were taking place in Britain. One significant design development was the placing of engines behind rather than in front of the driver. But Ferrari was the last of the Formula One teams to follow suit. It was also slow to introduce carbon fibre into the construction of the racecar. And while engine configuration moved on, Ferrari stuck too long to a V12 rather than a V10 powerplant. On top of this it had the financial and technical strain of two production tasks: building racecars *and* road cars. The appointment in 1981 of the British designer Harvey Postlethwaite was a belated and grudging admission that the technical expertise necessary to produce race-winning cars might lie outside Italy. The appointment in 1988 of John Barnard as technical director was confirmation that it did.

The ageing Enzo Ferrari was not a good manager, and the new organisational changes and flexibility that were sweeping through other teams left Ferrari behind. Enzo ran Ferrari from the heart, not the head. He was not an accomplished driver, nor one of the great engineers. He was a manipulator, who played games with the governing authorities, drivers, rival teams and the media. Ferrari was Enzo's personal fiefdom, and he inspired fear rather than admiration from many Ferrari workers. There were several highly public rows, which only went to fuel the legend. The Pope personally criticised him after the dreadful Mille Miglia race in which a Ferrari driver, Alfonso de Portago, and ten spectators died. Enzo suffered a split in the team in 1962, when chief engineer Carlo Chiti and several staff set up on their own. After one of many financial crises in the 1960s, Enzo almost sold 90 per cent of Ferrari to Ford, but the deal fell through when Ford would not accept Enzo's demand that he keep control of the racing division. The man himself was acutely aware that Ferrari's success depended on maintaining the mystique. This became more difficult in the 1980s. The quality of the road cars began to decline; the performance of the racecars was eclipsed by their rivals. Increasingly, Ferrari appeared backward-looking, its founder steeped in tradition and outmoded sentiment, and unable to adapt to the rapid changes taking place in Formula One.

Enzo's death in August 1988 was an occasion for national mourning. But it did release Ferrari from the grip of his idiosyncratic ways and offered a chance to move the company into a new era. Although, by this time, Enzo's role as head of Ferrari had been strictly honorary for several years, the man's shadow hung over the company and he was consulted about the racing team until his death. Fiat, controlled by the Agnelli family and one of Italy's largest companies, took majority control of Ferrari and set about devising a strategy to restore the glory days. The volume car producer already owned 50 per cent of Ferrari, having paid around L2.1 billion for the stake in 1969. At the same time Fiat acquired an option to buy another 49 per cent on Enzo's death. In the end, Fiat increased its holding by 40 per cent, leaving the remainder with the Ferrari family. The 40 per cent stake cost Fiat about L19 billion ($13.8m). This was a pretty good deal at the time, given that Ferrari had net capital of L127 billion and profits the previous year of L15 billion, from a turnover of L360 billion. However, the new executives from Fiat who took control found Ferrari in more disarray than they expected. The road car division was cushioned by a 1980s boom in the demand for luxury vehicles, but when that economic bubble burst this operation's shortcomings were exposed. Both arms of the company were now in trouble. Fiat was condemned in the early days for installing a collection of faceless executives at Ferrari who had no motor racing background. Ferrari had lost direction, and now it was losing its personality, the critics said. Yet, what happened to Ferrari is no different from what happens when other ailing companies are taken over. Ferrari had been swallowed by a larger empire. It became a profit-centre within Fiat, and a team of businessmen were installed to sort out the problems and, if necessary, wield the axe. If traditionalists were upset, then so be it.

By 1991 Fiat had a clearer idea of its plans to restore Ferrari to profitability, and in December that year it announced the appointment of Luca Cordero di Montezemolo as chairman and managing director. In many ways he was the ideal choice. With his aristocratic name, blond hair and fine clothes, the dashing Montezemolo was portrayed as the Prince Charming who could rekindle the Italian love affair with Ferrari. But Montezemolo was more than a pretty face. He also had a very impressive curriculum vitae. A law graduate, Montezemolo was brought to Ferrari as Enzo's personal assistant in 1973, at the tender age of 25. Remarkably, within a year, he was appointed head of the racing team, helping to steer Niki Lauda to the 1975 and 1977 championships. Montezemolo moved on to other things within the Agnelli's family business empire: director of external affairs at Fiat, head of Fiat's publishing interests, and managing director of Cinzano, part-owned by Agnelli. He was chosen to organise Italy's first entrant in the America's Cup yacht race, and he planned the 1990 football World Cup. It was an impressive CV, but then Ferrari needed a heavy-hitter. Although Montezemolo reports to a Fiat executive, he is given a large degree of autonomy to steer Ferrari as he wishes. Professor Garel Rhys, a motor industry expert at Cardiff Business School, believes this is just the set-up that an operation like Ferrari should have. 'The company requires careful marketing, as its exclusive cars do not sit comfortably alongside Fiat's mass market products. Fiat had proved itself to be a benign owner, giving Ferrari the freedom to operate. That is exactly what the company needed. Having found the man to do the job, Luca di Montezemolo needed space to impose himself on the company.'

Montezemolo's aim was to rebuild both divisions of Ferrari, and return a profit to Fiat. To do this he faced two challenges: one engineering, the other cultural. On the engineering front, Montezemolo wanted to bring the racing and production car businesses into closer harmony. This was not only more economic, it was also good for the marketing of Ferrari road cars. He explained the plan: 'Our strategy is to continue to develop very innovative products. My first priority is to invest and to work a lot in advanced research in new technologies. In engines, in aerodynamics, in new materials, in safety, driveability, brakes. Most of all, I will carry out research into engines. We have improved the link between racing and production departments, mainly in three areas. First, in aerodynamics; we have a new wind tunnel. Second, in engines. Third, in new composite materials. We are going to introduce new materials in the next Ferrari cars. All our activities – our new marketing initiatives, our racing, our production improvements, our product development – are strictly planned and implemented with the aim of improving our bottom line. To be sure, we have a rich shareholder in Fiat. But the reason he is rich is that he does not like holding shares in unprofitable companies.'

The cultural challenge facing Montezemolo was just as daunting. He inherited an apathetic workforce and management, and an antiquated factory. Maranello is a small town near Bologna, an area of Italy where the passion for red cars is matched by the passion for red politics. The total workforce in 1977 was 1,900, with 1,550 working on the production of road cars, and the rest assigned to the racing department (Gestione Sportiva). Although working on the racecars is regarded as the most prestigious job in the factory, there is discontent. Employees in the division are governed by the rules and bureaucracy of the factory as a whole. Workers complain that there is little involvement with the end product. There is dissatisfaction about pay and anxiety about the future. The atmosphere is more reminiscent of a traditional industrial shop-floor than a high-tech operation at the cutting edge of development. Ferrari workers earn the same as other car workers in Italy, where pay rates and working conditions are based on a national contract and the incorporation of European Commission employment legislation. The mechanics are governed by a seven-grade pay structure, although Ferrari workers start at grade four. The differentials are kept to a minimum, as management believes it improves the harmony of the shop-floor. The average basic pay is around £10,000 a year for an eight-hour day, plus overtime payments. Average pay at a UK Formula One factory is about £7,000 more. The racing department is located in two places, a bleak and featureless main plant at Maranello and a newer site next to the company's test track. Michael Schumacher, recalling his first visit to the factory, was alarmed at what he found: 'To be honest, I did not think about how special or atmospheric it was. Instead, I was quite shocked when I first saw the factory. I just thought everything looked very old and very out-of-date. It was a bit like visiting a museum.'

The factories of both the road car and racecar divisions are being upgraded. Ferrari has built its own wind tunnel, a £6.6 million investment, designed by renowned architect Renzo Piano. (The tunnel allows racecar models up to 65 per cent of their full size to be tested at wind speeds up to 150mph, powered by a 1000kW fan.) New personnel were brought in, too. One of Montezemolo's first personnel changes for the racing team was to bring back former driver Niki Lauda, this time as a consultant. It was Lauda who pressed Ferrari to find the money to lure back driver Gerhard Berger from McLaren. In July 1993 the Frenchman Jean Todt, previously director of Peugeot Sport, was appointed head of the racing team, the first non-Italian to take charge. Asked at the time where it had all gone wrong for Ferrari, it was clear that Todt thought the blame lay at the door of the former management. 'There was a lack of professionalism, an underestimation of what was needed to succeed in Formula One in the present era, a tendency to be too short-term,' he said. Ferrari desperately needed an injection of new personnel, and Todt persuaded the company to buy the best. John Barnard, by now regarded as one of the most important designers since Colin Chapman, was induced to return to Ferrari. Other appointments came in 1994: Osamu Goto, the Japanese engineer behind the powerful Honda V10 of the late 1980s, and the Austrian engineer Gustav Brunner. By the mid-1990s the Ferrari old guard had gone and all the pieces were being put in place for a competitive assault on the world championship. Or so Montezemolo thought. Unfortunately, the whole did not live up to the sum of its parts. Ferrari's ability to draw on finances and resources outstrips every other team. It has the biggest staff and the biggest budget. It even has its own test track to allow unlimited testing. (Ferrari has such deep pockets that it was able in March 1997 to soak the track with 250,000 litres of water to help Goodyear conduct some wet-weather tyre testing.) But the team failed miserably to make any impression on the Formula One championship. The performances were ridiculed by the Italian press. 'Ferrari: un altro disastro' was a headline that summed up the situation. There were calls for the management to go. Caesar Romiti, the Fiat managing director, was forced to make a public statement backing Montezemolo after the two Ferraris failed to finish the 1995 Italian Grand Prix.

The 1996 season was even more dispiriting than 1995, because this time Ferrari had Michael Schumacher on board. It was Montezemolo's masterstroke to have lured the reigning world drivers' champion from Benetton. Hiring a top driver was to be the last piece of the jigsaw. Ferrari, with a little help from its sponsors, was paying top dollar for his services, $24 million a year for two seasons, with an option to extend the contract. The deal made the German driver one of the three highest paid sportsmen in the world. What makes Schumacher so good? He can squeeze an above-average performance from an average car. But then, all quality drivers know how to do that. More important is that Schumacher has a way of raising the performance of even the best team. He has an ability to feed back valuable information to his technicians that more limited drivers do not have. As Montezemolo explained at the time of signing Schumacher: 'I need a "huge" driver. I need his intelligence. I need him to push and improve the team.' Whereas Enzo Ferrari employed drivers to prove his theory that the cars were better than the man at the wheel, Schumacher's performances were far superior to anything he was driving. The problem was that superb driving matters little if the cars keep breaking down, and the Ferraris did so with monotonous regularity. For three races in a row during the 1996 championship, the two Ferraris (the other being driven by Eddie Irvine) retired with mechanical problems. The newspaper headlines continued to pour scorn. 'Ferrari: Red Only From Shame' said the Rome newspaper *Il Messagero*. When Ferrari recruited Schumacher, Giovanni Agnelli, chairman of Fiat, left Montezemolo in no doubt that he expected a return on his investment. 'If you do not win when you have somebody like Schumacher, then it is the team's fault.'

Cracks were appearing in the Ferrari structure as the highly charged atmosphere began to intensify. One of Ferrari's problems seems to be the constant politicing. The company's reputation as a nest of vipers has dogged it for years, making attempts to streamline and change doubly difficult. Murray Walker, the celebrated television commentator who has reported on the good and bad times at Ferrari for three decades, summed up the problem: 'There are a lot of good people at Maranello, but a political atmosphere permeates the walls. There are too many self-interested groups. They have got the people at Ferrari, but they have not got it together. I have wondered sometimes if the whole damn edifice will collapse.' Calls for heads to roll resurfaced during 1996, with team manager Jean Todt joining Montezemolo on the list. John Barnard also became the target for criticism. He had an arms-length relationship with Ferrari – he operated from England, not Italy. Having refused to work at Maranello, Barnard persuaded Ferrari to finance an operation called Ferrari Design and Development (FDD), a 50-strong team of engineers operating in a factory at Shalford, near Guildford in Surrey. FDD worked on racecar design, and the cars were shipped to Maranello to be fitted with the engine and be refined. It was a set-up that Todt recognised as necessary because of the lack of specialist engineers and designers in Italy. But he clearly felt it was not an ideal arrangement. Former driver Michele Albereto described the situation as being like a surgeon operating by telephone. Todt blamed the aerodynamics for a large part of Ferrari's under-performance, an

implied criticism of Barnard, who had taken on the challenge of designing the completely new F310 car, rather than develop the previous
year's model. The set-up between Maranello and Shalford appeared
to be slowing down the process of developing a race-winning car.
Development of the gearbox, for example, was a joint programme,
but frustrating for both sides because it was taking too long. The
Barnard/Ferrari arrangement went completely against organisational
trends in industry, and was quite the opposite of what other teams
were doing. While Ferrari was struggling with its dual system, Williams
was in the process of fully integrating its plant under one roof and
installing a state-of-the-art information technology system. Williams
has a flat structure, with a highly skilled and compact workforce that
is given the autonomy and initiative to respond quickly. Above them
are the strong figures of Frank Williams and Patrick Head, providing
the leadership and discipline, who can simply go down on to the shop-
floor and tell people what to do. It was the opposite of what went on at
Ferrari, where changes had to be preceded by a round of committee
meetings, memos and telephone calls.

Much of the tension stemmed from the ill-defined nature of what
Barnard was supposed to be doing. He had worked for Ferrari in the
1980s, also based in England, and experienced the strains in the organisational structure at Maranello. He did not want a repetition of that.
For his second tour of duty he thought he had made it clear that he
wanted to be involved in forward-looking projects only – designing
cars, shipping them to Ferrari, and then moving on to the next year's
model. In fact, he got involved in the day-to-day operation just as before.
Ferrari had never plugged the gap in its management structure left by
Harvey Postlethwaite, the technical director who departed in 1992.
Barnard felt he was effectively thrust into that role, something he did
not want. 'I was put into a job I had never taken on. And there were all
sorts of expectations that I had come back in the same sort of capacity
as before,' he explained in a press interview after his departure.

Furthermore, although Barnard thought he was working on long-
term projects, he soon felt under pressure to cut out innovation and
produce a car quickly. 'It was clear from my point of view that I was
supposed to set up a base in England, and be in charge of designing the
racing car. Someone else would pull it all together at Maranello. That
used to be Harvey's role, but when he left there was never really anyone
put in to do that job.' At some point during the summer of 1996 the
decision was made to take all aerodynamic work in-house. Barnard

believes Fiat probably told Montezemolo to change the strategy.

Today, Ferrari's structural turmoil seems to be over. Some long-awaited organisational efficiencies have been introduced, and these are clearly paying off. The team's performance in 1998 proved that it was once again in championship-winning form. Schumacher was instrumental in pushing through some of these changes, including the recruitment of his former technical team at Benetton, Ross Brawn and Rory Byrne. Brawn was appointed technical director in December 1996 on a pay package worth £2 million a year. Acknowledged as an excellent co-ordinator with good managerial skills, Brawn plugged a hole that had really remained open since 1992 – and he is based at Maranello.

Montezemolo is steering a narrow course between modernising Ferrari while trying to avoid diluting the mystique that makes the marque so great. Sponsorship, except from technical suppliers, had been held at bay under Enzo Ferrari. Under Montezemolo, however, the racing division has to pay its way. The constructor still has fewer sponsors' names on its cars than other teams, but, now that Formula One is a business, Montezemolo wants the racing division. Even the colour of the racing cars has gone a shade more orange, a reflection of the link-up with Marlboro, the tobacco giant that switched from McLaren. And the rather modest decals of the past have been replaced by a large Marlboro chevron on the rear wing, and another advertisement down the nose cone. It is the shape of things to come. Before traditionalists complain too loudly, however, it is worth recalling that Enzo once went further than Montezemolo. In 1964 the cars raced in the official blue-and-white racing colours of the USA, after Enzo fell out with the Italian racing authorities. He thought nothing of abandoning 'red' if it was in his interests. The new Ferrari team is part of Montezemolo's strategy to put the road car division at the heart of the business. Enzo could be very contemptuous of the wealthy clients who bought the road cars. For him, racing was what mattered. Not so Montezemolo, who uses racing as a valuable promotional tool and engineering test-bed for the production car operation.

There is no direct link between success on the track and success in the sales showroom, Montezemolo maintains. He recalls that in the 1970s, when he headed the team that won two drivers' world championships, it was one of the worst times for car sales. The reverse happened in the 1980s, when track success eluded the team, but Ferrari sales boomed, even though the quality of the cars was not always up to standard. Motoring journalists at the time described the Testarossa as wide and cumbersome, the Ferrari 348 as poorly engineered, and the Mondial as unattractive. Porsche, and Honda's NSX, were regarded as better cars. But this was an era of City slickers and big bonuses – the age of the Yuppie – and luxury cars of all types were selling fast. Ferrari production rose to a record 4,400 cars a year. If, then, there is no direct connection between Formula One success and road car sales, is there much point in maintaining a racing team? Well, yes. It is the indirect spin-offs that makes the racing so valuable to the brand. Ferrari has only a small marketing budget. The free promotion that comes with newspaper and television interest in Formula One is worth tens of millions of pounds each year. As Montezemolo explained: 'Racing is our form of advertising. It supports our brand by expressing our courage; our daring to put our reputation to the test 16 or 17 times a season.'

Montezemolo has been keen to bridge the gap between racecar technology and Ferrari's road cars. It is good for marketing and good for economies of scale. The F50 proved that racing technology can work on road cars. Adapted from Alain Prost's 1990 racecar, the F50 has 520 horsepower and a carbon-fibre chassis. In particular, the suspension, with almost horizontal shock absorbers, was incorporated from the racing cars. It is, however, a car for the specialist Ferrari enthusiast only. More general race technology is filtering down to other models. Ferrari's transmission control and gearbox, Selespeed, has been fitted on the F355 and looks likely to become commonplace on all Ferrari road cars. Its F1-style steering wheel is fitted with a paddle to change gear, similar to that used by every Formula One team. The paddle was introduced in racecars to speed up gear-changing, but Ferrari maintains that research among its road drivers shows they prefer its ease of use. Ferrari is also working on new plastic composites and metallurgical materials, developed for racing, but which will increasingly be used in the road cars. Montezemolo explained the connection between road and racing cars: 'Our road cars have always been directly inspired by our racing cars in their technology, their dynamics and their appearance. Many times throughout our history they have even shared the same components. This close integration is possible because we are – and have been for some time – the only team in Formula One that makes the entire racing car in its own facilities. We manufacture the complete car, from the engine and the transmission to the frame and suspension. This gives us complete control over every detail of the car and allows it to be fully integrated and optimised for best performance. We were the first to fit a semi-automatic gearbox to a grand prix car, an advanced technology which we have just introduced on the F355 with great success. We have also been the first to introduce true ground-effects aerodynamics on our production cars, derived from Formula One. We have always challenged our engineers to do all they can to introduce features and technologies in our road cars that were derived from racing. This is a tradition to which we are wholeheartedly committed.'

Although Fiat owns its own huge aluminium foundry, one of the most advanced of its type, to cast its engine blocks, Ferrari has had a smaller-scale foundry installed for itself. It is good for Ferrari's marketing if a purchaser knows that the workers pouring the molten metal for his car's engine block may have been doing the same for Schumacher and Irvine the previous week. Ferrari does, however, work closely with Fiat on technological projects. Outwardly the two companies are marketed as separate entities. This is really for Ferrari's benefit, in order that its image is not weakened. Inwardly, though, the transfer technology from Ferrari to Fiat is increasing. The racing division has developed advanced plastic composites, which are now being developed for Fiat road cars. Ferrari also has its own consultancy division, but this works exclusively for Fiat. The value of owning a company like Ferrari is that it can test-bed prototypes in low volumes; running tests in small batches would simply not be economical for Fiat. Ferrari's developments in computer-controlled active suspension and steering systems have all been passed to Fiat. Montezemolo believes that technology and the computer are bringing uniformity to motor manufacturing. What will determine which companies succeed in the future will be creativity. For Ferrari – and for Fiat – a lot of this creativity will be coming from the racing division.

When recession last hit the luxury car market in the late 1980s, Ferrari's flaws were exposed. With the era of conspicuous consumption over, Ferrari could have retrenched. Instead, getting newer and more appealing models on to the market became an urgent part of Montezemolo's strategy. He has replaced every model since he took over. In recent years the cars have been engineered for consistency and reliability, and modern manufacturing methods have been introduced to improve efficiency and quality. The latest V12-engined 456GT and 550 Maranello models show that Montezemolo is prepared to broaden Ferrari's appeal. It is part of the image that a Ferrari must be fast and packed with driving pleasure. But Montezemolo recognises that the cars must also be easy to use. With Enzo, consumed as he was with racing only, there was little deference to consumers' tastes and requirements. Today's Ferrari is making some concessions to practicality. The Ferrari range now includes cars with trunk space, and for the first time a model with back seats. The F355 is a cheaper entry-level model, helping Ferrari to compete with top-of-the-range Mercedes or BMWs. A typical Ferrari owner is aged between 45 and 55, and, of course, very wealthy. The F355, Ferrari hopes, will entice the young rich on to the company's ownership ladder. Recent rises in Ferrari's annual profits are due to the sales success of these 'more accessible' models. Pre-tax profits in 1996 were L12 billion (£41 million) compared with L3.8 billion the previous year. With car sales rising year on year (in 1997 UK sales rose 28%; Japan 24%; US 14%), Montezemolo expects profits to rise still further and turnover to break L1,000 billion for the first time, a remarkable improvement on the L445 billion in 1993. 'Our road cars are our core business, but a business that must earn the funds that we need to support our racing,' Montezemolo said. So this continuing rise in profitability bodes well for the racing division. Ferrari merchandising, much of it sold on the back of racing successes, makes an important contribution to the bottom line, though separate profit figures are not stripped out. Turnover from merchandising was close to £30 million in 1997.

One of Montezemolo's most important appointments was that of marketing director, Michele Scannavini. The former food industry executive, who joined in 1993, brought with him new ideas about brand value and adjusting to a changing market. He regards the cars of today as more 'client friendly'; not trophy symbols to be brought out on rare occasions, but cars to be used on a regular basis. His fresh approach is timely, given that consumer attitudes to products like Ferraris are changing. For many people, the Ferrari is an emblem of wealth, but for others it symbolises greed and opulence. Environmental legislation and restrictions on noise and speed penalise the type of cars made by Ferrari, especially in America. Researchers are also finding that car-buying trends are changing. Increasingly, purchasing decisions are made on rational grounds, whereas Ferrari appeals to the emotions. For Scannavini the task is to adapt, but somehow retain the original features. No longer is Ferrari interested in selling to a few thousand ageing would-be racing drivers. Scannavini knows the company must broaden its appeal, yet remain exclusive. Just two Ferrari cars were produced in 1948, rising to 300 by 1960. More than 3,300 road cars were manufactured in 1996, up from 2,639 two years earlier. Production is now capped at 3,500 for the foreseeable future (1,000 below its peak in the late 1980s), a restriction which ensures the exclusivity of the vehicle and maintains residual values. It also avoids the speculative buying and selling which harmed Ferrari's image in the late 1980s.

Ferrari in the late 1990s is a very different animal. The racing team's fortunes have not only been linked to those of the road car division but to a certain extent, to Fiat's. Racing has to pay its way, if not in profits then in engineering and marketing terms. It would seem only a matter of time before Ferrari again wins the Formula One world championships. So much money, so much time, has been invested in pursuing this challenge that victory must be inevitable. It has been a long time coming, and will consolidate everything Montezemolo has done during the 1990s. In terms of Ferrari as a business, however, it may well mark a step towards a new financial future. Regaining the world championship would be an ideal time for Fiat to cash in on Ferrari's popularity and get a return on its investment. A partial flotation of Ferrari shares on a stock market is becoming a distinct possibility, according to financial analysts in Italy. Fiat has already begun loosening its ties. In September 1996 a group of Italian banks, Mediobanca, Banca di Roma, Credito Italiano and Banca Commerciale Italiana, bought 3 per cent of Ferrari from Fiat for L22.4 billion ($14.7m), leaving Fiat with 87 per cent, and 10 per cent in the hands of Piero Lardi Ferrari, Enzo's son and Ferrari's deputy chairman. Fiat may have been planning a flotation in 1997 on the back of an expected triumphant season in Formula One. The season did not fulfil expectations, and the flotation never went ahead. The smart money says that Fiat's intention is eventually to combine Ferrari with Maserati, another famous Italian marque, of which Fiat took full control in July 1997. A merged company would be a more viable stand-alone business, and an attractive proposition for investors. One of the biggest challenges facing Formula One teams is the search for money to finance research and development. As a general rule, the richer the team, the more successful it will be. Most constructors get their money from sponsors. Ferrari can also call on finance from the road car division. If, in the near future, Ferrari is also able to call on funds from stock market investors, it could satisfy the team's fund-raising requirements for many years. That would not only boost Ferrari's drive to win the Formula One World championship, it could help the team to maintain a stranglehold on grand prix racing for the foreseeable future.

Benetton: F1's Upstarts

BENETTON FORMULA LIMITED has done more than any other constructor in the 1990s to raise the profile of Formula One. Run for most of the decade by the buccaneering Italian, Flavio Briatore, Benetton kept alive the glitz and glamour in a sport that had been somewhat dulled by inward-looking concerns about technology and computers. Three decades ago, the long-haired Jackie Stewart made driving fashionable. Briatore did a similar thing for team ownership. Suddenly the style magazines and the colour supplements wanted to know about the lives of the Formula One bosses. Benetton in the era of Briatore seemed to chime perfectly with Formula One in the age of television entertainment. For him, grand prix racing was not about cars racing round a circuit. Formula One, on and off the track, was a colourful, fun-packed experience. Briatore would have loved to supplant Ferrari as Italy's national champion. In the latter years of his reign there were attempts to 'Italianise' Benetton, even recruiting two ex-Ferrari drivers. But the team never had Ferrari's history, its location (it is based in England), nor its gravitas. What it did have, however, was shock value, and that is no worthless commodity in a sport where image and publicity are everything. With his all-year tan and crocodile-skin shoes, Briatore cut a colourful figure among the cosy club of sober regulars who attended the FOCA meetings.

When he joined Benetton, Briatore knew nothing about Formula One. His peers, steeped in the heritage of racing, treated this newcomer with suspicion, but Briatore just ignored them and set about putting together a championship-winning team. But with the triumphs came rows about breaking safety rules and allegations of cheating. And there was the small matter of a bomb discarded outside his London home. Things just seemed to happen around Briatore. What sort of man is he? Volatile, according to the team's former marketing director John Postlethwaite. 'He's like dealing with a baby. He's very nice and happy one second, and the next second he's a complete bastard. He's unpredictable.' Perhaps Briatore might even agree. He once said: 'I am forty-six, but, in my head, I think I am only eighteen.' Whatever it was that motivated Briatore – volatility, immaturity, a sense of fun – it kept him and his team where he wanted both to be – in the media spotlight.

Benetton Formula is owned by Benetton Group, the Italy-based international clothing empire. Briatore was drafted in to run the racing team in 1989 by his friend, Luciano Benetton, co-founder of the fashion business. When Briatore arrived in England from his Benetton Group job in America, Formula One was about to enter a new era of global television and showbusiness. Briatore was a marketing man; he knew about business and he knew about putting on a show. His ignorance of Formula One, its history and technology, was irrelevant for the project he had for Benetton. As he said in 1994: 'I am not against technology. But in Benetton's philosophy, Formula One is an event. People don't come to the races to see our latest piston. They come to the races to see the fight. Benetton is in Formula One because it is about global communication. Noise and lifestyle, that is what Formula One is about.' The importance of marketing and media to the growth of Formula One were at that time alien to other team owners. They just wanted to race. Bernie Ecclestone's vision was to turn Formula One into an international business, financed by sponsorship and the sale of television broadcast rights. Briatore understood this strategy. Some teams languish on the sidelines for years unable to get into Formula One's charmed inner circle. Briatore was able to establish himself with relative ease, probably because Ecclestone was prepared to open doors for him. Journalist Norman Howell, who followed the Formula One circus for the *Sunday Times*, believes Briatore and Ecclestone were natural soul mates. 'The sport had become stale and Ecclestone wanted to shake it up,' Howell said. 'People like Ron Dennis and Frank Williams didn't care about Ecclestone's grand plans, they just wanted to race. In Briatore, Ecclestone saw this guy come into the sport who could help him shake things up.' There was a time when the two men seemed inseparable, together at breakfast, lunch and dinner during the race weekends. If you went to the fashionable San Lorenzo restaurant in London's Knightsbridge on a Thursday, the chances were they would there having lunch. Curiously, the closeness can even affect who Briatore talks to. When the author tried to arrange an interview with

Briatore, Patrizia Spinelli, head of publication declined – because I had not sought Ecclestone's permission to write this book.

Once installed at Benetton, Briatore moved fast, disposing of the old guard, rebuilding the team, and putting the shaky finances in order. Very soon Briatore had won the backing of rich sponsors, hired in controversial circumstances the services of an up-and-coming driver called Michael Schumacher, and become a powerful player in the Formula One firmament. Benetton Formula signed up, traded in, and profited from some of the best young drivers of the 1990s. The Benetton Group's investment arm, 21 Investmenti, bought just under 50 per cent of Tom Walkinshaw's TWR Group (which owns the Arrows racing team) and put Briatore on the board of directors. Briatore bought the French Ligier team and a 50 per cent stake in the Italian team Minardi (both of which have now been sold). At one time Briatore controlled almost one-third of the grid. That meant three sets of competition and prize money, and an important say in the annual round of musical chairs involving drivers and engine suppliers. It gave him substantial leverage with Formula One's authorities. It was Briatore who turned the annual pre-season launch by constructors of their new racecars into an extravaganza. Not for the Benetton team the standard unveiling of the car in a London hotel or club. Briatore's *folie de grandeur* came in 1996, when the team took over the town of Taormina on the island of Sicily. Around 10,000 people, many of them travelling at Benetton's expense from England, watched the cars stage a mock race, complete with pit-stops. The event lasted two days. Formula One, a sport used to superlatives, had never seen anything like it. And the sponsors loved it. Such events helped turn Formula One into an all-year event and provide publicity for sponsors during the 'close' season.

On reflection, it perhaps should come as no surprise that Benetton Formula would have an idiosyncratic approach to grand prix racing. The constructor is, after all, owned by a company whose iconoclastic advertising campaigns were controversial and sometimes distressing. Like the footwear company Nike, Benetton Group have successfully exploited bad behaviour for advertising purposes. Now the Benetton Formula team were to become the bad boys of motor racing, revelling in the heady mixture of power, politics and publicity. Nor was it bad for business. Benetton Formula's pre-tax profits for 1996 doubled to £2.68 million, on turnover (principally sponsorship and prize money) up £8 million to £47 million, despite heavy investment in facilities. Benetton Group entered Formula One as part of a move to diversify and end its dependency on the clothing business. Motor racing was ideal, giving the company a global marketing platform, while costs could be offset by sponsorship. Benetton Group's first foray into the world of grand prix was in 1983, when it became a sponsor of the British team Tyrrell. The deal was that Tyrrell would get a one-off payment, plus a performance-related bonus. The following year Benetton switched to the Italian Alfa Romeo team, but after one mixed season it was clear that it was going to be one of Formula One's also-rans. The idea of actually buying rather than sponsoring a team began to appeal to Luciano Benetton, though at this time no decisions had been made. He was looking for involvement with a constructor on the cusp of success. And Luciano thought he had found it with Toleman, a team which at the time was showing all the signs that it was going places.

The Toleman Transport Group, a haulage contractor run by Ted Toleman, entered motor racing in the 1970s, first at club level and then through running a Formula Two team. By the end of the decade Toleman was designing and building its own cars. Powered by engines developed by British engineer Brian Hart, and driven by Derek Warwick and Brian Henton, the racecars achieved notable success in Formula Two. These achievements were not repeated, however, when Toleman moved up to Formula One in 1981. The team failed to make the starting grid at many of that season's races. The 1982 championship saw an improvement, and also some sponsorship from Candy, the Italian electrical goods manufacturer. There was another incremental improvement the following year; another sponsor in the form of Magirus, a manufacturer of trucks and heavy vehicles; and a partnership with Italian tyre company Pirelli. Although Derek Warwick was to depart to drive for the Renault team in 1984, Toleman signed up a 24-year-old Brazilian, the great Ayrton Senna. If Ted Toleman really knew what a star driver he had on his books, he obviously did not try hard enough to keep him. Senna stayed only one year at the team before signing for Lotus to challenge for the 1985 championship. That year was a disappointing one all round for Toleman. The team missed the first three races, and finished in only one of the rest. Yet again, Benetton was linked with an under-performing team, but Luciano was not put off by failure. In 1986 a new company was formed, Benetton Formula Limited, which paid Ted Toleman an undisclosed sum for the team and its factory at Witney.

For Luciano Benetton, owning a Formula One team was an ideal medium through which to promote his brand of bright and youthful clothing. It united colourful products with a colourful sport; an international company with an international sporting series (which at this time was holding races in Benetton's all-important American market). The decision to enter motor racing was also a defensive move to protect the company's image. As Benetton emerged from its traditional, family-based roots in the 1960s, and grew a larger corporate structure, Luciano was worried about diluting the brand image. A decision was taken to concentrate on just a few trademarks, one of which was 'United Colours of Benetton', a slogan which was developed into a now infamous television and poster campaign. In an article entitled 'How Brand Power Works', Luciano explained the ideals behind the phrase, and its link with Formula One. 'United Colours of Benetton is rich with meaning; it suggests among other things the United States, united races, a united Europe and a united world. This is consistent with the philosophy of our company, which is truly global and generates the majority of its revenues and profits outside Italy ... A global company should, however, reinforce its image through a variety of communications media and not just through advertising. Sponsorship is one such medium and Benetton owns and directs its own Formula One motor racing team. All the characteristics of grand prix racing – speed, colour, internationality, excitement, plus the irresistible combination of high technology and the human factor – are a perfect expression of our corporate philosophy. The affiliation has been effective in creating an image for us in a number of countries even before we have established a commercial presence.'

Benetton Group's marketing campaign stretched advertising regulations to the limit, and brought the company into conflict with all manner of organisations and pressure groups. In Formula One, too, the approach was causing concern. Benetton Formula's eight-year engine supply deal with US car manufacturer Ford came to an end in 1994. It was the year Michael Schumacher took the Benetton-Ford racecar to the world drivers' championship. There had been an undercurrent of tension for some time. But relations were stretched to breaking point when one of Benetton Group's idiosyncratic poster adverts featured a car-bomb explosion – presumably meant to be a Mafia attack. The car was clearly seen to be a Ford Escort. The American motor giant was outraged, and when Ford protested the German poster campaign was pulled. Jac Nasser, then chairman of Ford of Europe, was beginning to question whether the company was getting value for money. There were worries that Benetton and its drivers lacked a commitment to get involved in the endorsements and promotions that normally go with the big sponsorship deals. In the end, it was Benetton which declined to renew the engine contract. Briatore had, remarkably, secured a deal with Renault to supply his team with the best engine on the market. The Williams team, which until then had the Renault engine to itself, was not pleased. But everyone, including Frank Williams, had to admire the speed with which Briatore had established Benetton Formula.

Around Benetton Formula were staged a series of promotional activities designed to reinforce the racing team's activities. Patrizia Spinelli, the publicity head who had worked with Briatore in America, was from a fashion rather than sports background, and it gave her a different perspective on Formula One's marketing potential. She was not interested in getting the Benetton name into the sports press. Spinelli wanted wider exposure in the general press. Money seemed to be no object. The occasional race-weekend football knock-about between the media and a few mechanics was once turned into a full 11-a-side event organised by Briatore and Spinelli. A stadium at Jerez was hired, and drivers and three Italian professional footballers took part. As editor of Benetton Formula's in-house magazine, John Lovesey was part of this whirlwind image-building enterprise. He described Benetton's role as 'to besiege Formula One in a marketing storm the like of which it had never before experienced. Benetton seemed to be everywhere at the track. When you got back to your hotel, the Benetton magazine would be lying around. Close the door, it seemed, and Benetton climbed through the window. Once, a Benetton mechanic even appeared on television in *Noel's House Party*[1] in some sort of caper.' The Benetton team was often used for fashion shoots, another innovation by Spinelli. Briatore loved them, as they would always involve someone famous – a footballer or film star, perhaps. There was a particularly memorable shoot at the famous Cumani thoroughbred stables. In flew the Benetton helicopter, managing to unsettle several million pounds' worth of horseflesh, and out stepped Briatore and a stunning blonde. Spinelli was on hand to comb Briatore's hair before the photographer got to work. Lovesey recalls the remark of a stable boy: 'Cor, it's just like the movies.' At each grand prix the Benetton motorhome was never without a film star or sportsman on show. Briatore did not start the practice of bringing in celebrities, he just took it to an extreme. Now it is *de rigueur* for team bosses to have a famous face around the team.

Luciano Benetton's brief to Flavio Briatore was to put the racing team

---

[1] A hugely popular British light entertainment programme involving members of the public.

in the spotlight, and it was working. Benetton Formula was making waves and making a profit. Luciano is an unlikely tycoon. With his unruly mass of curly white hair and ability to create controversy – he once posed naked for an advertising campaign – he neither looks nor acts like a mainstream businessman. Which, of course, he is not. It is the ability to think and act differently that distinguishes the entrepreneur from the ordinary businessman. In the mid-1950s, young Giuliana Benetton showed her brothers a multicoloured jumper she had made herself. What was nothing more than a germ of an idea, grew into a multinational fashion business. From a base in Treviso, northern Italy, the Benetton family has expanded from one factory in 1965 to 14 factories in eight countries, serving 7,000 shops and stores. The holding company, Edizione Holding SpA, has diversified sharply and now controls four main arms: manufacturing, which includes the fashion division; property; retailing and restaurants; and a miscellaneous collection of businesses that include financial services and Formula One. Luciano is the president, brother Gilberto is vice-president, Carlo is the production director of Benetton worldwide, and Giuliana is the creative force. The group is 72 per cent owned by the family, with the rest of the shares held by Italian and American institutional investors. Numerous members of the Benetton clan work in the group, including Alessandro, Luciano's son and possible successor, who is chairman of Benetton Formula.

The Benetton family rarely welcomes outsiders into the top echelons. An exception was Flavio Briatore. For those who thought Benetton's entry into Formula One seemed a strange move, the appointment of Briatore to head the racing team was nothing short of bizarre. But then these people misunderstood both the company's intentions and Briatore's talents. One of his close aides in the early days confessed to being somewhat bemused by the Italian's arrival. 'You know what the English are like. If you can't speak the language properly they think you're stupid. And Flavio's English was all in the present tense. He knew nothing about Formula One. I think the ignorance was an advantage. It meant he would say and do things the others would not try. Because of that, I suppose, he pushed back the boundaries in Formula One. The other teams saw him as an outsider, and they treated him that way. That is, until they discovered he was going to make himself a serious player. Then they treated him like a threat.' Briatore does not talk much about his background, which is no doubt why he has been the subject of so much gossip. Is it true that he used to run casinos? Was he forced to leave Italy? Where did he get the money to invest in Formula One? Briatore was not answering. Some people believe all the mystery is because he has something to hide; others that it is just a ruse to make him appear more interesting. In February 1993 the rumour mill went into overdrive when a small bomb exploded in the doorway of Briatore's rented Georgian house at the exclusive Cadogan Place, in Knightsbridge. The 8oz semtex device blew out windows, but no one was injured. Just as the whispers about organised crime began to grow, the police issued a statement that IRA terrorists had dumped the bomb because they feared they had been spotted. Briatore was an innocent victim, but the incident added more currency to his growing celebrity status.

Briatore was born in 1950 in Cuneo, near Turin in northern Italy, the son of teachers. A former ski instructor on the nearby slopes of the Italian Alps, he began working officially for the Benetton Group in 1982, but has told colleagues that he first met Luciano in 1974, when they established a strong friendship. Briatore had worked for RAS, an Italian insurance company, before moving to the Milan Stock Exchange, at a time of great financial turmoil and corruption in Italy. In 1977 Briatore fulfilled a childhood ambition to live in America. He ran a real estate business, and subsequently joined Benetton as a marketing executive, employed to look for suitable locations to open new shops in America. In the mid-1980s Briatore married a New Yorker, but they were divorced by the time he moved to Benetton Formula in England in 1989. Former colleagues say he rarely talked about his ex-wife, nor his family back in Italy. And although Italy is a country to which Briatore returns infrequently, he gets the newspapers sent over every day so as to keep up with events. When, as Briatore once told an interviewer, 'it was time to move' from his job in America, Luciano placed him at Benetton Formula. His lack of engineering experience was irrelevant as far as Luciano was concerned. Benetton Formula was a business proposition, and Luciano wanted a deal-maker to run the racing team; someone who would ensure the investment paid off.

Changes were swift at Benetton Formula. The English driver Johnny Herbert, struggling after a brutal accident, and team boss Peter Collins were among the first casualties. Briatore may have lacked Formula One experience, but he had the budget to surround himself with people who had. This gave Benetton a reputation for being political and overstaffed. But there is no doubt that Briatore bought the best. John Barnard, arguably Formula One's leading designer at the time, was recruited from

Ferrari to become technical director on a five-year contract. Barnard was given the money to turn Benetton's backward technical facilities into a modern research and development centre. His brief was simple – to give Benetton cars the edge in all areas of Formula One: in aerodynamics, composites, design. Barnard left suddenly in 1991, and in July that year Tom Walkinshaw (who now owns the Arrows team) was appointed engineering director to complete the job. Walkinshaw, an ally of Benetton's engine supplier Ford and a man respected as much for his ability as an organiser as for his engineering expertise, became the driving force behind the team's reorganisation. He hired staff from the defunct Reynard F1 project, including Rory Byrne as chief designer, and Ross Brawn was transferred from Walkinshaw's own Jaguar sports car programme. The Brawn/Byrne team gave Benetton one of the best technical double acts in Formula One, and it remained the team's core until the end of 1996. They also had one of the best-equipped factories to work in, the Whiteways Technical Centre, at Enstone, stuffed with more than £30 million worth of the latest equipment, and more than 200 staff. Not for Benetton a factory on a featureless business park, like Stewart Grand Prix or McLaren. Whiteways is built on 17 acres of beautiful Cotswold countryside. Screened by trees, a lot of the headquarters is below ground level, giving the impression that it is some secret establishment out of a James Bond film. Security is tight.

Much of Benetton's strategy in its early years was shaped around the hopes for its star driver, Michael Schumacher. By this time the young German had been the subject of the first of many high-profile rows over Briatore's tactics. Schumacher made a dazzling Formula One début in 1991 for Eddie Jordan's fledgling team, but was quickly lured to Benetton. Walkinshaw knew Schumacher from the driver's days in sports car and Formula Three racing. Schumacher's first outing for Jordan convinced Briatore and Walkinshaw – and anyone else watching – that he had something special to offer Formula One. There then followed three weeks of bitter rows that exposed all of Formula One's Machiavellian standards. Eddie Jordan, also in 1991 embarking on a Formula One career as a constructor, thought he had signed the services of one of the sport's future stars for himself. However, Briatore and Walkinshaw had other ideas. It turned into a messy affair, with allegations of dishonesty and double-dealing being levelled. On the Thursday before the 1991 Italian Grand Prix at Monza, Eddie Jordan tried to get an injunction preventing Schumacher from driving for any constructor except Jordan. The attempt failed, and Schumacher was free tu drive for Benetton – or so the team thought. Benetton's plan was that Schumacher should replace Roberto Moreno, Benetton's number-two driver. Moreno, however, was deeply angered by the move and during the Monza weekend sought – and won – an injunction preventing any other driver taking the number-two car. It was Bernie Ecclestone who eventually mediated a resolution among these warring parties, in a hotel on the Saturday night before the following day's race. The settlement was that Benetton would pay Moreno compensation, thought to be $500,000. And Moreno took a seat in the Jordan the following day. 'Eddie has not forgotten the affair,' one of his closest colleagues at Jordan was to say six years later. 'It taught him a lot; helped him in a way. But there was a lot a bitterness.'

The affair established Briatore and Benetton as an outfit with ambition, though it would be another couple of years before celebrity off the track was matched by success on it. In 1992, with the Williams cars having mastered active suspension, no other team was a serious challenger for the championship. Progress was made in 1993, when Benetton introduced its own active suspension and semi-automatic gearbox. The following year, however, was the year of triumph. Benetton and Schumacher were to sweep all before them. And they did it in controversial style. In fact, the 1994 season was to be the most momentous in Formula One's history, as it included the deaths of two drivers at the same race meeting. For a lot of people involved in Formula One the incidents that year were cause for shame and unease. But a by-product was to be a spectacular rise in global interest in the sport. At the start of the season there had been worries about falling television viewing figures. To spice up the season Nigel Mansell had even been brought back from America's Indy racing for a one-off drive in the French Grand Prix, his return fare paid for by Renault. Such attempts to heighten television audiences now look somewhat mild compared with the actual events that really sparked interest in 1994. For the first time in many years, Formula One received as much coverage on the news pages as it did on the sports pages.

Benetton's contribution to this remarkably eventful season began at the British Grand Prix, when Schumacher was disciplined and suspended for two races for ignoring a black flag (an order from the race stewards for an immediate return to the pits). Later, at Spa-Francorchamps, Schumacher was disqualified after Charlie Whiting, the FIA's technical director, discovered that the newly introduced compulsory 'skidblock' (a plank bolted to the underside of the car to reduce the aerodynamic effect) was worn below regulatory limits. Briatore said the plank was damaged when Schumacher's car ran on to the kerb. The stewards disagreed. Then there was the occasion at Hockenheim when Benetton's number-two car, driven by Jos Verstappen, was engulfed in flames during re-fuelling. No one was hurt, but news footage of this terrifying moment was beamed around the world. The FIA launched an investigation into the Benetton re-fuelling rig, and soon concluded that the fire could have been caused by the deliberate removal of a filter. The removal of the filter speeds up the fuel flow, saving perhaps half a second on a pit stop. But taking it out had probably allowed a piece of dirt to jam a valve open. Briatore hit back strongly, maintaining that the filter had been removed with the permission of the FIA technical delegate at the race. At the following grand prix, in Hungary, Briatore produced an independent report from experts at Accident and Failure Technical Analysis Ltd, which concluded that removing the filter did not cause the fire. At an FIA hearing in Paris into the incident, Briatore used the distinguished English QC, George Carman, to defend the team. His defence centred on the fact that another team had also allegedly been given permission to remove the filter, and that in Benetton's case the action was carried out by a junior member of the team. Benetton was cleared, but the whole affair left a sour after-taste.

Benetton's year of controversy had not yet ended, however. After the suspicions over poor safety standards came suggestions that the team was cheating. The use by constructors of computers and driver aids had become a worry to the sport's authorities. Serious fans, too, were getting less enjoyment out of their sport. The skill of driving was taking second place to the computer. The FIA acted in 1993, slapping bans on teams' attempts to give their drivers a computer-controlled advantage. But, there was more than a suspicion that some teams were not playing ball. It all started at that year's grand prix at Imola, when Benetton and McLaren were each fined $100,000 for trying to stop the FIA getting hold of the codes that access their in-car computer programmes. When Charlie Whiting, the FIA's technical director, eventually got inside Benetton's computers, what he found was sensational. Buried in the system was a software programme, called Launch Control, that would have enabled Schumacher to make near-perfect starts off the grid. Once a driver floored the throttle, the computer would take over to prevent the wheels spinning or the engine stalling. To find Launch Control, the FIA technicians had to select an apparently blank line on the menu programme and press a secret key. Benetton's claim that the system had not been used during the 1994 season could neither be proved nor disproved. But why had Launch Control been left in the software in the first place? Benetton said it was because removing it from the system was complicated. The programme, the team argued, had been concealed simply to prevent somebody switching it on by mistake. There was no conclusive outcome, but Briatore's critics seized on the issue as proof that Schumacher's successes were illegally aided. Niki Lauda, the ex-driver who became a consultant to Ferrari, was blunt in his assessment. 'When you build a car on the threshold of legality, which Benetton has apparently done all year long, and you get caught out again and again, it is simply not right.'

Even at the very last race of the 1994 season, Benetton was embroiled in controversy. Michael Schumacher started the Australian Grand Prix just one point ahead of Damon Hill in the Williams. The build-up was intense. Rivalry between the German and the Briton brought a new audience to the sport; people who had never been interested in racing. Sponsors loved it, the authorities loved it, and the television broadcasters pulled in the advertisers. The grand prix lived up to its billing, and the ending has gone down in Formula One history. Mid-way through the race Schumacher slid against a wall, damaging his car. At the next corner he hit Hill, taking them both out of the race, giving Schumacher the drivers' championship. Was the crash deliberate? Most probably, yes. The fact that Schumacher was blamed for a similar incident three years later involving Jacques Villeneuve confirmed many people's suspicions that the earlier crash was deliberate. The 1994 season was a traumatic one, though television audience figures and media monitoring prove that interest in the sport rose dramatically. Sponsors, too, got value for money from wider coverage of the sport. Even so, because the deaths, the scandals, and the excitements of 1994 had caused such controversy both inside and outside the sport, Formula One in the following season was on probation.

The 1995 season was another successful one for Benetton. With Schumacher again at the wheel, the team took both the drivers' and the constructors' titles, helping to dispel suggestions that Benetton could only succeed if it operated at the margins of legality. However, Schumacher's departure to Ferrari for 1996, followed later by technical duo Ross Brawn and Rory Byrne, left Benetton's superb facilities in the less experienced hands of Nick Wirth and Pat Symonds. Briatore's signing of drivers Jean Alesi and Gerhard Berger, whose partnership at Ferrari produced little success, always looked like a mistake. The team failed to win a single race in 1996. Briatore described the lack of competitiveness as a blip. He was wrong. The 1997 Benetton racecar was barely an improvement, winning only one grand prix – despite having the same Renault engine as its rival Williams.

One of Briatore's biggest headaches during this time was that title sponsor Mild Seven had a performance-related agreement with Benetton. Lack of success meant a reduction in sponsorship funds, leaving Briatore unable to throw money at problems like McLaren and Ferrari. When Mild Seven began sponsoring Benetton in 1994, the deal included a bonus of $1 million per win. That was good news in 1994 and 1995 while Schumacher reigned supreme, but in the following seasons both sponsorship and prize money suffered. Meanwhile the new Benetton drivers were costing about £4 million each in salaries. At the end of April 1997 members of the Benetton family gathered at the team's headquarters in Oxfordshire to consider their options for the future. A sale of the team, in whole or part, was on the agenda. An additional problem was Renault's announcement that it was withdrawing as a Formula One engine supplier after 1997. The same engines would be available via another company, Mecachrome, but they would cost £13 million a year. Until then Benetton had been receiving them free. Audi and Porsche, the German car companies, both looked at Benetton, not just as engine suppliers but as outright purchasers of the team. In the end Benetton Group kept faith with the racing team – though not with the manager, Briatore. His other business interests were taking up more and more time and, despite the public bonhomie, his relationship with his drivers was strained. Jean Alesi, now with Sauber, was blunt in his condemnation: 'Benetton were in a mess. Briatore spent no time at the factory.' In September 1997 it was announced that Briatore was being replaced by David Richards, chairman and 70 per cent shareholder of the British-based Prodrive, a £50 million turnover engineering company with 400 staff, that runs the successful Subaru world rally team. Richards had considered making an outright offer for the Benetton team, but the deal did not come off. Instead, he spent six months in talks with the Benetton family about joining the constructor's management team.

Asked what ingredients would make the best Formula One team, Richards replied: Ferrari's passion, Williams engineering, and McLaren's slick marketing. Oh yes, he added, and Benetton's image. Not, that is, the image of Benetton as rule-breaker, but the image it had before this started going wrong: sharp, fun, risk-taking, innovative.

Benetton in recent years had become stale, as Richards acknowledged. 'The image of the team had become a problem. You would look at a red car and say it was a Ferrari, the silver car you could say was a McLaren. Now you can spot Eddie Jordan's yellow car, but ours didn't communicate anything.' He believes the fans and employees lost a sense of attachment to Benetton. 'It was something Benetton had always been keen on, and in Italy they recognised that some of those core values had been allowed to slip away too far,' Richards believes. At Prodrive, Richards got a reputation as a control freak. In Formula One he admires, above all else, McLaren's Ron Dennis, a man with an obsessive attention to detail. At Prodrive, everyone had to use similar red mugs, keep their desks tidy, and park their car the same way round. There will be no slacking at Benetton under Richards.

The image created around Benetton during its heyday will probably be the team's lasting contribution to the development of Formula One in the 1990s. The Italian team became fashionable, in the way that some football clubs become fashionable, bringing millions of new fans to the sport. No longer did Formula One fans have to know the ins-and-outs of racecar technology; to be 'nerds' or 'anoraks' about the finer points of engineering. Benetton was a team to be followed simply because it was entertaining and stylish. If publicity is the measure, then Benetton has probably been the most successful team of recent years. Was it all part of a deliberate grand plan devised by Briatore, or the fortune of circumstances? The answer lies somewhere between accident and design. Several factors converged to make Benetton an extremely powerful and competitive force: there was a brilliant and determined driver in Michael Schumacher, and a team owner that relished controversy in Benetton Group. Both wanted to establish themselves quickly. No less important was that Benetton was locked into performance-related deals with Mild Seven, making the need to succeed still more intense. Also, the sport itself was ripe for change, and Briatore was skilful in the way he took advantage of this situation. He stamped his mark on Benetton, but also made a lasting impression on Formula One. Briatore took the cult of personality further than any other team boss in recent years, so inevitably Formula One seems less adventurous without him. He rocked the boat and made enemies, but that did not really matter in the closed world of Formula One. However, the man who did so much to raise the profile of grand prix racing is arguably not the kind of team boss that will be needed if Formula One becomes a company listed on the stock market. This is an important point, financier Nicky Samengo-Turner believes: 'Briatore was great value for money. But if Formula One had been a public company when he caused all that fuss, I can see how it might have unsettled investors. The buzz words in Formula One these days are transparency and respectability. Shareholders want stability. Formula One will not be a place for such high-profile entertainers as Briatore in the future. Richards is a completely different animal.'

Chapter Four: RACING ENTREPRENEURS

Introduction

APART FROM BENETTON'S brief spell as the leading team in the mid-1990s, Formula One has been dominated in recent years by McLaren and Williams. If there is an 'English approach' to Formula One, it is epitomised by these two teams. Ask executives in Formula One to name the team bosses they most admire and the answer is likely to be either McLaren's Ron Dennis or Williams Grand Prix Engineering's Frank Williams. These two are certainly no Flavio Briatore or Eddie Jordan, men for whom grand prix racing is about having fun. Indeed, if it was not for the fact that Dennis and Williams have been so enormously successful, they might appear odd fellows to be involved in a sport like grand prix racing. Dennis and Williams are somewhat austere, even humourless individuals engaged in what is a very dynamic and colourful enterprise. Yet, both have contributed enormously to the technological advances that have been made. And each has also brought a new professionalism to the job of running a Formula One team. When it is said that grand prix racing has become more businesslike and professional, it is because of what men like Dennis and Williams have done. They have, in short, significantly raised the standard over the past ten or so years. The factories at McLaren and Williams are models of engineering efficiency; spotless, high-tech, flexible – model businesses for the business sponsorship they are trying to attract. Impressive though this is, there are many racing fans who feel that Formula One has lost some of its intrinsic qualities because of this shift towards commercialism; too much business and not enough sport. Maybe this helps explain why there is so much public support for the fledgeling team that Jackie Stewart formed with his son Paul. Stewart Grand Prix is a commercial enterprise, just like the other constructors. But father and son talk about Formula One as a sporting passion as much as they do about it as a money-making operation. Jackie Stewart, a famous driver long before he became a successful businessman, is bringing a fresh attitude and integrity to the sport, and fans are responding positively to this. It is no easy job building a Formula One entrant, as countless failed team owners could testify. Inside the paddock, Stewart Grand Prix has still to win its spurs. Outside the paddock, however, the Stewarts are having an influence on the future of the sport, most notably because of their objections to tobacco sponsorship. Later in this chapter we look at the difficulties of building a new team, raising sponsorship, and carving out a niche in the highly competitive world of Formula One. But first we look at the influence of two seasoned constructors, and how concentrating on the right organisational and business environment turned them into two of the most successful teams in grand prix history – and role models for the rest of the grid.

McLaren: Big Ambitions

IN 1991 RON DENNIS, managing director of McLaren, featured on the front cover of *Management Week* magazine under the heading: 'Is This the Best Manager in Britain?' It was an era when McLaren cars, powered by Honda engines and driven by Ayrton Senna and Alain Prost, surpassed everything else on the grid. It was also an era when 'the entrepreneur' was king, when those individuals prepared to strike out on their own and build a company in their image were fêted by politicians and business leaders alike. Dennis proved that the principles of business were as applicable to grand prix racing as any other sphere of enterprise. And McLaren's success made Dennis an obvious choice to include among the cream of British management. While he was setting new standards in Formula One management, the team was setting new standards in innovation: the first carbon-fibre monocoque, money to use the best wind tunnel and test rig, the slickest pit-stops. Dennis did not stop at Formula One. Out of the racing operation grew electronics, marketing and manufacturing divisions. Today, most Formula One teams are only just beginning to explore how they can diversify and exploit the brand name. Dennis was doing it ten years ago. In the process he turned McLaren into the most profitable of all the Formula One teams. In 1996 the group as a whole, TAG McLaren Holdings (40 per cent owned by Dennis), saw pre-tax profits rise from almost £8 million to £11.9 million. Sales rose from £75 million to £86.4 million. The racing operation itself is now the largest in Formula One after Ferrari.

Success is rarely humbling. McLaren had the biggest and the best of everything – and Dennis had the ego to match. Rivals found his triumphalist public statements insufferable. (His comment to the media 'we make history, you write about it' is part of Formula One folklore.) Former McLaren driver Niki Lauda, in his autobiography *To Hell and Back*, did not pull his punches: 'To me, Ron's weakness resides in a sort of chip on the shoulder complex. It hurts to be reminded he started life as a humble mechanic. This is why he overreacts as team boss. His arrogance can be unbearable.' It might have been unbearable to some people, but it is what drove Dennis on to achieve bigger and better things. In any case, Dennis confined such criticism to the dustbin of professional jealousy. By 1993, when McLaren's remarkable run of success was coming to a shuddering halt, that dustbin was getting pretty full. The Formula One paddock is a claustrophobic and cruel place, and Dennis's rivals watched with barely disguised glee as McLaren lurched from one crisis to another. Flavio Briatore, the former Benetton boss who was initially shunned by Formula One's élite, mocked McLaren's fall from grace. 'It used to be that Dennis wouldn't want to say hello to me. Now, it's exactly the opposite.' If the arrows hit their mark, Ron Dennis never showed it. Even so, McLaren's fall from reverence to ridicule must have been a painful experience for Dennis. The nadir was a farcical episode involving Nigel Mansell's 1995 racecar. The car had to be redesigned because the former world champion was too big for the cockpit. Had McLaren not been known for the brilliance of its design work? Such incidents raised questions about Dennis's management. Had Dennis lost his touch? Or had he just got bored with Formula One? Was he distracted by other projects? Or had the brilliance of the team for years disguised a rather mediocre manager? Endless column inches in the magazines and newspapers were devoted to the downfall of one of Formula One's most historic names. The conclusion most often drawn was that McLaren's expansion into other fields meant Dennis had taken his eye off the ball. Watching McLaren's various commercial schemes take shape, Patrick Head, technical director of Williams Grand Prix Engineering, once observed: 'It begins to look as if they might be biting off more than they can chew. I do hope so.' Head got his wish.

McLaren is now back on top. The 1998 season saw a return to glory, with the West-McLaren-Mercedes racecars leaving their rivals in the shade. During the low years, Ron Dennis rebuilt the team: new staff, new chassis, new engine, new approach. Now his plans are all coming to fruition on the racetrack. Of all the team bosses to have come up through the ranks of Formula One, Dennis is still regarded as the most enterprising businessman among them. It may have something to do with Edward de Bono, the psychologist whose ideas about lateral thinking encouraged people to think independently. Dennis studied lateral thinking in the 1980s and was strongly influenced by the ideas. Management, its theory and practice, also holds a special interest for Dennis, who will happily talk for hours about his way of running a company. He does, however, have a tendency to drift into convoluted management-speak, a language irreverently known as 'Ron-speak', which makes it difficult to follow the thread of his argument. Dennis has no formal business training, but has gleaned his ideas from management books, and from the two journals he most likes to read: *The Economist* and *The Harvard Business Review*. The office joke is that he never reads them, but leaves the magazines lying around to make an impression. But Dennis certainly acquired a financial literacy from somewhere, something that gave him an edge over many other team bosses. This knowledge enabled him to talk to sponsors (a word he dislikes, preferring to call them investors) on their own terms; and it helped him crystallise his strategy to diversify McLaren into an engineering business. Many of Dennis's peers might not have liked him, but they admired him, and they eventually copied him.

McLaren's image tends to look sterile and unemotional. Dennis himself gives the appearance of being rather strict and somewhat aloof. Even when McLaren's cars came one and two in the first race of the 1998 season, a triumph that heralded a renaissance in the team, Dennis could barely raise a smile. 'He looks as though someone has given him £5 and taken £10 back,' quipped commentator Murray Walker. The bonhomie that comes out of Benetton or Jordan seems alien at McLaren. 'Ron even gets uncomfortable if people arrive at the office late,' says Norman Howell, a former employee. 'He'll trust his managers with huge budgets, but worries about them turning up on time. It's his business work ethic.' Dennis is famously meticulous, and obsessed with cleanliness and efficiency. When each new racecar is built for the following season, the last job is to stick on the sponsors' decals. Dennis likes to do this himself, not because it is some symbolic gesture to 'sign off' the car after the hard graft of development, but because he wants to ensure that sponsors get the exact positioning they paid for. All this attention to detail is probably no bad thing in modern Formula One, where presentation is all-important. For Dennis, the only *sport* in Formula One is those two hours between the start and finish of the race. 'Everything else is business,' he said. 'Never forget that.' The company's headquarters embodies his style. The overwhelming colour of the offices and fittings is grey, because, said Dennis, it conveys smartness. The furnishings resemble the first-class cabin of a jumbo jet. The only sparkle is in the impressive trophy room, lined with dozens of cups. Unfortunately, it has been a constant reminder of the difficulty of living up to a glorious past. There are not many trophies from the mid-1990s.

Born in 1947, Ron Dennis began his working life as an apprentice at Thomson & Taylor's, then a well-established British motor trade business. It was taken over by Chipstead, which had also just bought the Cooper F1 team, and Dennis ended up as a mechanic on the racecars. In 1967, Dennis moved to Brabham, run by Sir Jack Brabham, one of Formula One's legendary drivers and later a successful business-man. Although Dennis was head mechanic, he also found himself doing a lot of the managerial work. He left in 1971 to run a successful Formula Two outfit called Project Four, and in 1973 Dennis began to consider setting up a Formula One team. He was close to securing major sponsorship from the French oil company Motul, but was foiled by the economic recession caused by the Gulf energy crisis. It would be seven years before he got another shot at Formula One. It was Philip Morris, owner of the Marlboro cigarette brand that gave Dennis the break he craved. McLaren had been sponsored by Philip Morris, Formula One's single biggest sponsor, since 1972, but by 1980 the company was losing patience with the team's poor performance. The founder, Bruce McLaren, had died ten years earlier, and the glory days were long gone. Teddy Mayer, who became McLaren's principal share-holder, had run the team since the death of Bruce McLaren, but Philip Morris thought it time for a change. The tobacco company had talent-spotted a 34-year-old Ron Dennis running Project Four in Formula Two. In 1980 Philip Morris, demonstrating its already enormous power within Formula One, orchestrated a merger between McLaren and Project Four. In 1981 Dennis and Crichton Brown bought 50 per cent of McLaren, and the following year the celebrated racecar designer John Barnard also bought a stake in the company. The old management was swept away, and the new management set about revolutionising Formula One racecar construction. The McLaren MP4, with its all-new carbon-fibre chassis, laid the foundation for McLaren's dominance during the 1980s. The combination of Dennis and Barnard was suc-cessful, but explosive; these were two working-class boys with difficult temperaments. In the end McLaren was not big enough for both of them, and Barnard went off to join Ferrari in 1987. But the McLaren success story kept rolling on. Between 1981 and 1993, the team won 80 races, and the constructors' championships on six out of ten seasons from 1984. McLaren was runner-up in the other four seasons. A remarkable record.

Technical superiority, combined with great drivers, lay behind McLaren's success. But behind even these is a more important factor – McLaren's financial stability. Marlboro's three-year rolling contracts were providing around $45 million a year. Still more cash was coming in from other sponsors and prize money. The company also had a strong and loyal shareholder in Techniques d'Avant Garde (TAG Group). McLaren International, the racing arm and principal division, is owned by TAG McLaren Holdings. TAG McLaren is controlled by Dennis and the wealthy TAG Group whose chief executive is Mansour Ojjeh. An absence of serious money worries made long-term planning possible – a luxury in the ever-changing world of Formula One, and another reason for rival team bosses to be jealous of Dennis. With all that money and support, how could he fail to win, carped the critics. When McLaren did begin to fail to win, in the 1990s, the chorus of disapproval grew louder. TAG, a Franco-Saudi holding company with assets of about $500 million, began buying into McLaren in 1986, and increased its stake when John Barnard sold out. The rumour-mongers have fixed a For Sale sign outside McLaren's Surrey headquarters many times. Roger Penske, the constructor of Indy racecars, has persistently been tipped as a likely buyer, as has Philip Morris itself. And Tommy Suharto, son of the former Indonesian president, also looked at McLaren, before going on to head a group of businessmen who bought Lamborghini, the Italian sports car company, from Chrysler in 1993. Through good times and bad, however, Mansour Ojjeh has remained faithful to his investment.

TAG was founded by Mansour's father, Akram, and has been an important business link between the Saudi government and the rest of the world. The company has property and farming interests in the United States and South America, is a distributor for the Canadair Challenger executive jet, and used to own Diners Club in the Middle East. TAG Heuer, the watch division, is better known to Formula One fans as the official timekeeper and provider of race data to the teams. It was the flotation in 1996 of TAG Heuer, in which Dennis had a stake, that took him into the realms of the super rich. TAG's entry into Formula One was as a sponsor of Williams Grand Prix Engineering, whose boss Frank Williams had worked tirelessly to open up a new source of revenue from oil-rich Saudi Arabia. A young Mansour Ojjeh, who had been attracted to motor racing while studying law and business in Europe and America, was part of a high-powered Saudi delegation to the 1978 Monaco Grand Prix. It was Ojjeh who persuaded his family to support Williams. Dennis, however, spotted that Williams was on to a good thing, and it was not long before he was wooing TAG. Alan Henry, in his official history of Williams Grand Prix Engineering, recalls: 'Dennis arrived on the scene and virtually hijacked TAG from Frank's clutches. McLaren had committed themselves to the extremely ambitious Porsche turbo engine programme for the team, but they had not got the necessary finance available to follow the project through on a long-term basis. Mansour Ojjeh was targeted as a likely investor and Ron's judgement proved spot-on.' Frank Williams was very unhappy about losing one of his key sponsors in such a way. 'But that's Ron's modus operandi,' Williams told Henry.

It was a sharp manoeuvre, and one that marked Dennis out as a man with ambition. But the move was not as ruthless as some people like to pretend. Dennis was pushing at an open door with TAG, because Ojjeh too was looking for a change. At Williams, TAG was just a sponsor. Ojjeh wanted more involvement, and McLaren's Porsche engine deal was the ideal opportunity to get involved on the research and development side of Formula One. Ojjeh persuaded his father to finance the engine programme, subcontract it to Porsche, but retain the intellectual rights. For Ojjeh, the deal 'put the TAG name up there with Ferrari, BMW and Renault'. TAG viewed McLaren not as a 200mph advertising billboard (as it had seen the Williams team) but as a central part of the group's investment strategy. While other constructors remained pure racers – Williams GPE being the prime example – Dennis and Ojjeh had a vision of building on McLaren's Formula One expertise. Competing in Formula One can be a feast or famine business: one season the team is at the front of the grid, raking in sponsorship and prize money, but the next season might be a disaster. Dennis's strategy was to reduce the uncertainty by creating new money-making ventures on the back of McLaren's grand prix success. 'The idea was to address the logic of Formula One,' Dennis explains. 'And that logic is, you are never going to win every race and every championship. We are realistic enough to know that it is just too difficult. As you rise and fall in competitiveness, so your commercial success pretty much tracks those ups and downs. Strangely enough, it is when you are down that you need to spend the most money in order to get back up again. I was looking for ways of equalising those peaks and troughs.'

McLaren is now something of a role model for other teams looking to develop their racing divisions into diversified businesses. Several teams currently have management consultants drawing up business plans, including Williams. Why does Dennis think it has taken teams so long to see the logic of growing into mature businesses? 'Lack of opportunity? Lack of vision? I don't know. My corporate ego is pleased that we left them all in the dust when it comes to growth.' And what does he think of his rivals as businesses? 'Let's just say, they all need those management consultants – though you must promise to qualify this statement with the fact that I had a smile on my face when I said it. Some of these people are my friends.' McLaren's emphasis on a strong management structure is also being copied. Until recently, Jordan Grand Prix's senior personnel were content to hold 'corridor' meetings, decision-making on the hoof. When Eddie Jordan started in Formula One in 1991 he said he wanted to be like McLaren. But it was not until five years later that he formalised the executive structure. 'Why are we not performing as a company?' he said to John Putt, a management consultant with 15 years' experience in the automotive industry. It took Putt just minutes to come up with the answer: it was because the decision-makers never sat down together long enough to thrash out the problems. Now they meet religiously once a week.

There are four main divisions to TAG McLaren: electronics, racing, road cars and marketing. McLaren has invested heavily in the electronics division, drawing upon expertise in Formula One technology and engine management systems. The division supplies automotive electronic control systems to several Formula One teams, and has a customer base of 60 clients. Dennis explained: 'We had the know-how in automotive electronics and other industries, so it made sense to exploit this. For example, we are big in carbon fibre, and it made sense to build on these techniques. We are not interested in McLaren clothes, and branding of this sort. We are a high-tech company. It is possible to have a series of satellite companies that supply Formula One, but also spin off commercially from Formula One. Vertical integration has put our Formula One operation in a unique situation. The racing team has access to an electronics arm which is stronger than anything any other team has developed. We subcontract the services, including to other Formula One teams. It is all done in the strictest confidentiality. I have to make an appointment even to go into the factory. We have been able to invest in electronics to a level that we could never have justified if it was only for the McLaren racing team.' TAG Electronics, as the division is called, has a list of clients that includes the Italian motorcycle manufacturer Cagiva, and car manufacturers Peugeot and BMW. Figures for the year ending 1995 show pre-tax profits of £1.65 million, up from £358,868. Turnover was £10.595 million, against £7.33 million.

One of the most interesting projects that McLaren has started is a five-year partnership with British Aerospace (BAe), one of Britain's biggest manufacturers, for mutual exploitation of their technologies. McLaren has had strong links with the aerospace industry ever since Robin Herd was recruited from the Anglo-French Concorde supersonic aircraft project in 1965. Herd's Mallite chassis – basically an aluminium/balsa wood sandwich, as used in aircraft – was probably the stiffest of its day and took racecar construction to a new level. Formula One cars still share many of the technological features of advanced aircraft, such as using advanced composites and high-spec engineering. Having mastered aerodynamics, McLaren is now experimenting with fluid dynamics, and is already applying data to its own engineering design programmes. Where big business can learn from Formula One teams is in the fast turnaround times: new ideas can be taken from the drawing-board to the track in a matter of weeks, whereas for industry it can take years. However, competitive pressure is forcing aerospace companies to reduce their long design and development periods, and BAe believes it can learn from McLaren. Dennis calls it a cross-pollination of ideas. 'British Aerospace are quite interested in our management style and our mechanisms for motivating our workforce. They have some technology we are interested in, and we have some fast prototype strategies they are interested in, specifically, how we conceptualise an idea.'

A second McLaren division, Marketing Services, has also expanded rapidly. 'In fact,' said Dennis, 'the speed of growth alarms me. I do not want a dilution of effort, I want controlled growth.' Marketing Services 'handles the search for investors in the surface of our cars'. It looks after advertising and promotions, design, hospitality and general after-sales events. With 30 staff, it is by far the largest marketing unit in Formula One apart from Ferrari's. Once again, Dennis's professional approach to the task of raising sponsorship and servicing those clients is paying dividends. The division's financial performance has been impressive. Pre-tax profits were £1.6 million, rising from just £101,808 the year before. Turnover rose from £3.06 million to £6.18 million. The third important division of the group is McLaren International, the racing operation itself. Despite some poor performances on the track, the division still made profits of £9 million in 1995, down from £11 million. Turnover, made up largely of sponsorship and prize money, rose just over £3 million to £48 million. The fourth arm of the group is McLaren Cars – and it is probably the one Dennis would most like to forget. This is the division that built the McLaren F1 road car. Conceived in the yuppie boom of the 1980s, the vehicle did not reach the market until recession had hit in the early 1990s. Technologically, the car achieved everything McLaren hoped. But the F1 was a financial disappointment. Cash bled from the operation, which in the year ending 31 October 1995 made losses of £2.28 million on a turnover of £17.094 million. Dennis spent months sorting out the problem.

Ron Dennis and designer Gordon Murray had the idea for the McLaren F1 in 1988, while at the airport waiting for the plane home after the Italian Grand Prix. The late 1980s were the time to think such grandiose schemes. By 1993, when the road car went on sale, Western and Japanese economies were in recession and the demand for exotic cars had dried up. The F1 cost £634,000, and McLaren lost money on every one of the 100 cars made (the target had been to build 300). Motoring journalists lauded the McLaren F1, with its carbon-fibre chassis and racecar technology. Not for nothing did this car have F1 after its name. Economically, however, the McLaren F1 was a very expensive mistake, even if, as Ojjeh maintains, the development programme was extremely beneficial and good for McLaren's image. Final losses on the car are expected to reach many millions of pounds.

Dennis is always bubbling with bold plans and new ideas. But some proposals just look impulsive. No sooner has he dreamt them up, than he has abandoned them. One plan, conceived in 1991, was to challenge for the land speed record. Project Maverick was a 42ft-long vehicle, powered by a Rolls-Royce RB199 Mk140 gas-turbine engine borrowed from a Tornado fighter aircraft. The aim was to take the car from standstill to 850mph in 40 seconds. McLaren was looking for a new project: the two criteria were that it had to be world class and it had to capitalise on the company's core talents. A separate company was set up, McLaren Advanced Vehicles, headed by aeronautical engineer Dr Robert Bell. Staff were deployed to begin raising sponsorship and prepare the groundwork. After many months of hard work Project Maverick was just dropped. Dennis had learned that Richard Noble was preparing his own attempt on the record, and felt that McLaren was in a no-win situation. Noble went on to break the record in 1997 with his *Thrust SSC*. Norman Howell, a former motor racing journalist at the *Sunday Times*, who worked at McLaren, said the irony of the whole thing was that Noble's plans were not that far advanced until he heard of McLaren's interest. 'Noble received a telephone call requesting some tapes of the last land speed record. Being a clever guy he worked out that it was McLaren. Eventually, Ron pulled the plug and that's the last anyone ever heard of it.' Despite the abandonment of Maverick there were a few spin-offs from the project. It raised McLaren's profile, gave it a database on the design and construction of supersonic vehicles, and access to a new range of super-computers. But it is an expensive way to go about it, and incredibly frustrating for those involved.

To Dennis's detractors these activities were frivolous and, more importantly, a distraction. If there is a single explanation for McLaren's decline it was that the man who took the team to greatness was now more interested in other things. Nigel Mansell, the former Formula One drivers' champion is in no doubt that Dennis's pre-occupation with growing McLaren engineering businesses left a vacuum at the top of the racing team. In his autobiography, Mansell describes what he found when he joined a dispirited McLaren racing team in 1995, following two years as an IndyCar driver in America. 'To my dismay ... some of the people in the McLaren team hadn't a clue what to do about problems. I could see that until they put some new blood into the team and new direction in the design department, they would be in trouble for some time to come. McLaren's problem today is that Ron Dennis has got involved in so many other business ventures that he has increasingly left the running of the Formula One team to other people. Although he has got some great people in the team, some are living in a fool's paradise and resting on past glories. I think Ron became out of touch and only started to realise early in the 1995 season just how big a problem he had.'

Those problems started with, perhaps, the biggest one of all – the loss of McLaren's extremely successful five-year engine supply deal with Honda in 1992. The Japanese motor group was facing deep financial problems, and Honda's withdrawal from Formula One looked likely as part of a retrenchment strategy. But Dennis seemed to have a blind spot about Honda, and simply did not see Honda's withdrawal coming. At least this is what many McLaren staff felt at the time. 'Ron just would not believe it was going to happen,' said one of his associates. 'He flatters himself that he can read people. But he didn't read Honda.

If he had had his eye on the ball, he would have seen it and made some contingency plan.' When Honda ended one of Formula One's most profitable partnerships, McLaren had to find a replacement urgently – hardly the best circumstances for choosing the most important and expensive component of a racecar. Dennis was forced to buy an off-the-shelf engine from Ford, but was disappointed by the poor quality. It is not widely known that Dennis came close to doing a deal with the American car maker Chrysler, which then owned Lamborghini. Chrysler approached Dennis to see if McLaren could evaluate a Lamborghini V12 engine. The powerplant was secretly tested by Ayrton Senna, and according to those present the Brazilian driver was very impressed. Just as Dennis was close to securing a financial commitment from Chrysler, however, it was announced that McLaren would be getting its engines from the French manufacturer Peugeot. Mansour Ojjeh had been using his French contacts in order to privately broker a deal with Peugeot. Senna was said to have been 'flabbergasted'.

In addition to the engine problems, there was also criticism of McLaren's chassis design. It was a problem that went to the heart of the McLaren operation. Whereas McLaren had been able to disguise its decline in performance by blaming the quality of the engines, there was no way of exonerating itself over the chassis. The blame lay squarely at McLaren's door. Drivers are the best people to assess the quality of the chassis, and once again Nigel Mansell was stinging in his condemnation. Mansell said that McLaren had simply failed to maintain standards. The driver, who was being paid £1 million a race, competed just twice before calling it a day though McLaren was not unhappy to see him walk. Mansell's fault-finding, and the fiasco over the car cockpit that was too small for him, was highly embarrassing for the team. McLaren had been prompted into the Mansell deal by Philip Morris, which wanted a big-name signing to ride alongside the rising Finish driver, Mika Hakkinen. Inevitably it put further strain on the Marlboro sponsorship. Philip Morris wanted to cut its annual $45 million sponsorship deal by up to half. Dennis rejected the new proposal and switched title sponsorship to the German brand West, while Marlboro went to Ferrari.

Is there a lesson for other teams in McLaren's decline in the mid-1990s? Is it proof that the current trend towards diversifying and building the brand name is doomed to failure? After all, competing in Formula One requires a command and control approach to management, dictated by one man. When Ron Dennis got distracted by other things, McLaren's racing team fell apart. Not surprisingly, the man himself thinks such arguments are foolish. Dennis accepts that he got over-confident, too complacent perhaps, after the years of success. To have won 15 races out of 16 in one year alone must inevitably have sapped some of the motivation. Like any manager, he needs a challenge, and Dennis had already achieved it all. He puts the difficulties down to force of circumstances. 'It was not because I took my eye off the ball. Sometimes you just cannot do everything you want to do, because the timing is not right. You cannot just have the engine you want, or the driver you want. They may just not be available. You can only evolve into being the best. It is all about timing. What you need and what you get are two different things. That is why our resurgence back to competitiveness has taken longer than we would have liked. It is pitifully easy for journalists to look in from the outside and say, you need to do this or that. The skill is not in observing what a team needs, the skill is in actually getting it.'

At last McLaren has got the package it needs. A long-term engine deal, with Mercedes, and a five-year sponsorship (investment) deal with West, have re-energised the team. In 1997, Adrian Newey, the technical director so instrumental to Williams's successes, joined McLaren. His salary, at a reputed £2 million, was three times what he was getting at Williams. Martin Whitmarsh, meanwhile, has moved up from operations director to become managing director of the racing team. Whitmarsh, a former British Aerospace executive, is Dennis's anointed successor. Most Formula One executives have come through motor racing management. It is a school of management that is all about fire-fighting, rather than being planned, organised, controlled. Whitmarsh, like several of McLaren's top people, was brought in from outside the sport in an attempt to broaden and deepen the management. But he is not universally popular. 'Young, arrogant, but talented,' was how one employee described him. 'He knows just enough about everything to meddle in everything.'

It used to be a complaint that Dennis was reluctant to empower those around him because he always felt he could do things better himself. The best teams are those with flat management structures welded together by a charismatic boss. There is only room for one ego. Slowly, though, Dennis seems to have learned the lesson that in a company the size of McLaren he cannot do everything himself. McLaren's problem, perhaps, was not that Dennis lost interest in racing, but that he spread himself too thinly by taking on other projects. Now, however, he has finally found managers he trusts who can be put into positions of power. 'Martin is ten years younger than me,' said Dennis. 'And as he moves up, I would be very disappointed if in five years' time there was not someone coming up behind him. You have got to bring on new people. But you should try to avoid doing it from outside. The problem with bringing people in from the outside is that you can never be certain about them until they are actually on board. If they are not signed up to the culture, we could be in trouble. If I did nothing but run the Formula One team, and then fell under a bus, the team would be in a poor shape. Part of my responsibility is to ensure that the thing can work without me.'

In Dennis's philosophy, he must be a chapter in McLaren's history, not the book itself. 'The thing a manager has to remember, is that you are being a fool if you try to make yourself the beginning and end of the company. If you do not run it on the basis of being a chapter, your ego can run amok and your desire to be recognised will just get in the way. There is no reason why you should not aim to be the best chapter. But make sure you have competent second-level management who can pick up the values, add to them, and lead the company into another chapter. We are going through that process now.' Staff at McLaren are among the best paid in Formula One, and Dennis is regarded as a good employer. Annual staff turnover is low, at under 3 per cent. Dennis explains a possible reason: 'One of our company policies is that you can have any job you want in the group providing you are qualified for it. It is an unusual culture. We will only ever recruit from outside if we cannot find a suitable candidate within the company. This allows and encourages people to grow and develop their skills. My view is that when someone moves into a new job, the confidence might not be 100 per cent. But the difference between their current confidence level and reaching 100 per cent can usually be made up by motivation and a desire to broaden their horizons.' This desire for equality extends to providing drivers with equal equipment and equal treatment, unlike several other teams where the number-two driver gets a second-rate package.

The drawback of all this is that it can leave a lot of dead wood about the company. Norman Howell suspects that there is a soft spot in Dennis which makes it tough for him to make redundancies. He thinks part of the company's problem is that it has not had very much new blood for quite some time. The fact that McLaren has been rich enough to throw money at problems, instead of using a more surgical approach, has probably not helped either. Howell said: 'But this is the nature of the team, and for a long while it was a system that worked admirably. Undoubtedly, though, the McLaren tree could have done with a little pruning. Maybe then, the younger shoots would have come through faster and helped the team towards new thinking and new victories.' Dennis regularly briefs the whole factory. The underlying message is always the same: although staff may not be directly involved in the pinnacle of McLaren's activities, grand prix racing, they can still contribute to its success. Dennis said: 'Satisfaction comes from achievement, and staff may not feel they are achieving until the racing team is winning. I try to convey to people that if we try to be the best at everything we do, we can win in many ways. We can be the best presented team, provide the best hospitality. We constantly look at how the machinists operate, how the factory operates, and ask: are we doing it in the best possible way? Whether it be in the electronics division or the finance department, you have to get people to understand that a positive attitude contributes to the success of the whole group. You have got to convey those values through your management – it cannot be done through a disciplinary process. People must be carried with you, and persuaded there is a better way of doing things.'

To some ears, Dennis's ideas about running McLaren may sound like truisms from a third-rate book on management theory – except that, in the world of Formula One, fractions of a second can make a difference. And Dennis believes that fractional increases in performance on the track originate from attention to detail off the track, at the factory. He said: 'I have a view that every single thing in a company is important; the entire spectrum, from how a toilet roll dispenser functions, to who drives our racing cars. This way McLaren will be greater than the sum of its parts, and this will give you a performance gain in the design and performance of a racing car. A winning racing car rarely has one single thing that is lacking in the others. They normally have many tiny things that give them an incremental advantage. This makes the difference between winning and losing. The great companies are those that have the intention of being the best at everything. And this envelops the whole environment.'

Contrary to what the critics advised – that Dennis needed to roll up his sleeves and get involved with the racing team again – he now sees his role as supervisory, moving throughout all divisions of the company and dispensing advice to those on the shop-floor. Dennis admits that it probably sounds as if he is a megalomaniac, but it is not meant to convey that impression. 'I am very much the conductor these days. I am not in the orchestra. If any managing director is in a position where he can free himself of the day-to-day burdens, and yet use his experience moving around the factory and playing an active role in organisation, I am sure they would find it extremely satisfying. That does not mean I am becoming semi-detached. I want to play a constructive role in the group. I do not want some sort of token non-executive position.' Dennis does not need to work. Company accounts show that Dennis earned close to £4 million in 1996, and the annual *Sunday Times* survey of Britain's rich put his wealth at £45 million, making him joint 415th richest person in the country. He carries on because he enjoys Formula One, and because there is a renewed motivation to put McLaren back on top. Dennis still attends all the grand prix weekends, working out of a plush £800,000 motorhome that is fully wired-up to the head-quarters. He does not normally turn his attention to the team until the race day on Sunday. Howell, in his book on McLaren, recalls the confusion of one new McLaren driver, who had to deal with one manager running the factory during the weekdays, another when pre-paring for race practice at the grand prix, and then Dennis on the Sunday. 'He thought it didn't work too badly, but that the potential for confusion was greater than in other teams, where the lines of communication and command were more distinct.'

Much of Ron Dennis's time is now taken up with an ambitious project to build an all-encompassing technical centre on 125 acres of greenbelt land near the existing factory at Woking, Surrey. The oper-ation will be the catalyst to restructure the whole company, which has fragmented on to seven separate sites, with the Formula One operation on three of them. The plant will include a research and development laboratory, a design studio and a museum. It will also be home to a McLaren-sponsored university to develop young engineering talent. Formula One has been a big beneficiary of Britain's engineering appren-ticeship system, a form of training that has been in decline for years. Dennis said: 'There is a shortage of engineers in this country and we want to do something to reverse the situation. It will be a world-leading educational and training establishment aimed primarily at the automotive industry. One of the pioneering ideas is that the course will have university accreditation.' What Dennis plans is a sort of 'super-apprenticeship'. 'Students will be able to get a degree, but still be active members of the company. They will come out with academic qualifications, and with practical experience. The university will give us access to the *crème de la crème* of young brains.' And, yes, the students will get a chance to work in Formula One. 'We envisage something unique as far as engineering is concerned. There will be a lot of cross-fertilisation between different departments and different projects.' In its submissions to the planning inquiry, McLaren indicated that the £40 million centre would employ 1,000 people, and would take McLaren's turnover to £300 million by the year 2000. In 1997, the then Conservative government was clearly impressed. In approving the project the then Secretary of State for the Environment, John Gummer, described McLaren as 'exceptional both in the quality of its products and its achievement'.

At McLaren, Formula One has come full circle. The sport was born out of the auto and aerospace industries. Ron Dennis has been crossing over from the other side, using what he has learned in motor racing to build a hi-tech engineering business. Some people dismissed Dennis as 'an eighties entrepreneur running an eighties company'. But, now that Formula One has moved into the business mainstream and become purely profit-driven, Dennis's strategy to diversify seems to have proved correct. McLaren's racetrack achievements under Ron Dennis have gone down in motor racing history; but as a role model for how a constructor's activities can be deepened and broadened in the commercial era, Dennis has also been influential. Team bosses are discovering that over the next few years there will be tens of millions of pounds to be made from Formula One by using the brand name and engineering expertise in other areas. A wealth of new revenue streams are opening up, from subcontracting to entertainment projects. McLaren's founder, Bruce McLaren, was once asked if it would be easier if he had more money. 'No, we'd probably get in a terrible mess,' he replied. 'Each year it gets a little harder to keep things neatly and as nicely controlled as we did in previous years, because there's that much more administration, that much more to go wrong. You can get too big as a racing team, get too hidebound.' That was in 1969. The demands and conditions of modern Formula One make such attitudes look quaint. Grand prix constructors are now run by businessmen, with business instincts and business ambitions. And Ron Dennis is the epitome of this modern breed of Formula One entrepreneur.

Williams: Pure Racer

WILLIAMS GRAND PRIX ENGINEERING celebrated its 21st birthday in 1998. In keeping with the company's style, the occasion was marked in low-key fashion. Not for Williams GPE the extravagance of Benetton or Ferrari. Frank Williams, founder and majority shareholder of the business, lets the racing do the talking. In 1997 Williams GPE won the constructors' championship for a record ninth time. For Frank Williams there would be no better way to honour the birthday than to make it ten. (He failed.) His team's recent dominance in Formula One has won it two Queen's Awards for Export Achievement (designed to salute UK success in overseas markets). The business experts who made the awards were recognising the same quality admired by the Williams GPE's peers in Formula One – the team's consummate professionalism. This, above all, is the defining feature of the operation. Tom Walkinshaw, a successful businessman and owner of the Arrows team, believes one of Williams GPE's greatest contributions has been to raise standards. 'The Williams team's success comes from stability, from everyone knowing his own job and doing it 100 per cent – while trusting a fellow team member to do his job 100 per cent and not look over his shoulder. They've got utter belief in each other, and their performance shows it.' These are qualities other teams aspire to, but few achieve. Now, even the most focused team in Formula One is looking at how to exploit its expertise in other areas. Management consultants are drawing up ideas to broaden Williams GPE's revenue base. Subcontracting the company's engineering knowledge, something already done on a small scale, is the most likely diversification. But no idea to develop the brand has been ruled out (except a Williams eau-de-Cologne, say the consultants! One already exists). Such moves, as we saw with McLaren, carry rewards but also dangers.

Frank Williams's Formula One career bridges the old and new eras: starting in the 1960s as an ambitious young man, living hand to mouth in a time before commercial sponsorship, he emerged in the 1990s as one of the sport's most successful owner-entrepreneurs. That old cliché, rags to riches, seems an appropriate description. Having once resorted to a naked foot-race in order to raise money for his team, he has accumulated a personal fortune worth an estimated £85 million (according to the annual *Sunday Times* 'rich list') thanks to his 70 per cent stake in Williams GPE. The remainder of the shares are held by Patrick Head, the highly regarded technical director. Both men take home more than £1 million a year in salary and dividends. They have built an organisation dedicated to constructing the best racecar on the grid. Frank Williams would far rather spend money on research and development than pay some of the inflated salaries handed out to other drivers. Winning the constructors' championship probably means more to Frank Williams than to any other team owner. Williams loves the cars, and dislikes the financial power drivers exercise to get their multi-million-pound salaries. Damon Hill, a British hero after winning the world championship for Williams, was unceremoniously sacked for asking for too much money. It made Williams extremely unpopular, but such things do not disturb his sleep. Williams has had far more important crises in his life. There was the road accident in 1986 that snapped his neck and left him a paraplegic. There were the deaths of close friends. And in 1997 there was a long Italian court case where he faced – and successfully defended – manslaughter charges over the death of Williams driver Ayrton Senna. Compared with these incidents, a little opprobrium for a fickle public opinion over Damon Hill must barely matter.

Frank Owen Garbett Williams was born into a middle-class family on 16 April 1942, at South Shields, in north-east England. His mother, a schoolteacher, separated from her husband, a pilot in the RAF in the Second World War, when Williams was young, and she brought him up alone at nearby Jarrow. Frank Williams became hooked on motor racing while at boarding school in Dumfries, and spent much of his free time hitch-hiking around the country to various race meetings. After school Williams became a management trainee at the motor dealer, Rootes Group, in Nottingham. But motor racing was a bug that he could not get out of his system. In 1961 he entered his first race, at Oulton Park, in a Speedwell Austin once used by Graham Hill. Williams, however, recognised his limitations, and realised that if he was going to achieve anything in motor racing at all it would be as a team manager. The barrier, as is so often the case, was money. Serious competitive racing was at this time outside the reach of most enthusiasts, and commercial sponsorship as it is known today did not exist. Williams recalls his pre-commercial days in racing as a rather jovial affair: just messing about with friends like driver Piers Courage and Sheridan Thynne, preparing cars in lock-up garages. 'Racing for people like me – and many others – was all done on a shoestring. Rebuilding secondhand cars, bartering for components. Not taking it all too seriously.' From a flat at Harrow on the outskirts of London, Williams set up a small spare-parts business, using a public telephone box as his lifeline to customers. A talent for languages enabled him to do a lot of business on racing trips to the Continent, importing parts to order for his small network of contacts back in England.

In 1967 Frank Williams set up a business selling racecars. Frank Williams Racing Cars Limited became the official Brabham agent, offering Formula Three vehicles built by the racing ace Jack Brabham. It was a good training ground for sharpening up Williams's entrepreneurial skills for when he began running a Formula One team in 1969. Until then he had prepared a variety of cars for other people, and had also run his own Formula Two team with Piers Courage, helped by backing from Dunlop, the tyre company. Williams's foray into Formula One was with a Brabham, powered by a Ford-Cosworth engine, and driven by Courage. Their efforts were rewarded with eighth place in the 1969 drivers' championship. Frank Williams was proving adept at bringing in sponsors. Ted Williams, owner of a company making machine tools, TW Ward, thought Formula One would be good publicity for his business and succumbed to Williams's approaches for money. A little sticker placed on the windscreen of Courage's Brabham marked the first time Williams had found a sponsor from outside the world of the motor industry.

At the 1969 Italian Grand Prix at Monza, Williams met Alessandro de Tomaso, the Argentinian head of the eponymous Italian sports car maker. De Tomaso was making Ford-engined high-performance cars in an attempt to challenge Ferrari and Lamborghini, and he would later buy a controlling stake in Maserati. He had been impressed by Courage's performance at Monaco that year in coming second behind Graham Hill, and he offered Williams a deal: de Tomaso would build a new car and Williams would prepare and organise for Piers Courage to race in the 1970 series. Tragedy struck that year, however, when Courage was killed in the Dutch Grand Prix. It has been said that on that day a little piece of Frank Williams also died along with his friend. The deep personal loss came on top of years of financial struggle that was threatening the team's survival. It certainly knocked the stuffing out of the Williams-de Tomaso partnership – just when things had started to look up.

Frank Williams's team had a lorry, two engines and some components. 'But the heaviest thing we had was loads of debt,' he recalled. Such circumstances were not unique, and they broke many teams. Formula One entrants led a nomadic existence (and still do), travelling from one race to another, sleeping in vans or cheap hotels, just managing to secure enough points to warrant the occasional injection of sponsorship to finance the next leg of the series. In the early 1970s Frank Williams was surviving on about £60,000 a year, while the top teams were getting by on £250,000. Generally, a team's choice of driver depended on which racer could come up with the most money. In 1971 the French driver Henri Pescarolo came to Frank Williams with £38,000 in sponsorship from the oil company Motul, and Ted Williams stumped up another £10,000 to advertise his machine tool company. A third sponsorship, from Politoys, an Italian manufacturer, brought in another £10,000. The following year, 1972, Brazilian driver Carlos Pace contributed another £10,000 in personal sponsorship, which enabled Williams to field a second car. Yet, the team remained on a financial knife-edge, even though it was operating with a relatively small staff of ten. Today, Williams GPE operates with more than 200 staff, with the Formula One division bringing in sponsorship of some £30 million, excluding the free engines supplied by Renault.

The Formula One Constructors' Association, under the control of Bernie Ecclestone, eased some of the burdens facing team owners, by offering subsidised travel and negotiating with circuit owners. But becoming a FOCA member carried certain conditions. To join, teams had to be bona fide racecar manufacturers, rather than just privateers using vehicles built by someone else. From 1973 Frank Williams began building his own racecars. Becoming a constructor increased the costs, but the imposition of a professional structure on the UK teams helped the sport to be taken more seriously by sponsors. Frank Williams was one of the early beneficiaries of Marlboro money. Philip Morris, owner of the Marlboro brand switched its sponsorship from BRM to Williams for the 1973 season. Additional funds came from an Italian sports car company, Iso Rivolta, and Williams racecars entered the champion-ship under the Iso-Marlboro banner. However, sponsorship promised from Italian driver Nanni Galli did not arrive, and staged payments from Iso Rivolta were often late. Frank Williams was later to describe the Iso agreement as 'a bad deal'. Philip Morris moved Marlboro to McLaren in 1974, beginning a long and successful partnership, but nevertheless bailed out the Williams team that year with an extra £15,000.

By 1975 the costs of competing were forcing Frank Williams to look not just for sponsors, but for a partner to invest in the team. Enter Walter Wolf, a burly Austro-Canadian, who made his fortune selling oil equipment machinery. It turned out to be an ill-advised alliance, though as Williams said, it was the best available option at the time. In 1976 Wolf bought 60 per cent of the Williams team, leaving the founder with the remaining 40 per cent. Wolf bought the cars and assets of the Hesketh team for £450,000 in a package that included bringing Harvey Postlethwaite on board as designer. The team's fortunes barely improved, though, and with Wolf's patience at breaking-point he installed Peter Warr, formerly of Lotus, as team manager in 1976. From being the boss of his own team, Frank Williams had sunk to being a general fund-raiser. It was a massive dent to ego and ambition. The die was cast when Wolf took the team to the Argentinian Grand Prix in January 1977, but left Williams back in England.

The whole affair was a salutary lesson for Frank Williams, who vowed never to relinquish control of his business again. He left Wolf to set up Williams Grand Prix Engineering in 1977, recruiting designer Patrick Head who worked with Williams prior to the Wolf takeover. It was effectively back to square one. Williams even lost his FOCA mem-bership. Characteristically, he saw just one option – to bounce back. Williams bought a secondhand March 761 chassis from Max Mosley for £14,000, and four used Cosworth DFVs at a knock-down price. This got Williams GPE back on the grid. Meanwhile, back at the team's run-down factory at Didcot, Oxfordshire, Patrick Head was laying down plans for the future, starting with his development of the FW06 racecar. The team's driver, Belgian Patrick Neve, brought about £100,000 in personal sponsorship with him, but there was precious little other money around for research and development. Frank Williams estimated he had a budget to compete in about ten races.

When Williams Grand Prix Engineering was formed in 1977, Wil-liams owned 99 per cent, with his wife Virginia holding one per cent.

In 1988, 29 per cent of Williams's shares, along with Virginia's, were transferred to Patrick Head. The 70–30 split has remained to this day. The company made a profit in their first full year as a constructor of £593, on turnover of almost £487,000. (In 1995 it was £6.6 million profit on a £36.3 million turnover.) In the mid-1970s commercial sponsorship was still in its infancy. Formula One's top constructors were attracting sponsorship, but the number of backers prepared to support the second-division teams were few. Frank Williams decided to move outside the normal channels and looked to oil-rich Saudi Arabia. This proved to be an inspired strategy, though getting the deals done was extremely hard work. Williams said: 'Much of what we have achieved can be traced back to the sponsorship from Saudi Arabia. It set in train so much. Yes, it was a catalyst.' From the British Grand Prix in 1977 his cars carried the name of Saudia, the small but highly influential state-owned airline.

The Saudia sponsorship was very important for two reasons: first, it finally gave Frank Williams some financial security to plan ahead; second, it broadened the sponsorship base for Formula One, opening the eyes of chairmen from a variety of industrial sectors. Airlines had previously rejected Formula One as a marketing tool, fearful of the imagery that could link a racecar crashing in flames and a crashed aircraft. Frank Williams negotiated the Saudia deal through the company's London-based advertising agency and the airline's sales manager, Mohammed Al Fawzan. The airline advanced £30,000 in the first year, not a big sum. And although Saudia increased the sponsorship to £100,000 the following year, it was not so much the size of the budget that mattered as its symbolic significance. Formula One was a little-known sport in the Middle East at this time. News that Saudia was sponsoring grand prix racing opened doors for Frank Williams. When Patrick Head unveiled the Williams FW06 at Didcot in December 1977, the presentation was attended by Saudia's director general Sheikh Kemel Sindhi, later to become Saudi Arabia's deputy minister of aviation. As journalist and author Alan Henry wrote in his book on Williams GPE: 'By such a visit, the Saudi establishment was, in effect, bestowing its seal of approval on Frank Williams and his enterprise.' In 1978 Frank Williams was on a plane to Riyadh for a meeting with members of the Saudi royal family, arranged by a Ferrari-loving Prince Sultan bin Salman. That year Albilad, a trading company whose UK interests were represented by the now disgraced former Conservative Party MP Jonathan Aitken, contributed £200,000 to Williams GPE. A steel business, Baroom, and an aircraft maintenance group, Dallah, also provided funds. It was through Williams's Middle East connections that another of the sport's most enthusiastic sponsors got involved. For the 1978 Monaco Grand Prix, Prince Sultan brought along his friend Mansour Ojjeh. It was Ojjeh who was instrumental in bringing the family-owned group Techniques d'Avant Garde into the sport. The TAG-Williams link gave the team enough money to compete in all the races in the 1978 world championship and, importantly, enough money to finance much-needed aerodynamic research on the following year's car.

In 1979, Patrick Head's ground-breaking FW07 racecar won the British Grand Prix and another four races in the series. Frank Williams had proved that with sufficient funds behind it, the team could move up into Formula One's élite. In 1980 he won his first constructors' championship and the driver, Alan Jones, the world drivers' championship. Thanks to engineers like Head, racecar technology was surging ahead – and so were the costs. Colin Chapman's 1978 ground-effects Lotus, with its under-car aerodynamics, had been the car to emulate. For team's trying to keep up, wind tunnel research was a necessity. There was also the expense of new carbon-fibre chassis technology. On top of all this, Formula One was entering the battle between turbocharged and conventional engines. More money and resources were essential for the research and development. At the start of 1979, Williams GPE employed 18 people, but that number had trebled by the end of the year. There was a relentless cycle of raising money and spending money. Frank Williams said he used to 'scavenge car parts from anywhere and everywhere: nothing was wasted'. In his book *Theme Lotus*, published in 1986, racing historian Doug Nye describes the constant search for improvements that can soak up finance. 'Much of the expense of Formula One disappears into parts never used, and some idea of this "wastage" can be gained from experimental engineer Frank Dernie's wind tunnel programme. Of all the underwing profiles designed, developed and tested, only Marks 1, 4, 6, 7, 13, 18 and 24 were actually raced. The rest just weren't good enough.' There has been no let-up in the pace of technological research.

When, in the early 1980s, economic problems began to hit the Gulf region, all manner of projects dependent upon petro-dollars were affected. Frank Williams did not escape the impact, and it was not long before Saudi money began to dry up. Luckily, Williams had sensed that Saudi finance would not last for ever, and wisely set about broadening the sponsorship base. The competition between teams to raise money was growing fast, but then so was the number of companies prepared to sponsor Formula One. Leyland Cars, Mobil, ICI, Canon, Labatts and Camel all became major sponsors of Williams GPE, whose cars were taken to greater track successes by Honda, and then Renault engines. For Frank Williams, it is too simplistic to suggest that life in Formula One became easier once the team started winning. More money, better facilities, more technologically advanced cars: all these in their own way presented fresh challenges. 'Being in Formula One in the 1980s was no easier than it was in the '70s or '60s,' said Williams. 'If anything it was much, much harder. There was more money around. But the costs were higher. Everyone was in the same position, working at a tremendous pace to stay ahead, and trying to raise money to do so.' What about today? Is running a top team in the 1990s easier than the 1980s? 'No. The challenge to be quicker than the rest is getting harder than ever. It is incumbent on us to go for any small advantage, and achieving these costs money. We are already actively considering the practicalities of running a team in the twenty-first century. That means applying a fundamental principle that has always existed: the challenge is to be better, and more professional, than anyone else.'

What makes Williams GPE's achievement more impressive is that its founder has guided the team despite facing a crushing disability. Since 1986 he has been paralysed below the neck, the result of a car accident in southern France, which happened, as Williams himself admits, because he was driving too fast. Huge amounts of money are spent on enabling Williams's working life to continue. He has 24-hour nursing care, and various devices to keep him in the best health possible, including a hoist which lifts him vertically to aid normal circulation of his blood. A £4.5 million company jet and a £600,000 helicopter enable him to travel in comfort. Not once did he consider giving up Formula One. It was similar when Piers Courage died 16 years earlier. Although it was a personal loss, it did not change Williams's attitude to fast cars. He dislikes talking about himself, and particularly detests talking about his disability. He once told an interviewer that 'I don't give a fuck' about it. Was this just bravado from a man who did not want to discuss it? Probably not. Close colleagues say there is no self-pity about the man. But the real confirmation comes from his wife, Virginia, who wrote, in a little-known autobiography published in 1991, that her husband had never complained about the injustice of his accident. 'Motor racing is my life,' Williams said. 'Speed has a great fascination. The power of a man to control a machine fascinates me. That is what broke my neck. Every corner is a challenge, and I used to drive too quick. I made one mistake too many. I have one advantage over people who are in my position in that I have a business to run, and until I really screw up no one is going to fire me. You cannot fire the principal shareholder!'

Frank Williams's accident exposed one of the potential problems of owning and investing in a Formula One operation. And it involved an unpleasant dispute with the team's engine supplier, Honda. A successful team normally has to be fashioned around the personality of the man in charge. There is little place for democracy. The team has to be run as a benign dictatorship to function successfully. For staff and sponsors the fear is always: what will happen to the team when the dictator leaves or dies? The problem is not so great today, because most teams have more formalised management structures. Back in the 1980s, though, it was a factor to consider. Frank Williams's near-fatal accident brought home the dangers, though ironically the constructor had one of the best management teams around. Honda was clearly concerned about the team's performance now that it would be run by a paraplegic. This is another subject Williams prefers not to talk about publicly, but a good guide to his thinking comes in Alan Henry's book *Williams Grand Prix Engineering*, an official history of the team. There seems little doubt that Henry's views mirror those of Williams. The author writes: 'In July 1987, with some 18 months of its engine contract ... remaining, Honda managed to bring itself to tell Frank that the company would be terminating its supply of turbocharged engines at the end of that year ... This was a breach of contract by Honda ... It may be disturbing to those from a Western culture, but the apparent facts of the matter are that the Japanese company could not come to terms with doing business with a paraplegic.' Williams regrets not taking a tougher line, legally, with Honda. The termination of the engine supply agreement precipitated a crisis, with Williams urgently seeking a replacement deal.

Frank Williams was not to know it at the time, but the break with Honda was a blessing in disguise. Although in 1988 the team had to use Judd engines, which were well off the pace of the front runners, the search for a better powerplant eventually brought Williams GPE together with Renault. In 1989 the successful partnership between Renault and Williams began, lasting until 1997. The French car maker had run its own Formula One team until 1985. Despite some pioneering work on turbocharged engines, an unwieldy State-owned company like Renault was no match for the fast-moving owner-entrepreneurs of Britain – men like Frank Williams, in fact. Renault began supplying Williams GPE in 1988, though the alliance did not take off in a big way until Nigel Mansell returned to the team from Ferrari for the 1991 season. He came second in that year's championship, with five wins. By 1992 Patrick Head and the team had mastered active suspension and, driving the FW14B, Mansell was supreme. He won nine races that season and took the world championship, while Williams GPE took the constructors' title. The trophy cabinet continued to fill. Williams GPE took the drivers' and constructors' titles in 1993. The team again won the constructors' title in 1994, and would probably have done the double again had driver Ayrton Senna not tragically died at Imola. Williams GPE lost out to Michael Schumacher in a Benetton in 1995, but returned to do the double once more in 1996, with Damon Hill at the wheel. In July 1997 Williams notched up its 100th grand prix victory, the quickest century ever achieved, and went on to take the constructors' championship, with Jacques Villeneuve winning the drivers' title.

For Williams GPE to sustain this sort of success requires a continual cycle of investment in people and new technology. In its way, competing at Formula One is like competing at any leading-edge business – computing or pharmaceuticals, for instance. Such sectors are research intensive and once companies stop investing for the future they know they can kiss goodbye to any hope of being the best. The key to understanding Williams GPE's success – and why other teams try to emulate it – is that the company has always had the factory set-up just right. Other teams have bigger budgets, more staff and higher profiles: but Williams GPE knows how to get more out of less. Nothing illustrates the demands and changes in Formula One more clearly than a tour of the company's factory. If anyone needed convincing that a grand prix team is a modern engineering enterprise, here it is: an array of robotics equipment, clean rooms, advanced lathes for the machine shop. Some teams even have their own wind tunnel. The public perception of a motorsport manufacturing operation remains mired in an image of mechanics in oily overalls working out of dark and dirty warehouses. Such days are long gone.

Running a successful Formula One team means being successful at a number of complex elements: overcoming engineering challenges, finding the right drivers, raising sponsorship, complying with new technical rules from the FIA, and so on. Ultimately, though, it all comes down to two core elements – team effort and time. Bruce McLaren summed it all up in 1969: 'Experience is tremendously important and to build up a team with experienced people takes a long time. You can put any number of engineers together very quickly, but they're not going to come out with a race-winning automobile. They'll come out with a good car but they'll be too late; it may be unreliable and it may be underdeveloped. Putting together a group of people who can produce a racing car that will be ready on time and will work is the secret.' At its simplest, Formula One boils down to the time it takes to get a driver and a car around a circuit. But to achieve this, other personnel and departments are operating and co-operating at a pace unthinkable to most other manufacturing operations. Peter Roberts, a management expert with business adviser Andersen Consulting, has helped Williams GPE refine its working practices. 'Everything and everyone at the factory,' he says, 'works to the tightest possible deadlines. There is no room for slippage. A Formula One factory operates to a very unforgiving schedule. Once the racing season starts, that's it, the factory works flat out, 24 hours a day, seven days a week. Everything becomes focused on the car. Never can the engineers sit back and say: that's it, the car is finished.' Roberts, who has worked with some of the leading automotive manufacturers, believes Williams GPE operates the sort of 'best practice' found in any aerospace or car plant in the UK. 'There are not too many other similar businesses around to benchmark them against. But I believe that if you took these people, the way they work, the teamwork, the motivation, and transplanted them to another manufacturing company, you would find outstanding best practice.'

For the designers at Williams GPE the new season does not begin with the first race in March, but in the autumn of the previous year. With a computer mouse in one hand and a list of the latest FIA regulations in the other, they map out next year's car and the integration of the three thousand or so components that go into each vehicle. It is an expensive business. A design department for a top team will cost around £1 million a month to run. No more than about 20 people might be involved at the early stages of a racecar design, which involves mapping out various ideas on a computer. Such work is especially crucial when a team has to build a chassis around a new engine. Even before a piece of carbon fibre has been moulded, chassis designs can be tried out on computer, as can configurations of the car's internal layout. Once the chief designer has settled on a broad design, a scale model will be produced for aerodynamic tests in the wind tunnel and on a test rig which tries to replicate conditions of racing. Thousands of pieces of information have been distilled to ensure that as many problems as possible can be ironed out on the computer screen before the first full-scale chassis is produced. Patrick Head, Williams GPE's technical director, says it is a fine line between directing the production process with the necessary precision, and allowing engineers enough freedom to innovate. 'The best teams are the ones that do this successfully,' says Head. The first full racecars for the following season are usually made very early in the New Year, when Head will make essential final adjustments. The cars will be refined for the individual drivers, and will undergo stiff crash tests under the gaze of the FIA. Unless they pass, the cars cannot compete. Once a competition licence is given, it is the cue for a hectic couple of months preparing the four or five cars top teams need for a season.

In this type of fast-pace environment it becomes ever more important to create the right infrastructure at the factory. The whole culture must be geared towards quick responses. The critical importance of deadlines means that a team's strategy can easily be thrown off course by distractions. Given that most team bosses have only limited business and financial skills, many are now turning to management consultants for advice. In 1984 when Michael Heseltine, then Conservative Party MP for South Oxfordshire and latterly deputy prime minister, opened Williams GPE's new factory at Didcot, the complex was regarded as state-of-the-art. But no one could have anticipated the expansion in manpower and equipment that would have been necessary to compete in Formula One. Within ten years this factory was outdated. Williams GPE urgently needed to relocate and upgrade its facilities, particularly its computer design and information systems. This is when Andersen Consulting was drafted in. David Williams, Williams GPE's factory manager, told the firm: 'I do not want you to come in and tell me how to move a factory. I want you to come in and do it all for me.' Payment was a mixture of cash and 'free' branding on the helmets of the team's drivers.

The problem with the existing factory at Didcot was that it had grown in a rather haphazard way into a disparate collection of departments. New buildings and operations had been added piecemeal, with little thought given to the efficiency that comes from a fully integrated factory layout. To use a retailing analogy, Frank Williams was running a collection of corner shops when he should have been running a hypermarket. It did not help that the site was boxed in by a power station and a Ministry of Defence establishment, leaving no further room to expand. Peter Roberts, one of the two Andersen partners overseeing the project, described what he found: 'Departments that needed to be in close communication were separated from each other, or in some cases split in two. Williams had a bunch of computer systems that were operating in isolation. As the business grew in complexity, the systems were not talking to each other. Certain information was missing in the line and it caused, to some degree, chaos on the shop-floor. If Williams wanted to expand their core capabilities they were going to do it on the basis of poor information, which would cause them to employ a lot more people. The Didcot factory was not the sort of streamlined set-up a modern team needed.' Andersen began by finding a new site, an old pharmaceutical factory at Grove, in Oxfordshire.

Williams GPE designs and manufactures in-house almost all the components on its cars. Like McLaren, the team uses fewer of the services of Grand Prix Valley subcontractors than other constructors. And Patrick Head, the team's technical director, was adamant that it stayed that way during the factory move, even though it would have been easier to out-source some of the manufacturing for a limited period. Roberts said: 'Because of the secrecy around Formula One preparations, Williams were reluctant to share information outside the company. The team is so reliant on its own people and processes. We just had to work within that framework. Over the years I have done a number of these sorts of projects for blue-chip companies, but never within such a tight timescale.' Head's main concern was that nothing should disrupt development of the 1996 racecar. It was critical for him that Andersen kept to its deadlines, which essentially meant carrying out the move in the six-month 'window' between the end of the 1995 series and the start of the 1996 one. If the move had gone wrong, it would have jeopardised not just the 1996 season, but potentially 1997 and 1998 too.

With Patrick Head having his own strict engineering schedule designing the new car, he could not easily allow staff to be seconded to help Andersen. Because of this, frustrations developed, both during the move and during the installation of the new information technology system. Williams GPE is a lean organisation, which can be both a strength and a weakness. The weakness shows when a company is expanding fast, but is held back by its limited resources. This was one reason for completely overhauling the factory's computer network. Roberts explained: 'The idea was to take some of the mundane tasks out of the day-to-day jobs, like running around trying to find things, and release more time to be creative which, after all, is what this business is all about. But to create more time, you first have to introduce changes, and that can make things difficult. I wanted more resources from Williams. I did not want the changes forced on staff, only to introduce the new system with their co-operation and acceptance. When you are changing the processes and practices that people have been working with for years, it is vital to get their co-operation and involvement. We had to get a consensus that these were the right processes to adopt, and get them to buy into it.'

But how do you do this when engineers cannot be spared from the production line for consultation and training on the new system? This was, said Roberts, arguably the most difficult challenge Andersen faced. 'There were no spare individuals lying around to take off the production line to form project teams and working parties. Everyone was focused on the car. It was not like a traditional consulting assignment for us, in this respect.' The answer was to *become* part of the Williams GPE team and work alongside them. The ten Andersen people working on the move and the new computer system developed a 'buddy' system with key personnel. 'We had to become Williams people,' says Roberts. 'Only in that way could we tap into their skills and knowledge without disrupting the disciplines of the production timetable.' The Andersen team were urged to get under the fabric of the Williams culture (though just so they did not turn completely native, Roberts insisted that his people always wore suits). Andersen's job was not helped by initial resistance from the Williams staff to this group of sharp-suited City consultants descending on the factory. James Burton, Williams's deputy acquisitions manager, recalls: 'I can remember several people on the shop-floor having reservations about how a bunch of guys from London were going to mix with a bunch of engineers.' Andersen's Robert Baldock admits that his firm faced a credibility problem. 'What do you know about Formula One? What other Formula One teams have you been consultants to? These were the sort of questions we had to deal with. We told them they should be more open-minded about this, and just look at our credentials as consultants to industry. To a great extent Williams is like other manufacturing companies, producing a product. Once they accepted us, people became very open to our suggestions for reorganising the factory.'

When a company expands, it not only outgrows the premises, it also outgrows the way it is organised. The processes that were appropriate for Williams GPE in 1978, when it employed no more than 20 people, were under strain as the company grew to more than 240. Having made the factory move, with the loss of only one week of production time, the next project was to look at the way the computer information network was set up. All modern businesses work in competitive atmospheres, where continuous improvement and time-to-market become key competitive weapons. In Roberts's experience, Williams are perhaps the most extreme example of this. 'Fitting an improved component to a car before a race may only improve its performance by thousandths of a second, but that could be the difference between winning and losing a race. Fit that component one race later, and the competition may already have caught up with that improvement. Williams works on a continuous design-build-test-implement cycle. Cutting down this cycle can therefore have a crucial impact on race performance. Similarly, any delay or disruption to the design and production process means that vital seconds – or split second – can be lost on the track. Williams could be losing seconds on the track because it had outgrown the way it was organised.'

Williams had separate computer systems controlling different areas of the business. Because those systems were unintegrated, there was a high degree of duplication. This meant a lot of paperwork, and a lot of physical walking up and down to collect information. 'It meant costs were difficult to identify, allocate and strip out,' says Roberts. The aim was to bring control of the company under one computer software programme, though it had to be of sufficient sophistication to allow Williams GPE to take on third-party work under the Andersen business plan. Andersen had to install the system during the 'closed' season. The firm was given a fixed and non-negotiable cut-off point. The system was phased in, rather than go for a 'big bang' implementation with its consequent high levels of risk and disruption. First, the manual processes were automated and existing data transferred to the computer system. This immediately speeded up access to information and control of inventory. Stock control is one of a team's biggest financial headaches. It cannot be left with a stack of last year's parts, yet it must always have the right components in stock. A team wants to finish the season with as little stock as possible. The second phase linked the design and production departments, which had previously run separate systems. Finally, there was the integration of the manufacturing and

contracts system. This gave complete visibility of the entire manufacturing process. Williams has eliminated all the paperwork in the
factory, with the exception of technical drawings.

The whole project took between 15 and 18 months. 'It was not
without its stressful moments,' Baldock recalls. 'Williams not only
moved home, they completely changed the way they ran the house.
We challenged the way they did business. We questioned things. It was
not always acceptable to them at first, but we got there in the end. We
all agree that there is an improvement in the way things are done, and
that it provides a platform for the future growth of the business. I would
not say that the system is overly sophisticated. But the system they
have got today will accommodate the business of tomorrow quite
readily. In terms of the equipment we have introduced, it is not rocket
science. It is just good manufacturing and production equipment. What
matters is how it is applied and the people who apply it.' The jewel in
the crown of a business like Williams GPE is people and teamwork.
This is what gives it the competitive edge; not the kit, not the CAD-
CAM system. Baldock continued: 'In terms of talent, Williams is
probably one of the best companies I have worked for. Working with
some companies is not always a pleasure. Sometimes you have to drag
people to the trough. These guys are already at the trough, and you do
not really have to force them to drink. Some businesses are over-
organised; their disciplines, processes and procedures are enshrined in
stone. And to some degree you stifle creativity. But in Formula One
you have to put in a little bit more discipline, a little bit more procedure
to make it easier for them to enhance the time they have to be creative.'

Andersen's work is not finished. The firm signed another three-year
contract with Williams GPE to help the company expand and build on
the core expertise that has been accumulated over more than two
decades in Formula One. In 1980, when Frank Williams was still
uncertain about the team's Formula One involvement, he took on a
contract to produce a competitive rally car out of Rover's mass-market
small car, the Metro. More recently, Williams GPE has helped Renault
engineer a go-faster version of its Clio model called, predictably, the
Williams-Renault Clio. Baldock said: 'Certain areas of F1 are completely underdeveloped. Merchandising, for example, and other things
that enable the company to build on the name. Just take a look at
football. The marketing of Formula One teams is way behind football
clubs, which is odd given the world-wide popularity of Formula One.
Williams GPE is currently moving into a new phase of development.

It is a name known world-wide. And in achieving that success they have developed skills and technologies that would find application in many other fields – aerospace for example, or commercial car production. We will be working closely with the company to see where the name, the values and the abilities of Williams GPE can be taken next.'

Frank Williams has been mulling over a business plan containing some 20 ideas on how to take the company forward and open new revenue streams. Some are obvious, such as growing the subcontracting work; others less so, like branded clothing. You can now buy Williams GPE plimsolls, trainers and deck shoes. Baldock said: 'The business plan is not cast in stone. We have been trying to find out what exactly Williams GPE stands for. Ferrari stands for passion, as everyone in Formula One knows. Williams GPE stands for something more sedate, something like engineering excellence.' But is the company at risk of diverting attention, as happened at McLaren? James Burton, assistant manager at Williams, said: 'Some other teams have diversified, and while you could argue that the diversification has been successful, did it impact on the performance of the core product? We at Williams GPE have to be wise to the possibility of this happening, and make sure it does not. After the move and the reorganisation, the job now is to refocus back on the commercial side. Andersen has created a business plan to take us beyond the year 2000. We have worked on the factory to create efficiencies, and now we are looking at developing for the future. The philosophy of Williams is to design, build and run racing cars. But if there are other areas that are available for exploitation, ones that will not diminish in any way the success of the grand prix team, there are no reasons not to consider them. The test is: will they make money and be logistically possible?'

What are the qualities that made Williams GPE so good? In economic terms, Frank Williams provided the budget and resources. In personal terms, he provided the vision and the commitment. Essentially, he put the company in a position where it had no excuse not to construct a great car. There were no distractions, as at McLaren, and none of the internal politics of Ferrari that made simple decision-making so difficult. Williams GPE had always got the technology just right. While Williams was building his team, he invested heavily in the right personnel, bringing in experts in electronics and systems from outside Formula One. Once trained and experienced, these people were able to return the investment tenfold. Nor did the engineering department ever want for anything. Eghbal Hamidy, the respected former Williams GPE aerodynamicist, often felt the company's resources were limitless. 'Anything that helped the car was made available,' was his experience of eight years at Williams GPE. But it cannot only be money that accounts for the constructor's success, otherwise richer teams would not have been chasing Williams GPE racecars for so many years. Despite the dominance of technology in Formula One, the sport is a people business. Crucially, perhaps, there is no superstar system at Williams GPE, which means there is less chance of egos getting in the way. In this respect, Frank Williams leads by example. He is a low-profile man, whereas Benetton's Flavio Briatore craved publicity and McLaren's Ron Dennis craved to be understood. Frank Williams just wants to win races, and genuinely seems to care little about a media profile. That focus has rubbed off throughout the team. At the end of the day, believes team owner Paul Stewart, it is not that Williams GPE has anything that is absent from other teams. 'It is just that the range of qualities needed to win a championship are more in abundance at Williams than at other teams. Every team has what it takes, but Frank Williams has it in greater number.' Hamidy has now joined Paul Stewart at Stewart Grand Prix, and is certainly noticing the difference. The resources simply do not compare. Stewart GP has struggled to match the pace of its rivals since it entered Formula One in 1997. One of its cars even failed to qualify for the first race of the 1998 grand prix season. Creating a successful Formula One team is becoming a near impossibility for new entrants. The next chapter looks at what it takes to build a winner.

Stewart: Building a Winner

YOU COULD SEE the stress in Jackie Stewart's face on the eve of the 1998 grand prix season. All through qualifying at the Australian Grand Prix his team's cars had suffered engine problems. There was little to show after five months of refinement and testing during the winter 'rest' period. At the pre-race glad-handing in the hospitality tents, Stewart had some explaining to do to his sponsors and their guests. At least he could tell them that despite the mechanical problems, the engineers and drivers had pulled off a Herculean task in getting the cars through qualifying and on to the starting grid.

The anticipation before the opening race of a new season is always intense, and under a brilliant blue Melbourne sky 22 new cars in their multicoloured liveries screeched off in the searing heat. By the end of the first lap, one Stewart Grand Prix car was out due to engine trouble. By the end of the second lap, an ambitious overtaking move left the other car stranded in the gravel. If there is a lesson in all this for any would-be Formula One boss, it is: if Jackie Stewart cannot put together a credible team, who can? Despite his reputation as a former driving champion, extensive international business contacts, and the backing of Ford, Stewart Grand Prix continued to struggle. Formula One is now so prohibitively expensive that even established motorsport players like Jackie Stewart find it difficult to join the club. At the end of 1997, Stewart Grand Prix's first season, he described putting together the team as an 'almost impossible' task. And with the FIA planning to put tighter restrictions on new entrants, it is not going to get any easier.

Eddie Jordan thinks Jackie Stewart may well be the last individual to start a team from scratch. The barriers to entry mean that in future only large corporations will have pockets deep enough to contemplate entering Formula One. Jordan Grand Prix started out in 1991 with £5 million, and was £4 million pound in debt by the end of his first season. Several times the team nearly went under, and had to make some savage cutbacks to keep afloat. David Richards, whose company Prodrive has produced top rally sport champions, has for several years contemplated an assault on Formula One. But he decided it would be less risky to join an existing team, and was eventually installed as managing director of Benetton Formula by the Italian parent group. 'If you are starting a new team you need a minimum of £50 million pounds before turning a wheel, and at least 12 months to get ready,' said Richards. All that this time and money achieves is a possible entry into grand prix racing for a year or two. It does not guarantee glory. McLaren, Ferrari, Williams and Benetton have dominated Formula One since 1983. No other team has come close.

The paddock is an insular and spiteful place. Barely a dozen people run Formula One, and they meet every two weeks for eight months of the year to do battle. In such an environment egos clash and tempers fray. New boys are made to feel just that – new boys. As far as the public is concerned, Jackie Stewart, three times world champion, is a king of the sport. But inside the paddock he is just another chancer trying to succeed at one of the most challenging events in the world. Was this the reason that, at the 1997 Monaco Grand Prix, the team had to make camp in a car-park half-way up a hill, away from the main pack at one of the showcase events of the year? The feeling was that the team was being slapped down. Bernie Ecclestone deflected complaints with the comment: 'I thought Jackie Stewart would prefer being nearer the Royals.' Stewart Grand Prix had the last laugh, though. Driver Rubens Barrichello came a remarkable second in the race, which was probably worth £5–8 million in extra sponsorship and support. It was a result that drove Jackie Stewart and his son Paul, a partner in the team, to tears of joy. But there has been little cheer about since. Jackie and Paul always said that forming the team would be hard, but they could not have known just how tough it would be.

The latest chapter in Jackie Stewart's romance with Formula One began on 11 June 1995, aboard a Falcon 900 jet winging its way from Montreal to Detroit after the Canadian Grand Prix. The three times world drivers' champion was flying with executives from Ford, heading back to the motor giant's headquarters at Dearborn. Talk turned to Ford's disappointment with its existing Formula One involvement. The company was supplying engines to Sauber, but the team seemed to be going nowhere. And who remembered that it was Ford that had powered

Benetton to the world championship in 1994? What people did remember, however, was that Benetton dumped Ford in 1995 for a Renault engine. A high-profile manufacturer of cars with such a low profile in Formula One: the Ford chiefs at Dearborn were starting to get uneasy.

Stewart, a technical adviser to Ford for 30 years, told his companions to show more commitment; to spend more money, or get out. Dan Rivard, head of Ford motorsport, told Stewart that pulling out was not an option. Formula One was important for the Ford brand and good for the image of its dealerships. Ford marketing executive Bob Rewey and engineering chief Neil Ressler agreed. Maybe Ford should link up with a new team. Together they kicked around a few names and different strategies, until Rivard said to Stewart: 'How about you doing it for us?' By the end of the year Stewart and Ford had agreed a five-year partnership, costing the company £20 million a year. Ford would supply engines and technical expertise to a new team, run by Jackie and Paul, which would aim to begin competing in the 1997 season. It was a giant leap for both men. Jackie said he would never have committed himself to a Formula One team without first securing the backing of a major company like Ford. But fitting this part of the jigsaw was the easy bit. In the next two years the lives of Jackie and Paul Stewart would be turned upside-down as they struggled to 'give birth to our baby'. Stewart senior, executive chairman of the company, had the task of raising the minimum of £25 million a year in sponsorship that they would need. Paul, the managing director, had the job of organising the factory. (Ownership of Stewart Grand Prix is split almost equally, through Jersey-based family trusts.) Fifteen-hour, sometimes 18-hour days were not uncommon. Paul said he had to make a conscious effort to remember anniversaries, such as his wife's birthday. Jackie and his wife moved from their home in Switzerland so he could help plan the factory, on a nondescript industrial park on the outskirts of Milton Keynes, in Northamptonshire.

Formula One is often called the richest sport in the world. Most of the team owners are multimillionaires, as are many of the drivers. But anyone who goes into the sport for the riches is deluding themselves, Paul Stewart believes. 'If you are going into business purely to make money, then this is not the sport to do it in. There are many other businesses where, for the amount of effort and risk you put in, there are more financial rewards – like making bottle tops.' Formula One is littered with failures. The Simtek and Pacific teams folded in 1995, with debts of £6 million and £5 million respectively. The following year Lola Racing folded after just one race with debts of £6 million, and forced its parent company into administration. Because Formula One is such a seductive sport, people with more money than sense, or plenty of sense but no money, are constantly looking for a way in. Most projects are just Icarian flights of the mind. Keith Wiggins, who ran Pacific, said he knew from the start of his début season that the team 'was in the shit. And we never got out of it.' Money that had been promised never arrived. And Bernie Ecclestone impounded the cars because Pacific had not paid him the freight charges. Twelve teams have come and gone since Eddie Jordan launched his Formula One challenge in 1991. Jordan was the last 'new boy' to achieve any success, although the team has still not won a grand prix. It took Frank Williams ten years to win the world championship. Stewart Grand Prix hoped to do it in five. Paul Stewart summed up the challenge: 'You don't start a Formula One team from scratch and be competitive the first time you get on the track. We designed everything from scratch. Other teams have factories, existing designs and data from past races to build on. We had to design more than 3,000 parts, get them made and put them together. We had more than 100 staff who had never worked together. It all had to be done to a tight time-frame. The logistics were almost impossible.'

Life might have been simpler if they had bought an existing team. Arrows was on the market, before it was snapped up by Tom Walkinshaw. It would have meant instant FOCA membership, and brought the Stewarts a slice of the financial benefits under the Concorde Agreement. Instead, the team had to earn its spurs, and forgo benefits such as a slice of television revenues. So why did the two men start a team from scratch? Paul said his father's reputation had a lot to do with it. 'It is very difficult when you have Jackie Stewart involved. If it was just me it would not have mattered. But when Jackie Stewart is involved it is nice to preserve the Jackie Stewart image. Starting from scratch meant we had no baggage. It allowed us to create our own financial and reporting structures. We did not have to weed out people or wrestle against any funny shenanigans that might be going on inside the team.' Alain Prost, the French ex-champion who bought the Ligier team will, believes Stewart, for ever be associated with Ligier as its purchaser, not its creator. 'That might be a small price to pay in the great scheme of things. But we made the decision to start from a clean sheet of paper. It made it more expensive, more challenging. But it means the team has our identity, totally.' A feature of Jackie Stewart's psychological make-up has always been to think long-term. This was a characteristic in his driving days. He always knew it would not last for ever, which is why he always secured the best financial deals as a driver. Now, with Stewart Grand Prix, he is laying plans for a motor racing dynasty, that, just like Ferrari, has its roots in the Stewart family and not in some previous incarnation.

Jackie Stewart has forged his reputation over more than 30 years in racing and business. He was the first driver fully to exploit the growth in commercialism, and one of the first to have a manager. Integrity, fair-mindedness, an instinctive marketing man, well-connected: these are some of the words that crop up in any discussion of Jackie Stewart. They are also one reason why Ford backed him. He offered a fresh start in a sport that was changing fast. When he left Formula One in 1973, Stewart had built a fortune worth around £5 million. His personal wealth in 1997 was estimated at £30 million by the *Sunday Times* in the newspaper's annual 'rich list', though this is probably on the conservative side. He works 100 days a year for Ford as an adviser on its family cars, and uses his name to promote Rolex watches and Moët et Chandon champagne. He runs a shooting school in the country of his birth, Scotland (he is an excellent clay pigeon shooter, and came close to being in the team for the 1960 Olympics). He also owns a house in Geneva, worth about £12 million, which is rented to pop star Phil Collins while Stewart works on the Formula One team. But one of Stewart's biggest assets is his address book, which includes the names of royalty, prime ministers and the chief executives of some of the world's leading companies. It was this list of contacts that he hoped would open doors to potential sponsors.

It was Paul Stewart, rather than his father, who had the burning desire to form a Formula One racing team. As a child, Paul had ambitions to become a top racer. But he had, like his father, faced parental resistance to his becoming a driver. Jackie packed his son off to university in America, where he studied political science at Duke University. The racing bug never left him, however. Paul enrolled at the Brands Hatch Racing School, loved it, and in 1988 established Paul Stewart Racing to compete in Formula Three. He retired from racing in 1993 on the grounds that he would never be world champion, and there was no point in just making up the numbers. But that was not the end of his racing ambitions. While his father's business interests had pulled him away from grand prix, Paul still wanted to take a team to the pinnacle of motorsport. Paul explained: 'I had got to a point where I did not believe that my driving abilities were going to take me to the highest echelons of the sport. That was the only reason I became a racer. My first choice when I stopped racing was to create a Formula One team with my father. I had other options, but the desire was there from my side. I had gone through the lower formulae. It is like going through school: first grade, second grade, and so on. It was natural for me to want to progress to bigger and better heights. As for my father, he never had a secret dream to run a Fi team. It was just that one day, the right situation came along. He was in the right frame of mind, I wanted to do it, and it dovetailed nicely with Ford's programme for the future.'

Paul and Jackie Stewart had come close to putting together a Formula One team in 1994. They almost secured backing from the Malaysian government, whose prime minister, Dr Mahathir Mohamad, saw the potential of Formula One to promote his country's rapid industrial development. The team would, in effect, have been the official Malaysian Formula One team, fully financed by the government. Dr Mahathir sent representatives to England to meet staff at Paul Stewart Racing and tour motorsport subcontractors. In the end the deal was never done, the government getting cold feet about the marketing value of Formula One and the £20 million or so they would have to invest in the team. Paul Stewart then seriously considered a bid to compete in America's Indy racing, and also a challenge in touring cars. It was not until Ford sparked Jackie Stewart's interest that another Formula One project was considered. He told Ford that they would have to commit themselves long-term. Jackie Stewart did, after all, have something of a reputation to consider, and he was not prepared to risk it in a fast-track bid for glory. He explained: 'Too often sport is blighted by short-term thinking. Despite the vast amounts of money involved, Formula One has never been a truly focused business. It is a passionate pursuit and sometimes people allow their hearts to rule their heads. I watched others make the mistake of being under-financed, and came to the conclusion there was no point in going back to Formula One and risking financial disaster.'

When Jackie Stewart stepped off that plane in Detroit with the Ford executives, he had the germ of an idea only – and an invitation to return to the company in September for further talks. The Stewarts spent a busy few weeks outlining a business plan. It would be an important presentation, because they were not necessarily pushing at an open door in Dearborn. Not every car manufacturer thinks they should be involved in Formula One, and the Ford board contained its sceptics, executives who consider it a waste of time and money and of little relevance to the every-day car driver. The pitch had to be good. In the event the meeting lasted no more than an hour. Ford's executives liked what they heard. 'They have known and trusted Jackie for many years,' said Martin Whitaker, head of European motorsport for Ford. 'If he [Jackie] thinks it can work, I think the feeling at Ford was to put faith in his judgement.'

Jackie and Paul, along with Rob Armstrong, the commercial director, were asked to present a full business plan by the end of October, containing a detailed breakdown of the costs and benefits that would be involved. This was the big one, the meeting that would effectively convince Ford whether or not the strategy was worthwhile. Paul recalls an almost boyish excitement at the prospect. 'I really felt I was close to realising a dream. It was all very nerve-racking. We were all so busy, which helped, otherwise we would have worried ourselves to death. I could not have done it without my father.' The Stewarts had signed up the huge US-based advertising agency J. Walter Thompson, in Detroit, to help prepare the business plans. Jackie Stewart, a marketing man through and through, was leaving nothing to chance.

At the meeting on 30 October, five Ford directors, including Jac Nasser, chairman of Ford Europe, listened, asked questions and made observations. Jackie Stewart emphasised that long-term commitment from the company was crucial. Ford wanted assurances that Jackie could raise the additional sponsorship and hire the quality staff and drivers that would take the team to the top. Jackie Stewart left the room with absolutely no idea what impression he and his two colleagues had made. Five days later the two sides got together yet again. Good news. The Stewarts and Ford motorsport division were told to press on with the financial terms, and draw up plans to turn the Milton Keynes site into a Formula One factory. Macfarlans, the Stewarts solicitors, began work on the final legal documents. But it would be another month before Ford's senior executives gave the go-ahead for the creation of Stewart Grand Prix. On 6 December, after a very brief meeting in Detroit, Jackie and Paul Stewart were told that they had a deal. Paul Stewart cannot quite remember his feelings as he left the room. 'Elation, probably,' he said. 'But I was aware, obviously, that the job was not finished. Getting Ford's backing was only ever going to be one of many hurdles. It meant that a lot of other things would now fall into place, but there was still a tough job ahead of us.' The Ford package did not just include the engines. A huge amount of Ford know-how was available for the team to tap into: materials technology, the design shops, engineering and electronics support. 'Facilities of this kind would cost other teams a fortune,' said Paul Stewart. It led to claims that the company was effectively underwriting Stewart Grand Prix's challenge, a charge strongly denied by Paul Stewart. 'We make substantial use of the Detroit facilities, so we do not have to invest money in some things. But suggestions that we are dependent on Ford for our existence are simply untrue.'

As far as Ford was concerned, the motor giant felt it was backing more than a grand prix team. Martin Whitaker hoped it would be an opportunity to bring specialists and mainstream car engineering closer together. Just as Honda had done when supplying Williams and McLaren, Ford planned to use the project to 'hot-house' some of its best young engineers. There were other reasons, too. Ford was buying into Jackie Stewart's reputation: his position as one of Formula One's greats, the integrity he would bring to a frequently controversial sport, and some brilliant marketing skills that should ensure that Ford's large budget would be matched by a large profile. There are no performance clauses in the Ford deal, which is no great surprise since the team remains largely an unknown quantity. But Whitaker said Ford is consulted on all big decisions made at Stewart Grand Prix. 'That's because there is the potential for conflict between our business interests and racing interests, but that hasn't happened so far. It is only natural that we should have some input, but we do not make the decisions.'

Jackie Stewart has proved highly adept at marketing himself and the companies that employ him to promote their products. When he gave his driver Rubens Barrichello a prize for finishing fifth at the 1997 Argentine Grand Prix – a £3,400 Rolex Daytona watch – the motor racing world knew about it. It was a brilliant, calculated marketing job for one of Stewart's clients. He rubs shoulders with royalty and other VIPs. Jackie Stewart learned early on in his career the importance of networking. Barrie Gill, chairman and chief executive of CSS International, which arranges sports sponsorship, remembers a cameo which sums up Jackie Stewart's attitude to promotion. 'In 1966 I flew with Jackie Stewart to the Tasman series in New Zealand and Australia. Graham Hill, Jack Brabham and Denny Hulme were on the flight. We flew from the South African Grand Prix to Sydney, a flight which took 36 hours. Everywhere we stopped *en route*, Stewart bought a bunch of postcards. I was sitting next to him, watching him write card after card. He had a motor dealership in Scotland. And he said people came to his dealership because it was run by Jackie Stewart. He was not going to be there for two months. So he wrote a little note to his customers, every one of them. He just sat there and did it. I thought, what a smart little sod you are.'

Jackie Stewart never felt promotion and marketing were beneath his dignity. He was smart enough to realise he would not be driving for ever. So, he enjoyed his grand prix success while he could, and laid the foundations for his retirement by establishing a network of contacts. He had to call on a lot of these to find sponsors for Stewart Grand Prix. The search for backers began in earnest at the start of 1996, but it was not until nine months later that the first major contract was announced. The period in between was a gruelling schedule of meetings and chasing false hopes. The sound of heads banging against brick walls could be heard about the factory, one employee recalled. Jackie Stewart found it all a sobering experience, especially when promises of sponsorship were never translated into contracts. He targeted hi-tech and financial companies, as well as the traditional oil and fuel firms. He also went to see McDonald's, which listened carefully to the proposal, but decided it did not need a global advertising vehicle like Formula One. McDonald's is, after all, already one of the most famous brands in the world. Many companies refused to consider his proposal, something Stewart found amazing given that he was in effect offering a link-up with Ford, one of the world's biggest companies. Stewart was to discover that a deal agreed on a handshake meant nothing, which was a shock for a man who never bothered with contracts when he drove for Tyrrell during the glory days. Ask the Stewarts what they think of the business methods of some companies, and they are scathing. Ask them to embarrass the companies that let them down, by naming them and there is a blanket refusal. 'We want to be seen to be above that sort of thing,' said Paul Stewart, before adding that there was always a chance they might become sponsors a couple of years down the line. A Formula One team never shuts off a potential source of money.

Stewart Grand Prix's first big sponsorship deal, announced on 17 September 1996, came as a great relief. The banking empire of HSBC Holdings, which owns Britain's Midland Bank, was more used to sponsoring opera and museum exhibitions than exotic sports such as Formula One. HSBC's chairman, Sir William Purves, like Stewart born in Scotland, was initially sceptical about the value of Formula One. But the idea began to grow on him. There was also an Asian connection that HSBC could trade on. With its roots in Hong Kong, the bank was aware that interest in Formula One was growing fast in the Asia region, where several countries are bidding to stage grand prix races. The main strategy, though, was the bank's need to raise its international profile. Banking, like Formula One, is a global business. HSBC, one of the largest financial houses in the world, operates in 75 countries. But the company's problem was that while people recognised the names of its individual banks, HSBC itself was virtually unknown.

Purves invited Jackie Stewart to make a 30-minute address to the board of directors in June 1996. The planning and preparation had taken weeks, but he came away from the meeting with the promise of £25 million over five years. It was a modest sum by Formula One standards, but the largest sponsorship in HSBC's history. What mattered greatly to Stewart Grand Prix was the longevity of the deal. It contributed to the long-term financial stability that the young team needed if it was to grow. However, the sponsorship did not help dispel rumours that the team was having trouble finding backers and might have to delay its Formula One entry until 1998. The reports were dismissed at the time as paddock gossip put about by people who wanted their own engine deal with Ford. Some people pointed the finger at Sauber, whose supply of Ford engines was under threat.

It was not until more than two months after the HSBC announcement that the sniping over Stewart Grand Prix's financial position stopped, though it was to return before the start of the 1998 season. At the end of November 1996 a much-needed and innovative deal was announced with the tourist board of Malaysia. Despite failing to agree a sponsorship package with the Malaysian government in 1994, Jackie Stewart had kept in contact with the country's prime minister. This time Dr Mahathir Mohamad was persuaded to put a Visit Malaysia sticker on the car to promote tourism. Just as emerging nations like to advertise their modernity by building the biggest skyscrapers, so Dr Mahathir wanted to use Formula One to underline his country's technological advance. The prime minister had plans for his country to host its own race – a desire of several 'tiger economies' – so the link with a Formula One team was good publicity for its attempts to persuade Bernie Ecclestone to put Malaysia on the calendar. But the tourist board stayed for only one season, and the economic crisis that hit Asian economies has jeopardised plans to hold grand prix events.

There were continual reports that Jackie Stewart could not raise the sponsorship he needed. While Stewart wanted long-term financial commitment, potential sponsors did not want to get into anything from which they could not easily pull out. The announcements that Stewart Grand Prix had won backing from the Sanyo electronics group and Texaco, the oil major, came barely days before the official launch of the car. Paul Stewart admitted that raising enough money was a close call, and as late as early December he feared the team would have to delay the launch. He said: 'We could always afford to do whatever we were doing at the time. But we were realistic about the fund-raising. If we could not get the sponsorship needed to go racing in 1997, then we were not going to come in during the season. The Malaysia deal was done much earlier than it was announced. And Texaco was a long negotiation, but we were very confident about the outcome. However, until you have got the deals done, you cannot be sure you will be racing next year.'

While Jackie Stewart concentrated on the commercial side, his son dealt with organising the factory. The official announcement of the Stewart/Ford team was made in Detroit on 4 January 1996, and in England the following day at a presentation in Birmingham attended by Albert Caspers, chairman of Ford Europe. But for Paul Stewart this was only the beginning. There were a million and one things to do. First, they had to get planning permission to extend the factory. Only then could the new equipment that had to be bought be installed. In March 1996, with a year to go before the team's first grand prix race, a project control group was set up to organise the factory and identify subcontractors to make parts for the car. If the Stewarts had bought an existing team, most of this would have been unnecessary. Instead, they had to start from scratch, as Paul Stewart explained: 'We could not even transfer much equipment from my Paul Stewart Racing team. We had to set up new stores, inspection facilities, and design office. The whole place was turned upside-down. We leased a site in Milton Keynes, to do our carbon fibre work. The chassis is manufactured at the main factory. For the rest of the components, we effectively rely on sourcing them.'

Then came the job of finding staff. The Stewart name and the Ford engine made it easier to recruit than it might otherwise have been. Alan Jenkins, technical director, was hired from Tom Walkinshaw's Arrows, and Eghbal Hamidy, Adrian Newey's number two at Williams GPE, was brought in as aerodynamicist. Other people were recruited from Williams, Ferrari and Benetton. Some rival teams were unhappy at Stewart Grand Prix pinching their staff. But Paul Stewart said no poaching was done. The job applications came in response to adverts placed in the motorsport journal *Autosport*. The appointment of Jenkins was a coup, as two other leading teams also wanted his services. In all, staffing at the factory more than doubled to 120 people, with more than 200 people interviewed for jobs. The problem was that the best people naturally wanted the most money, and they were also used to working with big budgets. Paul Stewart said he had to do a lot of convincing, but most job applicants had faith in what he was trying to achieve.

David Stubbs, the team manager, and some other staff were dispatched to a couple of grands prix to look around the pits to see what equipment the team's future rivals were using. It is amazing how fast the set-up in the pits can change. After a couple of years away from Formula One the whole thing can look very different. So much equipment had to be bought, either new or secondhand: tool kits, fuelling machines, three specially designed articulated trucks costing £250,000 each, and so on. Some of the equipment came from technical sponsors, such as computer systems and software from Hewlett Packard and EDS. Most of the installation was done during the night, so as not to disrupt the Paul Stewart Grand Prix team, which throughout the changes was still competing. Once the CAD-CAM system was up and running, it enabled Jenkins to press on with the design of the new car. In fact, it was a mini-first for Formula One – the first grand prix constructor to build a car from scratch with totally computer-aided design. No baggage from the past, no pencil or paper; not a drawing-board in sight.

There is no blueprint for running a Formula One team. Every constructor is different, often fashioned around a single personality – the owner. In Stewart Grand Prix's case, it was a joint effort. Jackie and Paul would sit up late into the night, in discussion with the commercial and technical directors, trying to match the team's needs with the budget. Almost inevitably, they underestimated the finance and equipment needed. 'For example,' said Paul Stewart, 'we budgeted £20,000 for the racecar model that would go into the wind tunnel for aerodynamic tests. The real model cost us £300,000! Naturally, budgets for other things had to come down. It was a continual adjustment process. My advice to anyone setting up a grand prix team is, above all, keep a grip on spending. Don't kid yourself. If you cannot afford to do something, you cannot afford to do it. In an ideal world, you budget for the equipment and say, this is how much money we need. You must decide what amount of money is available, and then cut your cloth to suit.

But it is so difficult. For a start, how do you know the numbers are accurate? You can design a car that you think has included everything: then you discover that you have left out the springs in the damper system. So, it's another £60,000 for a full range of springs.' Borrowing heavily from banks or other financial institutions was not really an option for Stewart Grand Prix. As if Formula One was not risky enough, loans have to be repaid from sponsorship, and this is a precarious revenue stream, as those who survive on tobacco money may find out when it is outlawed. The key to surviving in Formula One is cash flow.

What distinguishes the good businessman from the misguided is having the guts to throw in the towel if the team looks unlikely to get the necessary funding. That goes for new entrants, as well as old hands. For all would-be constructors, entering Formula One is a dream come true, but few can recognise when the dream is over. Either they do not make it to the grid in the first place, or the shortfalls are exposed pretty soon into the season. The Pacific and Simtek teams both looked good, and had a professional approach. But they did not have money to do much testing or wind-tunnel work. As the money dried up, they had to rely on outdated equipment. Sponsors delayed deals for as long as possible, just to see whether they had backed the wrong team. A couple of poor races, and the teams looked uncompetitive. Pacific and Simtek sat at the back of the grid unattractive to existing and potential sponsors. While building Stewart Grand Prix, the two founders kept a tight grip on the budget, refusing to embark on each new and expensive development of the car and factory unless it had the next tranche of funding in place. 'The accounting is not very scientific, though,' said Paul Stewart. 'All you can do is make a solid guess of how much money you will need – then add some more. If you can only get half the money you need, you have to be brave enough to abandon the project. If you get 90 per cent, then you must make a judgement of whether it's worth taking the risk of going bankrupt. The history of racing is full of people who had ambition, but not sufficient funding.'

As Jordan Grand Prix proved, it is possible – though rare – to ride out the early years of financial deprivation. A truism of Formula One is that it is in the culture for team owners not to live within their financial means. Give a team a budget of £30 million, and it will spend £31 million. Carry this to an extreme, and it would be the end of the track for any constructor. Balancing income against expenditure is a juggling act, and in modern Formula One this task has to be in the control of professionals. Jordan Grand Prix, which for so long teetered on the edge of collapse, is now on the verge of joining the inner circle of top teams. The team's financial controller is Richard O'Driscoll, a former banker. He is not a petrol-head, like most Formula One executives. He leaves the passion and boyish enthusiasm to Eddie Jordan. O'Driscoll feels he does his job better if he has a sense of detachment. 'I cannot treat Jordan as anything other than a business. Eddie's objective is for Jordan Grand Prix to be world champion in Formula One. It is my duty, my obligation, to ensure that we are prudent with resources to enable that to happen. I am the only one in the company dealing with finances day-to-day. It is up to me to ensure that the alarm signals go up if we are pushing too far too fast. It would be easy for someone in my position to be emotionally attached to the business; to take a cavalier attitude to the business. When that happens, you see businesses go out of business.'

Paul Stewart thought many times of the hurdles Jordan Grand Prix had faced in its struggle to gain some sort of financial equilibrium. Even if Stewart Grand Prix got to the grid in its first season, it was no guarantee that there would be enough money to compete for a second season. Not all the sponsors would commit themselves to five years with the team. By July 1996, and with his budget approved, Alan Jenkins and his design team built a model of the planned racecar, and were ready to carry out the first aerodynamic tests in a wind tunnel. The tunnel used was the Swift facility in San Clemente, California, one of the best in the world. From July, until the moment the car was finished, designers spent two weeks of each month in the tunnel refining the vehicle. This is a crucial time. Much of a car's development is based around when a tunnel facility is available for hire, and the slightest hiccup can upset development plans. In one of those sudden rule changes that make technical directors go prematurely grey, the FIA banned a suspension design a month after the team started tunnel tests. A re-design was necessary. Even so, in that same month, August, the car passed the team's own crash tests, raising confidence that it was now ready for the official FIA tests.

As autumn approached there was still one major issue to be resolved: who would drive for the team. With money tight, the paddock view was that Stewart Grand Prix would not be able to afford any big names. On 18 September Jackie and Paul Stewart met Damon Hill and his lawyer Michael Breen. By then Hill was well on his way to becoming world champion, and could have expected to command an annual salary of anything between £4 million and £6 million. But Paul Stewart said he knew within days that Hill was not coming to the team, even though

Until defunct WWII aircraft bases in Britain were turned into race tracks, Brooklands in Surrey was racing's traditional home. Officially opened on 17 June 1907, it was was the world's first dedicated motor racing circuit. Here, Kaye Don (who came second) leads Count Czaykowsk (winner) in the 1933 British Empire Race.

Critics of modern F1 claim that the technical superiority of the racecar has made the quality of the driver virtually redundant. But Michael Schumacher has consistently proven that an above average driver can still win races in an average car.

TV commentator Murray Walker, who saw his first Grand Prix in 1948, disagrees with complaints that commercialism is driving out the excitement of F1.

Ron Dennis, who expanded McLaren from a sports team into an advanced engineering business.

Max Mosely, president of the FIA, has worked in partnership with Ecclestone to build F1 into a global enterprise. According to F1 folklore, Bernie carries the money, Max carries the contracts.

Paul Stewart (right) fulfilled his F1 ambitions with the support of his father, Jackie Stewart.

Luca di Montezemelo. The Ferrari president brought financial stability to racing and road car divisions. Racing is now effectively the marketing arm for the production cars.

Enzo Ferrari. Other teams may come and go, but without the legendary Ferrari, F1 would not be the same.

Jacques Villeneuve has split from Williams and will drive for British American Racing from 1999 – a team backed by his former manager and British American Tobacco.

Bernie Ecclestone pulls the strings in F1. But the riches he has made are largely tied up in family trusts linked to his wife, Slavica.

Flavio Briatore ensured Benetton stood for glamour. He was rarely seen without the company of celebrities or a pretty woman.

Frank Williams was an accomplished runner, until a road crash left him a paraplegic.

Beautiful women have become an essential part of the F1 scene. More evidence, say critics, of style over content.

Flavio Briatore (flanked by former Benetton drivers Gerhard Berger and Jean Alesi) cared little for F1's history and racecar technology. The sport was a great marketing opportunity for the Benetton clothing empire, and Briatore exploited its potential to the full through fashion shoots and celebrity-packed promotions.

Ayrton Senna in a Lotus. The black and gold livery of the John Player cigarette brand became one of the most potent images in F1 sponsorship.

A change of tyres and re-fuelling would take this McLaren crew 7–10 seconds on average. However, fuel stops are unnecessary. They were introduced to increase the excitement for television viewers.

The FIA's rule changes for racecar design were designed to limit the dominance of the top teams and increase competition between the teams. But the McLarens driven by David Coulthard (pictured) and Mika Hakkinen still looked like running away with the 1998 season. Only Ferrari kept pace.

The McLaren F1 road car. A technically brilliant cross-over from the racetrack to the road, but a commercial failure.

media reports continued to say that the dream-team of Jackie and Damon was still on. For sponsors Ford and HSBC, Hill was definitely the first-choice driver. In the absence of sponsors prepared to help meet the additional costs of bringing Hill to the team, however, everyone at Stewart Grand Prix had to lower their sights. In the first week of October the Danish driver Jan Magnussen, a star of Paul Stewart Racing's Formula Three team, was signed up, under a four-year deal. His salary was about £500,000. Two weeks later, the more experienced Brazilian Rubens Barrichello, who did four years with Jordan, agreed a three-year deal. Paul Stewart had said that having Hill in the team would be a fairy-tale, 'almost a dream come true for us'. But, with hindsight, he is glad Hill went elsewhere. 'Having the reigning world champion in the team would have put extra pressure on us. I think that this pressure is something this young team could probably have done without. The Ford negotiations, then the announcement, the build-up of the team and the car: it all meant an awful lot of stress. To have put Damon on top of all that would have meant carrying an enormous weight. We wanted the focus to be the team, not the drivers. It meant a healthier start to our life.'

It was widely reported that Damon Hill shunned Stewart Grand Prix because he wanted more money. In fact, Hill moved to Tom Walkinshaw's Arrows team because he thought it would be a risky career move to go to an unproven team. Hill accepts that it would have been a fairy-tale story to have teamed up with Jackie Stewart; and a marketing man's dream. But it would also have been a leap into the unknown. 'Damon came to see us,' explains Paul Stewart. 'I think he was impressed by what we had to say, and the things he saw at the factory. In the end Damon just decided it was too big a risk. I guess he was also impressed by what he saw at Arrows, and what Tom Walkinshaw had to say. He did not want to partner Ralf Schumacher at Jordan, which seemed to be the most obvious team choice at the time.' Hindsight shows that Hill might not have done any worse at Stewart Grand Prix than he did at Arrows. Tom Walkinshaw's team was geared up for a far better season than Stewart Grand Prix, but in the end both Damon's and his team's performance were slated for a disappointing season. 'That's racing. You do not always get what you want. Just don't take it personally,' Stewart said.

With the drivers in place, Stewart Grand Prix was ready to submit applications to the FIA for two cars to compete in the 1997 world championship, along with a $500,000 deposit. Approval came a week later. On 27 November, at the Marriott Hotel, London, the car was launched with the usual fanfare of glitz and glamour. The car's livery included a specially designed Racing Stewart tartan, now officially registered with the Scottish Tartan Society. Getting the launch out of the way is a watershed for any team. It signals an end to much of the backroom design work, the hiring of drivers, and negotiations with major sponsors. Next came the gruelling task of track-testing and refining the car before the season got under way the following March. Jan Magnussen did the initial shakedown runs, while Rubens Barrichello did development testing. Stewart Grand Prix was one of the first constructors to launch its car that year, so for the following few weeks the spotlight moved to the other teams. Stewart Grand Prix had much to be proud of. They had built a Formula One team from scratch. What is more, the Stewarts had probably secured the best start-up package of any grand prix entrant ever to begin competing. There was much optimism as the team, one of the few to use the new Formula One tyre supplier Bridgestone, improved on the car during the weeks of pre-season testing.

By the end of the season, however, there were mixed emotions about how things had gone. There were the jubilant scenes at the Monaco Grand Prix, where Rubens Barrichello drove a brilliant race in the rain to come second. It will go down as one of the most remarkable drives of the season. Little wonder that Jackie and Paul Stewart were too tearful for words after the race. The occasion was particularly sweet for other reasons, as Paul explained. 'Little games were going on, because we were the new boys on the block. Our motorhome was put in a parking lot on the other side of Monaco, that sort of thing. If there was a real will, the organisers would have looked after us. But people wanted to keep reminding us that we had not made it yet.' Monaco is a prestigious event, where levels of hospitality and corporate entertainment are at their highest. Jackie Stewart's marketing skills excel in such an environment, but no team boss wants to drag his VIP guests to a car-park away from the centre of the action. So it was poetic justice that the team received all the media coverage for its remarkable podium finish.

The 1997 season, however, also had many low moments. The Stewart Grand Prix was dogged by problems with the Cosworth-built Zetec-RV10 engine. The engine went through a surprising three phases of development through the season in an attempt to find some reliability. As the series moved on, the tension rose. Ford was unhappy. Its engines were being tested in public, in the full gaze of millions of television viewers. Jackie Stewart was blunt in his demand that Cosworth, the British company which supplies the engines to Ford, had to invest more and improve quality. Cosworth is one of the most famous names in grand prix engineering, but there was a definite feeling in the Stewart camp that the company, then owned by Vickers, the UK defence manufacturer, was sitting on its laurels. The Stewarts' concerns about the team's performance was not only mechanical, however. There was disappointment at the performance of the young Jan Magnussen, for whom there were high hopes at the start of the season. It is disappointing for sponsors as well as the team when things go wrong. Sponsors no longer enter Formula One for the fun of it. They want returns, and employ sophisticated marketing measurement techniques to track whether they get value for money. To his credit, Jackie Stewart never tried to convince anyone that his Formula One challenge could be anything other than a five-year plan. But it can be no coincidence that the Ford logo on the Stewart Grand Prix cars remains conspicuously low-profile, and will continue to be so while the team underperforms. Benetton boss David Richards's view of the money men who back Formula One is that they are all impatient for results, despite what they might say publicly. 'Most sponsors have a very simplistic approach. They are looking for a very quick and visible return – and that is an impractical wish.' A measure of goodwill and tolerance of mistakes helped carry Stewart Grand Prix through in its début season. The team had to start delivering results in its second year.

Life in the paddock had changed radically since Jackie Stewart was a driver. It had become hostile and secretive, he said. 'This is unnecessary. I do not know how it happened, the change in people, I suppose. But it does not have to be that way.' A legacy of the team's first season was to help smooth some of these sharp edges, and introduce a bit more honesty and openness in the way it went about things. It has not always done Stewart any good. His anti-tobacco stance did not win him any favours, nor did his outspoken comments after Michael Schumacher escaped with a slapped wrist for trying to shunt Jacques Villeneuve off the track in 1997. 'I don't think what Schumacher did is ethical at all,' said Stewart. 'And I don't think the governing body can allow it. I think behaviour of that type has to be not just discouraged, but eliminated. Otherwise, eventually it'll end in tears. There'll be one massive accident.' The FIA might not have liked Stewart rocking the boat, but his honesty won plaudits from the fans.

Paul Stewart, until 1997 an outsider, agrees with his father's observations that the sport must change. 'Each team has its own personality about the way it goes about business. It is nice that we are being seen to be doing business with integrity. That does not mean everyone else is not. But people do notice if you go about your business in a particular way. You get perceived in a particular way. We have already had an effect on Formula One, in lightening it up.' The Stewarts found some of the red tape frustrating. Jackie Stewart said joining Formula One was akin to joining a secret society – though in Stewart Grand Prix's case, the team is not yet a fully paid-up member. A particular irritant was that the team did not get a slice of the revenues from television broadcasting in its first year. Paul Stewart thinks the team deserves to be on the inside. 'The sport is now too big a business to continue its secretive ways,' he says. 'It will scare people away. Sponsors are going to think, am I going to get my hand bitten off, or am I in over my head? The antics of Formula One continue to bring up surprises. If the flotation goes ahead – and I hope it does – we have to start thinking about the image of the sport.'

The advice Eddie Jordan has for anyone thinking of starting a Formula One team is to tear up £25 million and scatter it to the wind. That way, they learn something of the futility of Formula One. Grand prix racing is not just the sport of broken dreams, it is the sport of broken balance sheets. Until Stewart Grand Prix began competing, Jordan's team was the most successful newcomer. And that was in 1991. Since then, however, it has become even harder to put together a team. Craig Pollock (Jacques Villeneuve's manager) and celebrated racecar constructor Reynard bought the Tyrrell team for around £20 million, but only with the promise of some £200 million from the tobacco giant British American Tobacco. In future only the big corporations will be able to afford to take the risk. Restrictions on newcomers will become even tighter if, as expected, the FIA begins charging a far larger deposit (a figure of $25 million has been mentioned) for Formula One entrants. Benetton's David Richards believes such measures will stop Formula One adventurers coming in and out of the sport, giving Formula One a bad name and upsetting the sponsors. But it could also mean turning Formula One into a closed shop. Already, the door to that shop is barely open. Stewart Grand Prix just squeezed through, but others may not be so lucky. Within a couple of years, the sport might consist of a league of no more than eight or ten permanent teams. The only opportunity to join the circus will be when an existing constructor sells up.

The race to start racing:

11 June 1995: Jackie Stewart and Ford executives have an informal chat about establishing a Formula One team

30 October 1995: Jackie and Paul make a formal presentation to Ford

4/5 January 1996: Official announcements that Ford and Stewart Grand Prix to enter Formula One in 1997 season

11 January 1996: First recruitment advert placed in *Autosport* magazine

4 March 1996; Alan Jenkins starts work as technical director. His job: to build the racing cars

30 March 1996: Designers complete layout of car

2 May 1996: Announcement of deal with XTRAC to build gearbox

1 July 1996: Wind-tunnel tests of 50 per cent model begin in California

9 August 1996: Construction of the racecar chassis begins

23 August 1996: Racecar passes in-house crash test regulations

17 September 1996: Relief as HSBC Holdings agree sponsorship deal worth £25 million over five years

18 September 1996: Discussions with Damon Hill about joining team, but it is clear they are going nowhere

3 October 1996: Jan Magnussen confirmed as team driver

22 October 1996 Rubens Barrichello confirmed as team driver

6 November 1996: Application to FIA to race in 1997. Approval comes seven days later

27 November 1996: Malaysian tourist board agrees sponsorship deal

10 December 1996: Racecar unveiled in London

9 March 1997: Both racecars retire during opening GP at Melbourne

11 May 1997: Barrichello achieves remarkable feat by coming second at Monaco

13 July 1997: Engine failures, again, force both drivers out of British GP

26 October 1997: Final race of the season, in Spain. Magnussen finishes ninth and Barrichello retires. Stewart Grand Prix finishes ninth in constructors' championship, one place behind Arrows

28 June 1998: Midway during the new season and the racecar's reliability is improving. But poor drives by Jan Magnussen mean that he is finally replaced by Jos Verstappen and rumours persist that Ford may dump Stewart Grand Prix for Benetton.

Chapter Five: OILING THE WHEELS

The Cost of Competing

FORMULA ONE IS a rich man's world. Only yacht racing comes close to Formula One in the amount of money needed to compete. The budget of a middle-raking constructor such as Stewart Grand Prix will be in the region of £25–30 million a year. Ferrari spends more than double that. To look at it another way: it cost the former Tyrrell team £750 a mile to run its cars; Williams Grand Prix Engineering, which has repeatedly won the constructors' world championship, was spending £5,000 a mile. The owner of a Formula One racing team faces expenditures similar to any other company. Huge resources have to be ploughed into research and development at factories employing between 100 and 300 staff. A team's travelling costs will reach many millions of pounds each season, as do the salaries paid to some drivers. Income from prize money, merchandising and television helps offset some of these costs, but the bulk of the team's finance, some 70–90 per cent for a typical constructor, comes from commercial sponsorship. It is no wonder that teams, therefore, devote substantial time and money to targeting, securing and servicing the sponsors that oil the wheels of Formula One. McLaren has more than 30 staff devoted to the task. In this chapter we look at the costs of running a Formula One operation and how teams go about raising finance. Of course, sponsorship is not a benevolent act. Sponsors demand a return on their investment and will soon withdraw their money if they do not get it. Why do companies spend such large sums sponsoring Formula One? 'Publicity' is the simple answer. But the marketing strategies behind sponsorships are all very different. This is especially true of tobacco manufacturers, Formula One's biggest backers. As we will see, Formula One and cigarette companies have always had a special partnership; indeed, 'dependency' might be a better description of their relationship.

There is much soul-searching in Formula One about whether the sport has 'sold out' to the marketing departments of the world's giant corporations. In truth, though, since motorsport's origins in the late nineteenth century, racing has always been beholden to sponsorship of one kind or another. European motor manufactures, and allied trades such as tyre and oil companies, were, for obvious reasons, backers from the outset. In the 1930s, the Fascist governments of Italy and Germany became indirect sponsors of national teams, believing that success on the racetrack could be used as a weapon to demonstrate technological supremacy. And after the Second World War a number of wealthy individuals came back into grand prix racing. By this time, however, the costs of competing were beginning to spiral upwards. Until the 1960s, motor racing was able to cloak itself in pretensions of amateurism, because the sport's governing body did not allow commercial sponsorship from outside the motor industry. By the end of that decade, however, Formula One was becoming a sophisticated technological sport, and the need to finance research and development made restrictions on sponsorship unrealistic. Formula One's governing body lifted its ban in 1968, opening the floodgates to a wave of new money, from companies as diverse as tobacco manufacturers, airlines and condom makers. Today, there is no pretence that Formula One is anything other than a commercially driven enterprise. McLaren's Ron Dennis sums it up thus: 'The "sport" in Formula One lasts for a couple of hours on a Sunday afternoon. Everything else is business, pure and simple. McLaren is in the business of enabling companies to get a message across to an audience. Winning races helps them achieve that. We set out to provide the best platform with the best image and the best environment for companies to maximise the benefits of their investment.'

When Formula One's critics try to dismiss the sport as a mere competition between 200mph billboards, they are simply stating the obvious. The *raison d'être* of modern grand prix racing is to be a vehicle for advertising, and few people working in the sport today feel any embarrassment about that. Flavio Briatore, the former managing director of Benetton Formula, was fond of saying that no sponsor ever gave him a cheque because they enjoyed seeing high-powered machines racing around circuits. Benetton's sponsors want a means of public exposure, and Briatore ensured they got it – otherwise the money would simply be channelled into another marketing opportunity. Benetton's racecars regularly carried more advertising than their rivals, sometimes

25 or so multi-coloured stickers promoting everything from Gillette razors to Kickers footwear. In 1996 Benetton Formula's turnover was £47 million. Up to £30 million of that came via direct sponsorship of the car, with the balance made up of other sponsorships involving the Benetton name and prize money from the team's successes in the previous season. On top of this, Benetton got free engines, a package worth some £20 million.

No two sponsorships are the same, so it is difficult to generalise about how teams raise cash. Contracts vary in length, and will contain complex get-out clauses for both sides. Some deals are straight cash transactions, while others might be for services in kind, such as consultancy or help with associated promotional activities, such as hospitality. Often contracts are performance related, with money paid out according to how many races are won or championships points accrued. In many cases contracts will be a mixture: a lump sum and bonuses. A dissection of the Benetton racecar gives some indication of the sorts of money involved. The team's full name in 1997 was Mild Seven Benetton Renault. The two title sponsors contributed the most towards the team, and so got their names in the best positions on the racecar; that is, the positions most easily picked up by the television cameras or in newspaper photographs. Until it pulled out of Formula One at the end of 1997, Renault supplied the engines free in return for its name on the car, plus other benefits including access to technical facilities and the use of the Benetton name and personnel for other marketing projects. This so-called works engine deal was Benetton's most valuable sponsorship. Renault – like all works suppliers – invested hugely in the research and development and in back-up. The majority of teams on the grid have to buy their engines, something which puts them at a distinct disadvantage. Again, the contracts vary, but it can cost £5–12 million a season, a third of the budget of a middle-ranking team. Under these agreements, the suppliers put far less effort into refining the engines for Formula One use, and the teams' ability to call on the manufacturer's vast resources of technical expertise is limited. The results speak for themselves: without a works engine deal, a team has no chance of winning the championship.

Mild Seven, a cigarette brand owned by the conglomerate Japan Tobacco, was Benetton's second most lucrative sponsor. Mild Seven joined Benetton almost by accident, after some initial inquiries about sponsorship led the company to call a contact who also knew Benetton. Flavio Briatore was a fan of performance-related deals, a form of contract he used with drivers as well as sponsors. When Mild Seven began sponsoring Benetton in 1994, the deal included a flat payment plus a bonus of $1 million per win. That year Michael Schumacher achieved eight wins and took the world championship, a feat he repeated in 1995. By the end of 1995 Mild Seven owed Benetton more than £11 million. In return, the light-blue colour of Mild Seven was splashed over the car, with the name posted on the nose cone, side panels and on the air box behind the driver's head. These are prime spots on any racecar and command the highest fee; Mild Seven shared them with Renault. Another key spot on the air box section was taken by Agip Petroli, a division of the Italian oil giant ENI, whose £2.5 million sponsorship included the supply of lubricants and fuels. The final spot on the air box was taken by A1, an Austrian mobile telephone company, which paid close to £2 million for the privilege. A second-division Formula One team would get little more than £1 million for these air box positions. Elsewhere on the Benetton car were large decals for Akai, the Japanese consumer electronics company, and the airline Korean Air. Their names were printed on the side panels, slots which sell for between £2 million and £2.5 million (£500,000 for lesser teams). Gillette, the shaving products group, took the rear wing of the Benetton at a cost of £1.6 million, while Kickers footwear paid £1.3 million for a red strip around the front of the cockpit and the wing mirrors. Other spots sell for between £500,000 and £1 million depending on the size of the decal. Magnetti Marelli traded electronic management components for a position at the base of the air box. Fondmetal Group gave components in return for a small decal just in front of the rear wheels. Such spaces are worth £500,000 to a top team, and no more than £50,000 for a team lower down the grid. Finally, there are the tyres, costing in the region of £900,000 per season to those who have to pay. Benetton got their Goodyear Eagles tyres free under a deal that included putting the manufacturer's name along a strip at the base of each side of the chassis.

The above gives a guide to the income, but what of the outgoings? The cost of running a Formula One team varies considerably. The following is a rough guide to the outlay during a season:

- **Drivers:** Ferrari driver Michael Schumacher is paid £16 million a year, with some of the money coming from the team's sponsors. This is an exception, however, and £3–5 million seems to be an average package for a quality driver. Other drivers might pay teams to give them a seat, for example Pedro Diniz at Arrows. A test driver might earn as little as £50,000.

- **Cars:** £3–5 million will be needed for aerodynamic testing, research and development, accident repairs, and so on. The nose cone on a chassis, the body part most liable to damage, costs around £12,000, while brake systems and gearboxes cost £100,000 each; suspension systems about £60,000. The in-car electronics and computers cost about £1.5 million.
- **Engines:** Unless the teams get them free, they are looking at a budget of £2 million at the very least.
- **Tyres:** Free for some teams, and about £700 each for the rest. Racing rules on tyres are changing, but with seven sets for each race plus more for testing, the budget will easily top £1 million.
- **Transport:** The Formula One Constructors' Association will transport the two cars and five tonnes of equipment needed for races outside Europe. Several large trucks are needed to transport equipment within Europe. Many teams take extra freight, mobile homes, or use private jets. The cost will be over £1 million. Between 20 and 30 staff will go on 'fly-aways' outside Europe. When hotels and hire cars are included, the cost will be about £1.2 million.
- **Factory:** Computer-aided design systems and lathes last several years, but a new team entering Formula One will have to spend an initial £2 million on such equipment.
- **Other:** Not all teams can afford to run a test team. Those that do will have to budget £1.5 million. Finally, fuel and lubricants, unless supplied free, will cost £250,000.

The costs of competing have exacerbated the gulf between rich and poor teams. During the 1990s the four richest teams were the only four serious challengers for the Formula One championship: Ferrari, McLaren, Williams and Benetton. Ferrari and McLaren have a 'spend what it takes' philosophy. In particular, Ferrari has in recent years decided that it must win the world championship at all costs, hence the company's willingness to pay Schumacher his record-breaking salary. Frank Williams estimates that in the early 1980s the total racing budget for his team was around £2.25 million, out of which came the money to buy Cosworth engines. By 1990 the costs had grown to more than £15 million, with free Renault V10 engines thrown in. In 1997 the budget had more than doubled to £35 million, again with free Renault engines as part of a sponsorship package. The FIA has attempted to contain the costs with rule changes that restrict racecar design and technology, but the expenditure just keeps going up. It is an iron law of Formula One there can never be enough testing or experimenting with new composites and components. Also, if the number of races on the grand prix calendar is increased, as seems likely, it will mean higher transport costs. Nor should anyone forget the simple inflationary costs that affect any company, from higher wage bills to more expensive components.

For the moment, and it would seem for the foreseeable future, there is no shortage of sponsors willing to help meet these spiralling costs. The popularity of Formula One as television entertainment means sponsors are prepared to pay a premium to get their names on the racecars. According to FIA figures, the 1997 Formula One world championship series reached 50.7 billion television viewers, compared with 41 billion in 1996. The figures, based on returns from television broadcasters, are cumulative and counted each time Formula One appears on a television screen. As we will see later, in the chapter on television, such figures should be treated with caution. Yet, what they do show is a consistent rise in the number of times a Formula One-related item appears on television. Advertisers have few opportunities to reach a global audience in a single hit, but Formula One is one of them.

So, how much do sponsors spend? The truth is, probably the only people who really know are the company directors and the senior executives in the marketing departments. There will be a headline figure of the amount of direct sponsorship. But on top of this will be help with the annual racecar launches, possibly a contribution towards the drivers' salaries, and corporate hospitality. The international rolling circus of Formula One means money might come out of different budgets in different countries. That said, it is possible to build up a picture of the sort of sums involved. The respected UK magazine *Marketing* puts the total direct sponsorship by six tobacco companies in 1997 at $168 million. In addition to this, as is explained in more detail later, in 1998 British American Tobacco bought a racing team and intends to invest $275 million over five years. Cigarette companies are generally prepared to pay a 15–20 per cent premium over other companies to sponsor Formula One. Having been excluded from mainstream advertising, tobacco companies have little choice but to spend heavily on other forms of marketing. The sort of sums being paid by non-tobacco companies are as follows: banking group HSBC is sponsoring Stewart Grand Prix for £25 million over five years; Danka, an office equipment company, is spending £11.2 million a year with Arrows; and Mercedes, which as an engine manufacturer is a slightly different form of sponsor, is spending an estimated £300 million over five years with McLaren.

Often, these figures do not include spending on related promotional activities. As a general rule, marketing consultants believe that for every £1 spent on direct sponsorship, another £1 should be spent on supporting it through hospitality, other advertising, and media events. However, in the case of Formula One, consultants advise sponsors to spend an extra £2 or £3 on related marketing. Barrie Gill, chairman of CSS International, a sponsorship consultancy, explains: 'Formula One is a very expensive sport, and a global one. These are the first things to remember. And now that the car launches during the winter months have become events in themselves, Formula One lasts all year round. There is no point in a company spending a few million to put its name on a car, and then failing to exploit it.' Taking valued clients to the Monaco Grand Prix, for example, or paying £1,000 per guest to entertain clients in the Paddock Club, the corporate hospitality tent erected at each race, are not cheap activities. Then there is the promotional literature, branded clothing and newspaper advertisements that are used to underline the message. All these are essential activities, Gill believes. 'A sponsorship needs to be worked at; a strategy needs to be developed over time. That costs. A company cannot buy space on a car and then sit back and let it happen.'

The onward march of commercialism through grand prix racing is not without its critics. Rather than add value to the sport, they say, sponsorship has now devalued it. For many fans the impact of large-scale sponsorship has been to alter radically the shape and nature of Formula One, to the point where it is unrecognisable as a form of sporting entertainment. Most racing enthusiasts accepted that the demands of technological development, staging races in far-flung corners of the globe, and the impact of television, would change the structure of Formula One. But they feel the pendulum has swung too far in favour of commercialism. Stirling Moss, one of the greatest post-war drivers, no longer talks about Formula One as a sport, but as a branch of showbusiness. It is not that the critics are against sponsorship. What concerns them is that by bowing to the ever greater needs of sponsorship, modern teams have changed their very motivation for racing. For instance, established national racing colours – green for

Britain, red for Italy, blue for France, silver for Germany – have long been consigned to Formula One history. Cars are now identified by the gold of a Benson & Hedges cigarette packet or Winfield red. Even Ferrari painted its cars a different shade of red when Marlboro became a sponsor. Formula One teams have become multinational enterprises, dependent on, and subservient to, the demands of international corporations. As a result, the excitement of competition between nation states which grip other sports has, in the case of Formula One, become diluted. Grand prix constructors, run by their multimillionaire owners, are now as profit-centred as their sponsors. It is the rules and language of commerce that drive Formula One, rather than any sporting principles. Or so the critics claim.

Even if this is true, the fact remains that Formula One has never been so popular. Under Bernie Ecclestone and Max Mosley, grand prix racing has been turned into an 'event' that is ideal for the television age – fast, colourful, glamorous. But it is not just the television audiences that are growing. Purists may regret the passing of the era when they could walk around the paddock, sharing a word with the drivers. Yet, there are more fans attending live races today than before. For Ron Dennis the value of sponsorship has been to allow the teams, the circuit owners, the television broadcasters and the administrators to develop the sport in a way that would have not been possible before. 'Basically, it is the money that has come in from investors that has enabled Formula One to give more to the fan. I cannot see how we could satisfy the level of interest without taking money from outside Formula One and using it to grow the sport.'

Nigel Geach, a director of Sports Marketing Surveys, has been monitoring the growth of Formula since 1984. One explanation for the surge in popularity of Formula One, he believes, lies in the fact that it has become part of popular culture and current affairs. No longer is the sport confined to the sports pages. Style magazines regularly feature the antics of the millionaire drivers; and Formula One is central to the news debate over tobacco sponsorship of sport. This broadening of the image helps broaden the range of sponsors, because the sport is appealing to a wider set of demographics. Geach said: 'Formula One used to be like any other sport, with people just interested in the action. But, in fact, I think that growing interest in the track action has spilled over into what goes on outside: in the politics and the commercial side, and all the things that go on around Formula One. Michael Schumacher's decision to leave Benetton and drive for Ferrari was news. But then so was Marlboro's decision to leave McLaren and sponsor Ferrari. Fans were interested in the reasons for these moves, the money and the strategy behind them.' Geach pinpoints the death of Brazilian driver Ayrton Senna in 1994 as a watershed in interest in the sport. 'The pictures made front-page news across the world. It brought Formula One into people's minds – for the wrong reasons, of course, but there was still huge publicity all the same. It made people think about the sport in general, not just about what went on on the track.' The result, said Geach, has been to broaden the Formula One audience base. 'We have seen a maturity of the Formula One viewer. People's favourite sports used to be football, or cricket, or Formula One. What we find in our surveys now is people saying: I like football and Formula One, and I like cricket and Formula One. No longer is it of secondary interest to the general sports fan.' So, grand prix racing has emerged as an extremely important vehicle for sponsors trying to reach an audience. But how have these companies sought to exploit this world-wide surge in Formula One's popularity? The remainder of this chapter explores in more detail some of the strategies adopted by sponsors, and in particular how the tobacco industry came to exercise such a tight grip over the sport.

The Art of Sponsorship

MOTOR RACING AND sponsorship have been inextricably linked for more than 100 years. As we saw in Chapter One, the first serious car race, between Paris and Rouen in 1894, was arranged and sponsored by a newspaper, *Le Petit Journal*. Six years later another newspaper, the *New York Herald*, sponsored a series of international races as part of a promotion to establish a French edition of the journal. However, patronage from the fledgeling motor industry was the main source of racing finance, and for more than 60 years car manufacturers and their allied trades remained virtually the only source of sponsorship. During the late 1950s and '60s, however, radical changes began to shape the development of motorsport. The heart of racing was moving to Britain from the Continent. And new engineering developments meant that the cost of competing began to fall, putting serious racing within reach of individuals, not just corporations. The traditions and rules that had governed racing, including restrictions on sponsorship, were to be swept away thanks to a new generation of British-based owner-entrepreneurs. Men like Colin Chapman and Bruce McLaren resented being told by a stuffy racing authority how they could finance their teams. Frank Williams, one of the pioneers of modern grand prix racing, recalls those days as a time of great change, but also great fun. 'Race meetings seemed to be full of Antipodean engineers and enthusiasts. Not just Bruce McLaren's crowd, but other less famous people. They came from Europe and America too. It just seemed as if a whole new scene was developing, which, of course, it was. These were people who were passionate about racing; people who did not really like being told which sponsors could back them and which could not. They were going to change things, though I am not sure if we all knew this at the time.'

Improvements in air transport meant that many grand prix enthusiasts had worked or driven in the United States, where they witnessed advances made in racing because of the availability of commercial sponsorship. It was so different in America, and Australia for that matter, where money called the shots and no one objected. Guy Edwards, who financed his racing career in the 1970s by arranging his own sponsorship packages, recorded his exploits in a fascinating book, *Sponsorship and the World of Motor Racing*, a 'how-to' guide for raising money and a pictorial history rolled into one. One photograph in the book seems to sum up the different attitude to sponsorship in America. A heavily built, stern-faced man, looking like Hollywood's archetypal Chicago mobster, is strutting down the pit-lane prior to the start of the 1964 Indianapolis 500 race. He is wearing a white suit, dotted with dozens of labels bearing the letters STP, the American oil company. The man is Andy Granatelli, boss of the company. He is a sponsor, and he is proud of it. Such a blatant display of commercialism, even from a company involved in the motor industry, would have been heavily frowned upon by the FIA, and probably banned by some television companies from being screened.

When, in 1968, the FIA's Commission Sportive Internationale bowed to commercial reality and lifted restrictions on commercial sponsorship, it was not the groundswell of grassroots pressure that had finally tipped the balance. It was the action of an important existing sponsor, Esso, which perhaps had the single biggest influence on changing the rules. In 1967 the company withdrew from racing, somewhat irritated that over the years the tyre manufacturers had usurped oil companies in importance as sponsors of Formula One. With a major sponsor pulling out, and with the prospect of others following suit, the CSI realised that racing would be damaged unless fresh money was forthcoming. Esso was an important sponsor of Lotus, and within months of the ban being lifted, the team's owner Colin Chapman was negotiating a landmark deal with the Imperial Tobacco cigarette company. Team Lotus became 'Gold Leaf Team Lotus', and Formula One sponsorship was never the same again.

In a curious way, Guy Edwards believes, it could be argued that Formula One probably benefited from advertising restrictions. In America, where commercial sponsorship had financed motor racing for decades, the sport failed to become a mainstream entertainment, except possibly at Indianapolis. As a result, sponsorship did not develop much beyond the level of putting a few stickers on the cars. There was no marketing strategy, no 'artistry' about developing an advertising programme. In Europe, however, motor racing had some snob value. It was an exclusive sport, 'untainted' by commercial sponsorship. As Edwards explains: 'Seventy years of racing had brought about an entirely different image. Royalty not only attended races but, in the case of Prince Bira of Thailand, competed. Interest and participation from the establishment has embedded racing into Europe's sporting culture as an upmarket sport. It had developed with 'old money' government money and manufacturers' money. Had commercial sponsorship been allowed from the early days, as it had in America, the development of the sport in Europe would undoubtedly have been different.' By the time restrictions on sponsorship were lifted, Formula One had become an upmarket sport which also had mass appeal – an attractive prospect for any marketing executive with a multi-million-pound budget to spend.

New money began flowing into Formula One, spurring research and an expansion of constructors' engineering departments. There was, however, one team boss who thought he could survive without corporate backers. The wealthy Alexander Hesketh, an ebullient member of Britain's House of Lords, dug deep into his own inheritance to finance a grand prix team in the 1970s. His motto was 'Racing for Britain and Racing for You'. 'It is a hundred times more rewarding to receive recognition from the people of this country, than to receive a cheque from a commercial sponsor,' he said. The Hesketh team, however, was the exception that proved the rule. The day of the wealthy amateur, able to fund a private team out of his own resources, was over. A new commercial era had arrived, and any team owner who thought he could work outside it was doomed to failure. It was Lord Hesketh, known as Le Patron, who brought James Hunt into Formula One. With its teddy bear mascot, the team was renowned for its partying and its fun-loving approach. At the races, Hesketh Grand Prix was never to be without its butlers, champagne and Rolls-Royces. But this affluent public face concealed a rather shaky operation. Hunt jumped ship to drive for McLaren for the 1976 season, going on to win the world championship that year. With a financial crisis looming, Lord Hesketh was forced into a change of heart about sponsorship (in recent years he has been a vocal supporter of the tobacco industry's right to sponsor racing). Driver Guy Edwards, later to become one of the sport's top sponsorship 'fixers', brought Hesketh a package deal involving *Penthouse*, the men's magazine, and Rizla, the manufacturer of cigarette papers. Under the sponsorship agreement, Rizla got free advertising space in *Penthouse* (on the pages where the advertising slots went unsold), and both companies had branding on the 1976 Hesketh car. However, with Lord Hesketh's other business hit by economic recession, the team folded soon after, his conversion to sponsorship coming too late.

The *Penthouse*/Rizla deal was an example of the increasingly sophisticated methods being used to bring sponsors into Formula One. Rizla paid £70,000 to have its decals on half the car, and got £70,000 of free advertising in *Penthouse*. The magazine would take the other half of the car, free. This strategy of linking one sponsor with another for mutual benefit (it does not have to involve a company putting its name on a car) is now commonplace. Jackie Stewart, for instance, excels at this corporate matchmaking. He promises his backers that they will make more in business-to-business deals than they spend on the sponsorship. Back in the 1970s and '80s, however, such deals were rare. Furthermore, little thought was given to how sponsorships were serviced. Adding value to a sponsorship, in the form of hospitality or cross-marketing deals, was never considered. Part of the explanation was that tobacco sponsorship was so readily available. Barrie Gill, chairman of CSS International, a sponsorship consultant whose clients include Williams Grand Prix Engineering, believes tobacco companies were just thankful to have a vehicle to promote themselves. Unable to advertise through normal media channels, cigarette manufacturers were eager and undemanding sponsors. But, Gill said, success with tobacco firms led constructors to believe that it would work with others sponsors. 'No thought was given to catering for a sponsor's individual needs in those early days, beyond a few pit-passes. There was no attempt to refine a package to a particular company. It was a scatter-gun approach: telephone enough people and eventually you will persuade someone to pay up in return for putting their name on the side of the car.'

These days, negotiations with sponsors have to be meticulously prepared. The big, multi-million-pound deals can easily take more than a year before both sides are ready to sign. Yet, if sponsor and client hit it off straight away, it is not unknown for an agreement to be reached within weeks. Rothmans' sponsorship of Williams, arguably one of the most successful of recent years, took just six weeks to complete. (Rothmans had already decided to enter Formula One, and contacted Williams after their telephone calls to the Swiss-based outfit Sauber went unanswered. Williams switched to Rothmans' sister brand Winfield in 1998.) Generally, about six to nine months seems to be the norm for securing a sponsorship deal. Much of that time is taken up in actually educating potential sponsors about the sport. Barrie Gill explains: 'It is often said that a company sponsors Formula One because its chairman or chief executive is a fan. That is a fallacy. Sponsorship is a business proposition, involving large budgets and large companies with shareholders' interest to represent. We have to persuade companies that Formula One might be better for them than other forms of promotion. We have to explain what Formula One stands for, and how it can be used. It is not like the car makers, and tyre and oil firms, who are already close to the sport.' However, it is not all about presentations, flip-charts and statistics about Formula One's global television audience. Any potential sponsor will also get the red carpet treatment: tickets to the races, factory tours, meetings with the drivers.

Guy Edwards, who now acts as a sponsorship broker from his base in Monaco, might target no more than three or four organisations a year. 'I do not just fire off dozens of letters to managing directors who might have an interest in Formula One. I have to do my homework: read the company's balance-sheet, the financial press, find out how the company sees its market position and how it wants to expand. Do the aspirations of the company fit with motor racing? A wasted pitch is a waste of money as well as time.' Giving the five-star treatment to a potential sponsor will cost a team many thousands of pounds, so good research is essential. McLaren has a large in-house marketing operation, the biggest of any Formula One team, employing some 30 people who specialise in finding financial backers and acting as consultants about the best ways to exploit their involvement. McLaren's managing director, Ron Dennis, does not use the term 'sponsor', preferring the word 'investor' instead, as he believes it more aptly describes the relationship between Formula One and its financiers. 'Companies that spend money with us are investors looking for a financial return. We give them media exposure on our cars. We know the value of that exposure, and we know how to enhance that value well above the cost. With 30 years in Formula One we think we are well equipped to get the most out of Formula One for our investors.' Headed by managing director Ekrem Sami, McLaren's Marketing Services Division is run as a separate profit-centre within the group. Sami's team have built a huge database on companies connected to, or interested in, motor racing and sports sponsorship. Any detail that might be relevant is logged, enabling the team to analyse and dissect every potential sponsor with care. With the competition for backers so cut-throat, even the smallest piece of extra information could give McLaren the edge, Sami believes.

McLaren has calculated that the total value to investors of their involvement with the team – in marketing and business-to-business opportunities – is around $4 billion each season. How come? Teams receive a constant feedback of information about their world-wide exposure on television and the print media. Ekrem Sami then works out how much it would cost to buy equivalent advertising on television or in newspapers. With some 200 countries screening and reporting on Formula One, it is easy to see how the value of the exposure mounts up. Of course, a lot of this advertising is worthless to the sponsors. Companies may not find it worthwhile promoting themselves in certain countries, or for the same length of time or in the same way. But the value put on McLaren's, or any of the other team's, total marketing potential underlies the power of Formula One as a promotional medium. And that matters when constructors are competing with others sports for sponsorship. Another factor in Formula One's favour is that the relative cost of sponsoring constructors appears to be getting cheaper. Nigel Geach, whose company Sports Marketing Surveys measures the success of sponsorship, argues that the price of buying space on racecars has in no way kept pace with the rise in public interest and coverage of Formula One: 'The costs of sponsorship have always been high in Formula One. But sponsors are reaching a wider demographic area and a wider age group. The monetary value of sponsorship relative to the return is actually very good. If someone were to ask, does Formula One deliver the goods to the sponsor at value for money, my answer would have to be: generally, yes.'

The first rule of Formula One sponsorship is that there are no rules. A deal might be struck after months of hard bargaining, or secured in the time it takes for a round of golf. Marketing executives fly the world in search of corporate cash, trying to persuade companies that they would benefit by basking in the reflected glory of Formula One. Yet, the vital first lead might come from a chance conversation, according to Ian Phillips, commercial director at Jordan Grand Prix. 'There is no science to finding sponsors,' he argues. 'You can spend £100,000 on a corporate video, £20,000 on glossy brochures, £50,000 on research: and the company you are targeting might not even reply. On the other hand, you might be standing in a pub, and someone will overhear the conversation. It could be a chairman interested in knowing more about Formula One. But a lot of business comes from being in the right place at the right time, so networking is crucial.'

Some sponsorships are one-off deals for a particular grand prix event. Maybe the company has a group of key clients it wants to entertain for a day. About £5,000, for example, might buy a small space on the front wing of a racecar for a single race. As part of the deal, the sponsor would probably get to take its guests around the pit-lane, meet the team boss and drivers, and then go off to the exclusive Paddock Club for lunch. Other contracts might last five years, like the £25 million deal struck between Stewart Grand Prix and the international banking group HSBC. Here, co-operation might extend to such things as tours to the Stewart factory for HSBC clients and appearances by Jackie Stewart at the bank's functions. Sponsorship is not just about selling space on a racecar. As long as the commercial director is imaginative enough, there is a sponsorship deal for every occasion. Drivers need kitting out in smart suits; food and wine is needed for a corporate hospitality bash. Cerruti, the Italian fashion company, signed a deal with Ferrari, while both Guinness and an Italian vineyard had special links with Jordan. In return, team principals might turn up once a year at these companies' promotional functions. Sponsorship is all about back-scratching, and in Formula One they have turned it into a fine art.

Why do companies spend such large amounts of money on Formula One? All the sponsors, of course, have something to sell. But there the similarities end. No two marketing strategies are the same. Some sponsors, such as tobacco companies, want blanket coverage. Others, such as Andersen Consulting, are targeting no more than a few thousand potential business clients. The best way to grasp why companies choose to sponsor Formula One is to look at specific examples. Before doing that, however, it is worth understanding what makes Formula One such an attractive marketing tool in the first place. Few marketing experts would disagree that Formula One offers a unique vehicle for companies wanting to position themselves globally or give their products international branding. The key to this is the power of television, which has been instrumental in building Formula One into a worldwide sport. This is explored in a separate chapter but one basic fact cannot be emphasised too strongly: without television, the hundreds of millions of pounds that pour into Formula One would dry up. The majority of the television audience is made up of men aged 18–35, a high-spending section of the population that advertisers want to reach. Meanwhile research also shows that female audiences are rising. According to Sports Marketing Surveys, the number of women watching Formula One rose by 10 per cent between 1994 and 1996.

Unlike World Cup football or the Olympics, two events that attract similarly large audiences (but which are four-yearly events), sponsors are not consigned to the margins of the action. 'Sponsors of Formula One do not have the restriction of having to place their message on a billboard at the edge of the football field,' Guy Edwards explains. 'They can communicate their message at the centre of the action, where the hearts and minds of the consumer are focused; that is, on the cars. It is the car and the drivers that people pay to watch. They are pictured in the newspapers and in the advertisements; are the subjects of the television programmes.' With Formula One, companies do not sponsor an event, they sponsor a competitor. Becoming an official sponsor of the Olympics costs around $30 million, and that is limited to using the five Olympic rings as a marketing tool. No advertising banners are allowed in the stadium, and sponsors probably have to spend three times that sum to get any advertising benefit. With football, and to a certain extent with the Olympics, there is no way of knowing who will be in the final. Sponsors of Formula One know that they will have a grid full of cars, with all the best teams and drivers taking part each season. And because Formula One racing takes place every two weeks for eight months of the year, it must have a better chance of succeeding, Edwards believes. In fact, sponsoring Formula One is no longer an event lasting eight months. All the hype around driver changes and the launch of new racecars means that Formula One is a 52-week promotional tool, enabling sponsors to build up an enduring marketing programme. As Edwards puts it: 'With Formula One, sponsors get a bigger bang for their buck than if they had spent the money on other sports.'

Corporations used to look upon sponsorship with suspicion, preferring straightforward advertising via television commercials, newspaper adverts and posters. Cigarette manufacturers, denied mainstream advertising in many countries, were forced into sponsorship. Most other businesses still prefer other forms of marketing. One explanation for this reticence is that sponsorship can be a far more sophisticated and riskier tool than advertising, requiring an ongoing relationship with those organisations being sponsored. In Formula One, that means getting team bosses and drivers to attend events, devote valuable time to help with corporate hospitality and, above all, spend a lot of time formulating a precise promotional strategy that can often last several years. For marketing directors, spending a lump sum on a television campaign is simpler, and the benefits are more easily explained to a board of directors and shareholders.

Two decades ago sponsorship would have hardly figured in a graph plotting a company's total communications expenditure, believes Guy Edwards. But advertising's share of total marketing budgets is slipping as companies go in for more sponsorship. The reason, Edwards argues, is that the cluttered and conflicting world of marketing images gets in the way of companies' efforts to carve out a unique message. 'How can a company make its cry heard above all the others when the world is becoming one large living-room? Unlike straight, paid-for media, a good sponsorship provides a company with an armoury of communications, motivation and image-enhancing weaponry as part and parcel of the overall package. Consumers are very sceptical of advertising bombarding them every day, and the sponsor must look for a vehicle that has enough depth to be believed.' It is sponsorship's ability to 'borrow' the imagery of an event that already has a presence in the human psyche that makes it powerful. And there are few events with a more distinctive imagery than Formula One. Management consultancy, banking, making electronic equipment, are essentially dull activities. Sponsors hope Formula One will bring their products to life. Edwards explains: 'An alliance with the right partner also underpins product statements, providing the sponsoring company with credibility and reassuring the consumer. Why pay through the nose to try and establish an image when it can be more effective and cheaper to borrow it through the right alliance?' A brand name means nothing until you give it the image that is created around it. Whereas good advertising becomes part of language, good sponsorship can become part of culture.

Some products lend themselves easily to have Formula One 'superimposed' on them. But all sponsors hope that motor racing will enliven and explain the essence of the goods or services they are trying to sell. Andersen Consulting, a London-based international management consultancy that sponsors Williams, has incorporated the language and imagery of Formula One into its general marketing. When Jacques Villeneuve won the 1997 British Grand Prix, the firm took out full-page adverts in the *Financial Times* newspaper to congratulate him and underline Andersen's part in the teamwork behind the win. At one time, wherever you saw the Andersen name, you also saw some Formula One imagery. Andersen's strategy was to present itself as an active partner in the Williams success story, not just a sponsor. The firm could lay claim to this contribution because it had helped Williams to relocate factories and install new equipment. Rather than pay hard cash to brand its name on the crash helmets of the drivers, Andersen took payment in kind for the consultancy work. Robert Baldock, the marketing partner at Andersen, explained: 'We were not interested in a straight cash deal in return for branding. We did not want our image to be parasitic on achievements we had nothing to do with. We wanted to be an active contributor to the success of the team we were sponsoring. We agreed that, instead of the usual pure cash-based sponsorship deal, we would contribute our skills, the strengths of our people, to help Williams build on their success. In this way, our relationship is one of partners, not sponsors.' Pictures of Damon Hill's eyes staring out from his helmet – with Andersen's name in full view – became one of the most potent images of the 1996 season, when Hill won the world drivers' championship. Andersen continues to advise Williams on how the firm might diversify its engineering business into subcontract work, and exploit its brand name. To have done the consultancy work looks good on Andersen's curriculum vitae, and the firm is in no doubt that other business has come its way precisely because of its Formula One association.

A typical television audience for a Formula One race will include a large number of ABC1 viewers, many of whom will be business people. This is the section of the audience that Andersen is trying to reach, not the millions of other people who watch grand prix racing. The firm has specific business-to-business objectives. Andersen is not targeting a broad customer base, like Marlboro. Andersen's exploitation of its relationship with Williams is narrowly focused, and based on event hospitality and customer relations. As Baldock puts it: 'We are not trying to reach 400 million people. Andersen Consulting's customers number, perhaps, 4,000. Formula One helps us reach those customers, as well as enhance our reputation. Here we are, doing something for a premier sport that is highly advanced and competitive. We are associated with a team that continues to lead. We will invite clients and potential clients to the races, or take them to the Williams factory. It gives us a chance to reaffirm our relationship with clients, and meet new ones.' Is Andersen convinced that it gets value for money? Sponsorship is an inexact science, but Baldock is convinced the relationship works. 'We know who we want to do business with in each country. We know, typically, who would be buying Andersen Consulting services in those countries. So, we went through an exercise of contacting those people whom we would call our target buyers. We basically asked them, had they seen our name at all? We were quite staggered by the result. In one year in the UK, 40 per cent of target buyers had seen our name on Damon Hill's crash helmet when he drove for Williams. We have not achieved that level of name recognition through other forms of advertising. On all measures, the relationship with Williams Grand Prix Engineering has exceeded our expectations.'

Henderson Investments, another Williams sponsor, was also looking to incorporate the theme of teamwork into its marketing. The firm, a private money management group, signed a three-year deal worth £3 million a year to put its name on the helmets of the Williams pit crew. The sight of a pit crew changing tyres and refuelling in seconds speaks volumes about teamwork, and Henderson wanted its name to be at the centre of this action rather than on the car. The sponsorship deal was viewed by many in the industry as expensive, even by Formula One standards. And the wooing of Henderson by Williams had its inauspicious moments. When Williams took the Henderson board of directors to the British Grand Prix, their vehicle got stuck in traffic. A helicopter was dispatched, but could not take off because of bad weather. Williams had to resort to ferrying the directors across muddy fields by tractor. It was not exactly the sort of magic Williams was trying to convey. Yet, after all, sponsorship contracts are not about glamour, it is about striking a good commercial deal, and the firm has absolutely no regrets. When Lindsay Firth-McGuckin, Henderson's marketing director, explains the rationale behind the deal, the benefits-vs-costs ratio becomes clearer. 'We spent months researching whether Formula One would be right for us. Now, we are just amazed that no one else from our field was already involved. It is amazing the reaction of people when they are invited to come in on the inside; to get invited to the pits.' What were Henderson's aims? Firstly, the firm was rebranding itself with a new name and logo. Corporate hospitality at the races became an important part of informing clients. Secondly, Formula One is a rich sport. Wealthy people work in Formula One; wealthy people from the world of business and entertainment are attracted to it. Such people are all potential clients for private fund management advice. Thirdly, there is the prospect of getting closer to Williams's other sponsors, Andersen Consulting perhaps, and maybe working with them on other projects. Another of Henderson's aims is to expand the business in Asia, particularly Japan, where interest in Formula One is growing fast. Finally, there is the link with technology. One of Henderson's investment trusts is a technology fund. Formula One provides plenty of scope to draw on hi-tech imagery of racing cars, as well as help from Williams executives in promoting the fund. 'When you consider all these elements,' concludes Firth-McGuckin, 'Formula One is an ideal fit with what we as a firm are trying to achieve.'

Andersen and Henderson 'borrowed' from Formula One to sell services, though it is much the same with manufactured products. Tyres and motor components lend themselves easily to a grand prix connection. Manufacturers of other products have to work a little harder. Danka, the office equipment maker, looked closely at sponsoring golf, athletics and football's World Cup, before choosing Formula One. The deciding factor, as is so often the case, was that Formula One is fast, modern and technology-driven. These intrinsic elements of the sport have become important selling points for a whole range of sponsors hoping some of the 'shine' will rub off on their products. Danka, which makes photocopiers, printers, and faxes for a global market worth £2 billion a year, bought prominent spots on the engine cover and nose cone of the Arrows Yamaha racecar. It was a three-year deal, with Danka expecting total spending, including corporate hospitality and other add-ons, to reach £40 million by the end of 1999. The aim of the promotion was simple: to reach businessmen who might buy Danka equipment. In fact, the global audience reached by Danka was far greater than it really needed, something accepted by Mark Garius, the marketing director who negotiated the deal. However, as Garius explained, Danka wanted to move quickly. The company had suffered years of relative anonymity compared to its nearest rival, Xerox. 'We did have some catching up to do,' said Garius. 'Danka has grown into a big company, yet our name was not as well known as Xerox. We wanted to address that state of affairs quickly. We are finding that you can generate awareness very quickly by sponsoring Formula One, and certainly a lot quicker than through traditional advertising.' If, after three years backing Arrows, the Danka name is more familiar to its target audience, then the sponsorship will have worked. If Danka also becomes a household name, then that will be a bonus.

On the surface, it might appear that Danka's first season as an Arrows sponsor did not go well. The team's performances on the track in 1997 were poor indeed. At times the reliability of the racecars were so bad that they were ridiculed. For Danka, however, disappointing races did not necessarily equate to disappointment with the sponsorship. Arrows were fortunate to have attracted Damon Hill, the reigning world champion, to drive for the team. No matter where he finished, there was always a lot of human interest in Hill's performance. So even when Hill did badly, Danka's name more often than not appeared on television and in the press. Danka wanted coverage, and they got it – whatever Arrows' result. At the British Grand Prix, where Hill came sixth and gained a single championship point, he featured more prominently than any other team or driver. When, against all the odds, he finished second in a race, there was massive coverage. Marketing expert Nigel Geach watched Arrows' coverage during the 1997 season, and believes that none of the team's sponsors would be too unhappy with the result. He said: 'For a constructor that had an under-performing car, Arrows got a remarkable amount of exposure in the media. This can be put down almost entirely to having recruited Damon Hill as a driver. Maybe that was part of the plan – to bring in sponsorship.'

Another example of a sponsorship programme also concerns a company trying to establish its brand name quickly. Hype, an energy drinks brand owned by Worldwide Beverages, has been a sponsor of Benetton and Williams. The drink firm's Formula One marketing strategy, however, was more subtle than Danka's. The plan was to establish Hype as a premier brand even before the product was generally available. Hype's fluorescent name was unmissable along the side of the Williams Renault FW19, as it had been on the Benetton in previous seasons. The drink currently had a limited distribution in a few fashionable clubs, but the plan was to turn it into a mainstream brand. The marketing brief given to Mark Lund, chief executive of Delaney Fletcher Bozell, Hype's marketing agency, was 'to make Hype rapidly famous and as much a part of the drinks topography as those that have been around for much longer'. In essence, Hype's strategy was to 'pretend' it was a big brand, which would lay the foundations for a world-wide launch on the drinks market. Formula One was ideal for this, said Lund, because there is a perception that small companies do not sponsor a rich, global sport like grand prix racing. Hype wanted to move fast, so the 'big' image helped open doors. Breaking into overseas markets is a tough job, and a link-up with a top Formula One team acted as a sort of advance guard in countries where Hype was about to launch its product.

What is important for a company like Hype is the business-to-business contacts it makes with other companies. Through its Formula One sponsorships Hype rubbed shoulders with oil giants that own petrol stations (potential sales outlets for the drink), restaurant groups, and distributors. Teams now put considerable effort into introducing sponsors to each other and looking at how they might work together. All the major teams run forums to help sponsors explore their mutual interests. This works particularly well if the constructor is part of a larger organisation, like Benetton or Ferrari. Both companies have clients unconnected to Formula One sponsorship, but which can nevertheless be brought into the business-to-business ambit. This kind of cross-marketing is something that team owner Jackie Stewart excels at. For 30 years he has worked tirelessly to build up a network of global contacts, and this certainly helped when trying to raise money to establish Stewart Grand Prix. Like McLaren's Ron Dennis, Jackie Stewart dislikes the term 'sponsor', preferring to talk about our 'partnership'. 'Sponsorship' implies that a company gives money in the hope of some unspecified or uncertain return, he believes, whereas partners have a clear commercial interest in getting a return on their money. If treated right, Stewart said, these partners will 'receive an increase in business that surpasses what they invested in our team. Most of the partners have committed to five years, because it takes that long to understand each other and how the business can be grown. Our philosophy is to offer our business partners much more than simply space on a car or a patch on the drivers' overalls, or merely lay on corporate hospitality. HSBC sponsors Stewart Grand Prix because they believe they get more out of this relationship than they put in. We expect partners to get more in the way of financial return than they have invested in the team, simply by networking their respective services as Formula One moves around the world. On top of that, there is whatever promotional benefit they can derive from their involvement with the team.' At a Stewart Grand Prix hospitality event, the chief executive of telecoms giant and sponsor MCI might rub shoulders with the man who control Ford's $300 million telecoms budget, who in turn can discuss interests in south east Asia with HSBC. All it takes is one deal, said Stewart, and it will probably pay for their sponsorship budget. Even when Stewart Grand Prix was struggling to raise money to get the team started, advertising space remained unsold because 'we wanted to get the right partner for our other partners. We have blue-chip organisations on the car, and we want to make sure we can maintain that.'

Jackie Stewart told HSBC that he could open doors on their behalf, which would result in a tenfold return on their initial investment. That makes £250 million over five years. The deal runs until 2001, so there is still some time to go before anyone knows whether Stewart is correct. But part of Stewart's success has been to stake his reputation on his ability to deliver. For Stewart, a proud man, personal credibility is everything. Today's commercial sponsors are often major corporations, with their own shareholders' interests to satisfy. 'When I go to companies with my proposals I have to be certain I can meet my promises. That is how Stewart Grand Prix has been able to get the money we have,' he said bluntly. At his son's Formula Three team, Paul Stewart Racing, the bottled water company Highland Spring won a deal to supply British Airways because of Jackie Stewart's contacts at the airline. He also helped Forte by persuading his contacts to send their executives to the company's hotels. This personal dimension is important for Jackie Stewart. It means that when companies back Stewart Grand Prix, they are buying Jackie Stewart. 'They are buying my name, my reputation,' he said.

Stewart's emphasis that today's companies demand a return on their investment underlines a new era in sponsorship. No company sponsors Formula One unless they think there will be substantial benefits. The old saying – 'half the sponsors do not know if their money is wasted or not; the other half do it in order not to be left out' – no longer applies. The so-called 'chairman's whim syndrome' – in which decisions to sponsor Formula One are made because the boss enjoys the sport – is very rare these days. Not that gut-sponsorship (those decisions made on impulse) will ever disappear completely, believes Mathew Patten, an executive at M&C Saatchi, the advertising agency which handles Benson & Hedges' sponsorship of Jordan. 'It is the nature of marketing that some decisions are done for emotional reasons. It is the same for sponsorship. You go into a company's boardroom to present the creative work, and the first thing the chairman says is: I like that, or I don't like that. But increasingly organisations in the 1990s cannot afford to conduct their business based on a single opinion like this. No chairman of any Plc will risk his position or shareholder anger on a whim. The decisions are often up to a board of directors, not an individual. A sponsorship strategy has to be carefully investigated, especially when you are dealing with money from a multinational company.' Increasingly, sponsors will have to justify the millions of pounds they spend on Formula One each year. In the 1990s shareholders and employees want explanations for such extravagance. Nigel Geach, of Sports Marketing Surveys, has noticed more companies seeking out research on attitudes among employees and investors. 'We have seen how shareholders can rock the boat. Hostility to what is perceived as waste or undeserved pay rises has been well documented in the financial press. Corporations are a lot more interested in what their staff think. It affects attitudes, and things like pay reviews. Any company with a large staff has to inform them of the reasons they are doing that sponsorship. Organisations today recognise the need to carry staff with them, because they are the best salesmen.' Some sponsors understood this many years ago. Geoffrey Kent, head of John Player in the 1980s, was well aware that the company's sponsorship of Lotus, £500,000 for five years, was expensive. 'As a public company you have to be able to justify that sort of expenditure to your shareholders,' said Kent. 'We have proved over the years that our involvement is well justified.' It certainly was. Public awareness surveys that measure the success of marketing programmes still named John Player as a Formula One sponsor long after it left the sport.

Sports Marketing Surveys has been measuring the success of Formula One sponsorships for 15 years, and is now one of the leading companies in its field. Its clients include Rothmans, Benetton, Goodyear and Shell. The most common way to measure the effectiveness is to track exposure on television, literally by counting the number of seconds a sponsor's name, image, or logo appears on the TV screen. It is long-winded and labour intensive, but governed by international industry guidelines which try to ensure that the methodology is as scientific as possible. For Formula One, Sports Marketing Surveys records television 24 hours a day in 28 countries. People monitor the broadcasts with a stopwatch, and that includes the highlights and magazine programmes, as well as the live race. Because television stations world-wide take a live feed from the host country's broadcasting unit, it is not necessary to monitor the race in every single country. But when monitoring the chosen broadcasts there is no substitute for having someone sit in front of a television screen with a stopwatch. Geach said: 'We have tried computer readers, scanning in the logos, but it is not feasible. You have to monitor all the major broadcasts because of different commercial breaks and changes to the feed.' Once the exposure has been calculated, Geach's team relates it to the number of people watching the television at the time. This is then measured against the cost of taking a 30-second television advert.

Successful teams attract the biggest sponsorship because their names appear on the screen longer, which is why there is much more at stake than a team's pride when a driver goes off the track early. Geach said: 'Most sponsors' marketing departments receive research reports every one or two months, and they can make painful reading if the team has not done well. Generally, the results even themselves out during the course of the season, but for those companies which sometimes embark on one-off sponsorships for a single race the risk can be high.' Similar analysis is carried out on coverage in newspapers and magazines. The size of pictures, the number of times a name is mentioned, and the size of print type are all measured. The result is then compared with the cost of a quarter-page newspaper advert. The shortcoming of using the 'stopwatch' method of measurement is that it records the level of coverage, but not whether anyone has actually noticed the product. A more sophisticated tool is the tracking study, which measures spontaneous awareness. This involves sending researchers into the high street to ask people if they can recall the names of Formula One sponsors. The method is used to determine the image and perception of the sponsor, and ultimately whether customers are going to buy the product. The last and most complex research method of all, and one likely to be used mainly by the largest sponsors, is the focus group. This asks detailed questions of a target audience. In Formula One's case the audience is likely to be males aged between 18 and 35, the most sought-after sector of the population as far as many sponsors are concerned.

When sponsorships go sour, the root cause is often a lack of initial planning. With so much money involved, expectations of success are high. But failure to lay the groundwork, argues Barrie Gill, a specialist in arranging sponsorship for Formula One, will only end in disappointment. 'Companies have to be educated about Formula One, and how to get the best from it. It is not a case of putting your name on a car, and just sitting back and waiting for the rewards to flow in. Both sides have to be clear why they are entering the partnership, and what they want out of it.' Sponsors and team executives have to work together closely, which will put pressure on time and patience. One common commitment required by the sponsor is that team principals and drivers make themselves available for the round of glad-handing that goes on in the hospitality tent and at other functions. But it can cause tensions when it gets in the way of the job in hand: getting the team ready for the race. 'Sponsors like their pound of flesh,' said Frank Williams, only half smiling. As we saw earlier Ford had differences with Benetton over the direction the alliance was taking. The US car maker was unhappy with the support it was getting from the Benetton team, and also with the parent company's infamous *United Colours of Benetton* advertising campaign. Sponsorship requires two willing partners, otherwise they may as well go their separate ways.

Some sponsorships look to be such perfect fits that they cannot go wrong. But as Sega Europe's experience proves, a half-hearted approach to sponsorship is doomed. The video games company wanted to use Formula One to help establish Sonic the Hedgehog. Sega signed a £2 million deal with Williams, and launched it with a fanfare. Sega branding featured heavily on the cars and helmets of Alain Prost. And there was added resonance, and publicity potential, because Prost's arch rival Ayrton Senna, driving for McLaren, was endorsing Sega's Formula One racing game, Super Monaco Grand Prix. The deal had all the ingredients of a successful sponsorship, but was pulled after just one season. Sega Europe said it could not justify the cost, and had no chance of recouping the outlay from increased sales. Others believe that it failed because Sega Europe was not fully committed. Nigel Geach, of Sports Marketing Surveys, believes Sega entered Formula One with its eyes closed. 'My opinion is that they probably did not exploit it to its full potential. From a marketing point of view I would have thought Formula One for an electronic games company was ideal. It is fast and furious. But if you are going to spend that amount of money you have to be fully committed and single-minded about making it work. My understanding is that Sega Europe did not have full backing from Japan. It was a great shame because it was an ideal fit. But people in Formula One just remember Sega as a company that pulled out.'

Generally speaking, if a sponsorship is conceived correctly it should work, Geach argues. 'But a lot of people expect to go into it for a year and have a major impact. It won't. Like all sponsorship it has got to have a planned entry, planned execution and planned exit. We always say, and more importantly our research always shows, that a minimum Formula One sponsorship should be three years. The first year is education, finding your way, your link-promotion; the second year is for consolidation and getting a response to the way you used the sponsorship in the first year; the final year is to exploit it. The sponsorships that have had no impact are the ones that have only gone on for a year.' Nokia, the mobile telephone company, wasted its sponsorship of Tyrrell, said Geach. 'The company had a great place on the car, but failed to exploit it. When you start looking at the reason why, so often it is because not enough planning was done at the outset.' Inadequate planning has been known to kill off a team. Simtek – standing for Simulated Technology – folded in 1995 while waiting on a promise of sponsorship from a private backer. Run by Nick Wirth, who at 28 years old was the youngest team boss in Formula One, Simtek competed in just one season before going under. It later transpired that the sponsorship was never likely to materialise. The individual concerned had a reputation for withdrawing from deals with other teams. It was because of the secrecy surrounding Formula One sponsorship that no one was in a position to warn Wirth that he was pinning the team's future on false hopes.

In an attempt to avoid such fiascos in the future, the Fédération Internationale de l'Automobile now takes a far closer interest in team's finances. Before Stewart Grand Prix was granted permission to compete in the 1998 series, the FIA demanded assurances from the team's auditors that it had the necessary resources to compete. It followed the loss of the team's $5 million sponsorship from the Malaysian tourist board. Jackie Stewart was not too pleased at being singled out, and there were suggestions that the FIA was attempting to embarrass him because of his outspoken views on Formula One's dependency on tobacco sponsorship. However, it may have had more to do with the racing authorities' fear of doing yet more harm to Formula One's flotation plans. Bernie Ecclestone and Max Mosley do not want teams rocking the boat by going bankrupt. Regulations governing teams' financial stability were tightened after the collapse of the Lola racing team soon after the start of the 1997 season. The Lola group, run by Eric Broadley, is one of the leading chassis manufacturers, but had never before competed in Formula One with its own team. Its foray into grand prix racing was backed by just one main sponsor, MasterCard, the US credit card company. Under the deal, sponsorship money was to be raised by inviting cardholders to subscribe to a Formula One racing club in return for tickets and hospitality. Advantage International, which handles MasterCard's marketing activities, said the deal was a 'breakthrough in the way that companies fund sponsorship programmes'. It should have raised $10 million for Lola Formula One. Instead, after just one race, the team crashed out of Formula One with debts of £6 million, amid accusations of broken promises about sponsorship that was not forthcoming and threats of legal action. Exactly what went wrong has still to be resolved. But the episode was an embarrassment for motor racing, and one that the FIA is trying to guarantee never happens again.

A lesson of the Lola débâcle is to ensure that the legal contracts between teams and sponsors leave nothing to chance. Easier said than done, of course. Contracts can be lengthy documents, and may go into minute detail, even, for example, spelling out what does and does not constitute 'a race'. Guy Edwards, who has been brokering contracts for 20 years, believes teams would be wise to remember that the signing of a contract is the start rather than the end of the partnership. After all, both sides have still to deliver what they promised. And the contract between team and sponsor might be just one of several interlinked deals, all of which potentially can undermine the original deal. Constructors generally prefer three-year contracts with sponsors. Ideally, several agreements will be overlapping, so they do not all have to be renegotiated at the same time. This gives the teams time to plan, and cushions the blow if a sponsor pulls out suddenly. The trickiest contracts are the performance-related ones, such as Benetton's deal with the Japanese tobacco company Mild Seven. In 1994, when Benetton was dominating, the team was cash-rich. But when the winning dried up, so did the money, and Benetton's financial problems contributed to the departure of its team boss, Flavio Briatore, in 1997. Under a standard sponsorship contract, payment is normally in instalments spread through the year. There will usually be a large tranche paid up front to help with the heavy initial investment needed to get the racecar ready for the new season. According to Edwards a typical payment schedule, on a £1 million sponsorship, might be £400,000 in January, and £200,000 in April, July and October.

Addicted to Tobacco

FORMULA ONE AND cigarette manufacturers have had a special relationship for some 30 years, starting with the landmark deal between Lotus and John Player cigarettes in 1968. The recent history of Formula One is also a history of tobacco advertising. On one side was a sport in need of huge amounts of money for research and development. On the other was a cash-rich industry facing tighter restrictions on how it could advertise itself. Grand prix racing and tobacco companies welcomed each other with open arms. In many countries Formula One is the tobacco industry's last link with television, and the sport is certainly its last global market platform.

From the outset, though, Formula One and tobacco faced attempts to sever their partnership. Former racing driver Guy Edwards recalls that when he signed a sponsorship contract with Embassy cigarettes in 1972, the company included a clause in the agreement: 'In the event of tobacco advertising being outlawed or restricted we reserve the right to terminate this agreement at any time.' Recently, though, the issue of tobacco funding of motorsport has risen up the political agenda. When Western governments speak of banning tobacco sponsorship, the cry from Formula One is that racing's very existence would be threatened by such a move. Such arguments are highly questionable, as we will see later. The British government, however, seemed to have fallen for them. After what looked like a conspicuous lack of consideration of the issues, Prime Minister Tony Blair went back on promises to include Formula One in a ban on tobacco sponsorship. It was an important victory for the tobacco industry and for Formula One bosses Bernie Ecclestone and Max Mosley. Indeed, after the controversy of the last couple of years, tobacco's grip on motor racing appears stronger rather than weaker. New long-term sponsorships have been signed. Jackie Stewart was a rare voice from within Formula One to speak out against tobacco funding. But, after rejecting cigarette money for his grand prix team, Stewart may be forced into a change of heart. The costs of competing have become so high that no team wanting to make a serious challenge for the championship can afford to reject tobacco money out of hand.

Six of the twelve teams that began the 1998 championship had title sponsorship from the cigarette industry. Tobacco companies only pay for the best. The six teams are also the top-performing six in Formula One. The minimum they received from tobacco company sponsorship in 1997 is, according to *Marketing* magazine: Ferrari (Marlboro, $50m), Jordan (Benson & Hedges, $17m), Benetton (Mild Seven, $20m), McLaren (West, $32m), Williams (Rothmans, $32m), and Prost (Gauloises, $17m). A seventh team, called British American Racing and jointly owned by British American Tobacco (BAT), bought the famous Tyrrell team in 1997, and has yet to prove itself a race winner. It begins racing in 1999. But, as BAT said: 'You don't think we've spent all this money to sit at the back of the grid?' BAT's Formula One budget is a minimum of $275 million over five years. Some of the smaller teams also benefit from tobacco money, as do the drivers. Marlboro is a personal sponsor of several drivers, and invests heavily in circuit advertising. All this makes it difficult to argue with Richard Branson's assessment that Formula One has nothing to do with sport, but is 'an advertorial designed to glamorise smoking'.

With hindsight, it is no surprise that Colin Chapman was the first of the new-generation constructors to sign what was Formula One's most important commercial sponsorship – a deal struck with Imperial Tobacco to advertise the company's Gold Leaf brand. He had an entrepreneur's eye for a good deal, and he spotted early on the potential to raise sponsorship after the FIA lifted restrictions in 1968. Chapman signed the Gold Leaf deal the same year, and transformed the colour of the Lotus cars from traditional racing green to the red-and-gold of Gold Leaf. The livery even bore the cigarette company's bearded sailor logo. It was a shock for the purists, but there was no going back. It is widely believed that the Gold Leaf deal was the first sponsorship of a racing car by a tobacco company. In fact, a Rothmans-sponsored Cooper, with a blue-and-white livery, raced in the 1965 and 1966 Tasman series. Nor was Lotus the first Formula One team to race under the tobacco banner. Team Gunston was formed for local events in southern Africa in 1967. Tobacco companies were then already looking at the sponsorship potential of top-level motorsport. But it was Chapman's deal that really opened the floodgates to tobacco money and pointed the way ahead for other teams in a world where sponsorship was still in its infancy. In 1972 Imperial Tobacco launched a new brand, John Player Special. Lotus racecars soon adopted the distinctive black-and-gold of the JPS packet, the cars and the colours becoming synonymous with Formula One world-wide.

The Lotus/John Player agreement came about by chance, but continued to survive thanks to a strong personal chemistry between Colin Chapman and John Player executive Geoffrey Kent. After the 1968 FIA rule-change, Andrew Ferguson, manager of Team Lotus, wrote to the 200 largest companies in Britain seeking their financial help. However, this random mail-shot proved fruitless. What unlocked the multi-million-pound John Player deal was the personal touch. Then, as now, networking was the key to securing and maintaining successful sponsorship. The journalist Gerard Crombac, in his biography of Chapman, recounts the way Team Lotus secured Formula One's first tobacco sponsorship: 'By pure chance, Dave Lazenby (the former chief mechanic for Lotus at Indianapolis, who was then managing Lotus Components) was looking, quite independently of Andrew Ferguson, for a relatively small sponsor for his two racing Europe Lotus 47s. One of Lazenby's mechanics used to go out with a secretary who was working at Sales Link, the company that handled the Imperial Tobacco public relations account, and she tipped him off that Imperial were thinking of sponsoring motor racing. The prospect was so good that Lazenby took it to Andrew. It very soon transpired that Imperial Tobacco were indeed very keen, and were prepared to spend a really large sum of money to promote their Gold Leaf brand of cigarettes.'

Geoffrey Kent, then marketing director (and later chairman) of parent company Imperial Tobacco, chose motor racing as a promotional tool because it seemed to him the only sport in which Britain was excelling at that time. The partnership between Chapman and Kent developed into a friendship, and the executive was later asked to join the board of Team Lotus. The alliance between tobacco company and Formula One team ran from 1968 to 1986 (there was a gap between 1978 and 1981), turning on a meeting of the minds between the two company bosses. Then, in 1982, Chapman died after a heart attack and Imperial Tobacco later became part of Hanson Trust following a bitter takeover battle, after which Kent left the company. The sponsorship was not renewed. A testament to the lasting success of the JPS/Lotus sponsorship is that, years after it ended, an image of the black-and-gold racecar remains embedded in the mind of the public. Nigel Geach, of Sports Marketing Surveys, said that when the public is asked an 'open' question – 'name a Formula One tobacco sponsor' – between four and six per cent of respondents still mentions JPS. 'It is the sort of reach that sponsors would die for,' said Geach, 'and impossible to put a true value on the enormity of its success.' Benson & Hedges, a tobacco company currently involved in a high-profile sponsorship of the Jordan team, might get no more than 15 per cent. One possible explanation for the lingering imagery is that the late Ayrton Senna drove a JPS Lotus, and photographs of the legendary driver are often reprinted. The JPS deal proves that sponsorships can have long lives if they are executed properly, says Geach. 'Many people still think Mars [the confectionery group] sponsors the London Marathon. Companies that work hard at their sponsorships will know just when to pull out, but still get some residual value from it long after it has ended.'

During his time at Imperial Tobacco, Geoffrey Kent repeated the success with Formula Two and Formula Three, motorbikes and powerboats; all of which proved an instructive lesson for Marlboro, the tobacco company owned by Philip Morris, and Formula One's biggest sponsor for many years. Today, Marlboro's red-and-white chevrons are omnipresent in all forms of motorsport. Aleardo Buzzi, an architect of Philip Morris's sponsorship strategy, summed up the involvement thus: 'We are the number one brand in the world. What we wanted was to promote a particular image of adventure, of courage, of virility. But our sponsorship is not just a matter of commerce, it is a matter of love. We don't just sign a cheque, we support the sport.' The Marlboro brand started life as a cigarette targeted at women, its cork-coloured filter designed to mask lipstick stains. But this new female cigarette failed to take off in America, and was almost withdrawn from the market. Philip Morris called in an advertising agency, Leo Burnett, to have one last go at a marketing strategy. Instead of trying to refine the image for the female market, however, the agency proposed turning the brand on its head. Marlboro, said Leo Burnett, should be promoted as a cigarette for men; but not just any man. Marlboro would be the cigarette for the rugged individualists, for the man who walked alone and faced the world alone. The Marlboro cowboy was born in 1955, and the brand became an instant hit in America. Ronnie Thompson, a Philip Morris executive, was sent to Geneva to investigate how Marlboro might go down in Europe. He quickly became aware of Formula One's place in the sporting heritage of Europe, and identified its cross-cultural nature as ideal for Marlboro. At the heart of Formula One is the driver, an individual doing battle with outside forces. For Thompson, Formula One was tailor-made for the Marlboro image. In 1972 the company started sponsoring the long-established British Formula One team, BRM. Two years later, however, Marlboro began its long association with McLaren, a sponsorship that survived until the cigarette manufacturer moved to Ferrari in 1997.

Former driver Guy Edwards remembers talking to Thompson at the time Marlboro was looking at the possibility of sponsoring motorsport in Europe. 'He said he was going to sponsor some Formula One cars. He eventually sponsored five of them. Lotus had two Gold Leaf cars, but he bought five! Not only that, he started buying into the structure of the circuits. The curbings were red and white, and they put up hoardings with the name Marlboro emblazoned across them. He had a vision about what Formula One could do to project the Marlboro brand. Philip Morris kept hold of that vision, and have basically become integrated into motorsport. The company never deviated from that original vision in almost 30 years. They had a clarity of purpose, not just dipping in and out of the sport like other sponsors.' The company's sports sponsorship strategy comes under the aegis of the Marlboro World Championship Team, which has bought into all levels of motorsport: single-seater racing, motorcycling, rallying, and the drivers themselves. MWCT sponsored Finland's Mika Hakkinen in saloon car racing in 1988, and then in Formula Three, and again when he went to McLaren. In Holland, the Marlboro Masters is now the most competitive Formula Three race on the calendar; and, in Dubai, the Marlboro Desert Challenge is one of the most demanding events in the FIA Cross Country Rallies Cup Series. In grand prix racing, MWCT is the title sponsor of three Formula One races: in Argentina, Hungary and Spain. Among some ten Formula One drivers with sponsorship links to Marlboro are the world's best, Michael Schumacher, and the world's richest pay-driver, Pedro Diniz. It represents a huge financial commitment, though just how much money is spent on these projects remains one of Philip Morris's financial secrets. What can be said is that Philip Morris would not do it year in, year out unless there was a return. Public opinion surveys on sponsorship in general, and Formula One in particular, consistently record Marlboro as the most famous brand name in motorsport. In a simple brand recognition survey, conducted in 1996 by Research Services Limited, Marlboro was the clear leader. Adults in five countries were asked to name brands associated with motorsport. Below are the top five names mentioned for each country (note the presence of John Player, which had not sponsored Formula One for more than ten years):

UK	France	Germany	Italy	Portugal
Marlboro	Marlboro	Ferrari	Marlboro	Marlboro
Rothmans	Renault	Benetton	Benetton	Galp
Benetton	Elf	Mercedes	Agip	Shell
John Player	Benetton	Marlboro	Pirelli	Mobil
Renault	Gitanes	Ford & Opel	Goodyear	Castrol

Even in France, where advertising regulations are the strictest of any country staging a grand prix, Marlboro is by far the most recognised Formula One brand name.

Name	awareness %	awareness in males %	awareness in females %
Marlboro	40	50	30
Renault	24	33	16
Elf	20	29	12
Benetton	13	17	10
Gitanes	11	16	7

In 1997 Philip Morris switched Marlboro sponsorship from McLaren to Ferrari, having become increasingly irritated by its long-time partner's lack of success. The cigarette company had supported McLaren since 1974, and can rightly claim a role in orchestrating McLaren's remarkable success in the 1980s: it was Philip Morris that forced a merger between an ailing McLaren and Ron Dennis's small Project Four Racing team in 1980s. Dennis took McLaren to seven constructors' titles and 97 grand prix victories. However, McLaren's star began to fade in the early 1990s. In 1994 the team failed to record a single victory in the series, something that had not happened since 1981. Further embarrassment followed in 1995, when Nigel Mansell was signed up to drive for the team. Marlboro had backed the signing of Mansell to drive alongside the up-and-coming Finnish driver Mika Hakkinen. The tobacco company had been looking for a big-name driver that year to help back a major promotion in South America, one of its biggest markets. But the McLaren car was built too small to accommodate Mansell in any comfort. What is more, Mansell had some uncompromising things to say about the quality of the McLaren car. It was clear to staff that Marlboro was becoming concerned. A McLaren employee involved in the sponsorship remembers it thus: 'Marlboro was run pretty independently, so we did not have much contact with their marketing team. But I can remember people in the McLaren office suddenly talking about Philip Morris, and how the big chiefs in America must be getting worried. Obviously, words were filtering down about whether we were giving them value for money. It was obvious some people were not happy about the performance, though I do not ever remember Ron (Dennis) appearing worried.' In August 1996, after Marlboro failed to agree a reduction in its sponsorship the tobacco company announced that it was going to Ferrari. Dennis, meanwhile had already been working on a replacement deal. He signed up West, the tobacco brand owned by Germany's Reemtsma. The tobacco company's five-year deal, worth £12 million a year brought West together with McLaren's new engine supplier, fellow German company Mercedes. And it will be no surprise if West and Mercedes one day bring another German, Michael Schumacher, to drive for McLaren.

Marlboro, West, indeed all the other tobacco sponsors, seemingly have long-term plans to continue funding Formula One. It is as if threats to cut tobacco's link with grand prix are non-existent. Are they right to be so relaxed? The biggest challenge to tobacco sponsorship of Formula One comes from governments within the European Union. There are no Formula One races in the United States, so for the time being tighter legislation from the Clinton administration has little impact, and in Asia and South America tobacco sponsorship remains largely unfettered. The issue of tobacco funding of Formula One became a major political football in Europe in 1997, particularly in Britain. Prior to the General Election in May that year, the Labour Party made a straightforward promise to ban the promotion of tobacco products throughout sport. Yet, seven months later, the government said Formula One would not be covered by the ban. It was the prime minister himself, Tony Blair, who personally intervened on behalf of Formula One after lobbying from Bernie Ecclestone and Max Mosley. As we saw in Chapter Two, the affair became a political hot potato, given added spice by the revelation that Ecclestone had donated £1 million to the Labour Party before it came to power. Condemnation of Blair's U-turn was swift, but the government's decision was final. While tobacco sponsorship of other sports such as darts and snooker would be phased out, Formula One looked to have been given an open-ended exemption. Labour's move did not just create a furore in Britain. The unilateral move threw the European Commission's own proposals for a Europe-wide ban on tobacco sponsorship into disarray.

Concern about the financial and health costs of smoking-related diseases has been snowballing for years. (The number of UK deaths from smoking-related diseases are running at about 121,000 a year, out of a total of 624,000 deaths – 19%. The National Health Service is spending between £600 million and £650 million a year treating smoking-related diseases.) A UK television advertising ban was imposed on tobacco products in 1965, and regulations have been progressively tightened. No tobacco brand name can be displayed on race-cars or circuits at the British Grand Prix under a voluntary code agreed in the late 1980s. (For obvious reasons, the code does not cover broadcasts being beamed into the UK from races where tobacco promotion is allowed.) The voluntary code also exists in Canada and Germany. In France, where there is a legal, not a voluntary ban, tobacco brand names not only have to come off the cars, they must come off all the equipment, from the transporters to the baseball caps. When making Formula One documentaries or using library footage, broadcasters are encouraged to use film from races where advertising is banned. The anti-smoking lobby expected the UK and other European governments to build on these restrictions, at the very least tightening up on loopholes. Instead, Tony Blair was persuaded that a sponsorship ban could mean the loss of the British Grand Prix and ruin Britain's motorsport industry, as Formula One would move to Asia. Labour politicians appeared on television and radio making absurd claims that 50,000 Formula One jobs were under threat.

Ecclestone and Mosley can be forgiven for wanting to paint a worst-case scenario in order to defend their sport and its main sponsors. But Blair can be forgiven little. Either he had a predisposition to favour Formula One, or he was badly advised by those around him. Much of the economic argument put forward by his ministers are groundless. Formula One does not employ 50,000 people in Britain. Even Max Mosley admitted that it employs no more than 5,000. Grand Prix Valley, that network of specialist motorsport firms outlined in Chapter Two, employs probably not more than 30,000. And, as we saw, the Valley is far more than just Formula One. It involves all kind of motorsport. The majority of Indy cars driven in America are built by companies in

England, proving that the businesses do not need to be sited in the markets they supply. One of the unique features of the motorsport industry is that it has strong cultural roots in Britain, and so will not be easily displaced. The teams, and the designers, engineers and entrepreneurs that make up motorsport's subcontractors, are not going to uproot and transplant themselves in Asia. It is true that a lot of motorsport firms are lightly capitalised and have small workforces, and so could be mobile. For many of these companies, however, motorsport is only part of their business. They also serve the engineering aerospace and UK production car industries. Two economic geographers, Nick Henry and Steven Pinch, spent 18 months studying the motorsport industry for the Economic and Social Research Council. Their report, published in December 1997, concluded that the industry only thrived because of the close interaction between firms in the Valley. 'To be outside the Valley is to risk your position within the knowledge community,' they said. Furthermore, McLaren, Williams, Jordan and Stewart are among Formula One teams that have all recently made large investments in new UK facilities. To think that they can just shift themselves to the East is fantasy. Besides, as the teams are already committed to travelling eight months of the year (to Canada, South America and Japan as well as inside Europe), they may as well base themselves in Britain as anywhere else.

In the future more races will be held in Asia. There is a thirst for Formula One in the East, and sponsorship money from companies in the region will grow. Also, importantly, these countries will be the tobacco industry's most profitable markets in the coming years. As some teams are objecting to an increase in the number of races each season, it is inevitable that Europe will lose one or two. The shape of the Formula One calendar is always changing, and some European races may go in order to make space for more Asian events. Such moves are not cast in stone and can always be reversed. A deepening of the Asian financial crisis that hit in 1997–98 could impact on plans to take Formula One into South Korea or Malaysia, in which case Europe will get its races back. Even a surge in the popularity of IndyCar racing could derail Ecclestone's Asia strategy. It is also worth remembering that Asian governments are not completely unaware of the social costs of tobacco. Laws on tobacco advertising are certainly not as relaxed there as many people believe. Thailand and Singapore have total bans on cigarette advertising. China and Malaysia have partial bans. Also, there is a vocal anti-tobacco lobby in the Far East.

Even though tobacco sponsors want more Asian grand prix races, there is no evidence that *all* sponsors do. Mercedes' reasons for involvement in Formula One are different from those of the tobacco companies. For technical reasons Europe remains very important, said Mercedes. 'We have our own priorities. We have our own strategies. We came into Formula One for our own reasons. You cannot just decide to move all your races to another part of the world without consulting all main sponsors.' Similar arguments are put forward by team bosses. Stewart Grand Prix, which gets by without the help of tobacco money, has very different priorities to, say Jordan, whose boss Eddie Jordan is a vociferous supporter of tobacco sponsorship. Paul Stewart, managing director of Stewart Grand Prix, said: 'I think going towards the East is healthy, but I do not want to be chased out of Europe because of the tobacco issue. It is very important to have a British or Monaco Grand Prix. These are part of the history of Formula One, and you just cannot ignore the history and expect the fan base to understand it. It would be a shame if it went totally to the East. We are in a world championship, and there has to be a balance of races throughout the world.'

If Formula One were forced to cut its links with the tobacco industry, would the constructors be damaged? Or, to put the question another way: is there enough non-tobacco sponsorship around to fill the gap? Not surprisingly, Bernie Ecclestone thinks it would be a problem. 'Very few other multinationals are capable of investing as much as cigarette producers. If they abandon the sport it will be a disaster.' Yet, privately, even team bosses who depend on tobacco money believe the sport could adapt, so long as no overnight ban was imposed. The problem, according to one team owner, 'is that there is not really the will to change all the time tobacco companies are willing to pay – and pay a premium – to put their names on our cars.' Stewart Grand Prix and Arrows have proved that there is non-tobacco money available if teams want to look for it. Raising sponsorship is tough, and non-tobacco companies will not pay as much. But as John Perera, head of sponsorship consulting at API, points out, more blue-chip companies are wanting to come into the sport. He said: 'The lack of availabile quality sports is the problem. A valuable sponsorship property like Formula One will have no difficulty in finding replacement sponsors. It will be more of a struggle for less mainstream sports like snooker and darts.' Compare pictures of Formula One racecars today with those of ten years ago, and one can see that there are few sectors of industry and commerce not now represented on the vehicles.

Some companies, meanwhile, remain outside Formula One *because* of its link with tobacco. Wealthy companies like Richard Branson's Virgin Group have already shown interest in a 'healthier' Formula One. Branson promised to back an independent British Grand Prix if Ecclestone carried out his threats to pull Silverstone from the calendar. He told a conference in London, attended by British health officials, that Virgin would help sports and arts meet a shortfall in money. 'I pledge today that Virgin will set up a rival spectacle [British Grand Prix]. And that goes for any sport that claims it cannot survive without cigarette advertising. Even an international sport like the grand prix need not suffer. The only reason it is heavily sponsored by cigarette companies is that they are so desperate to reach a young TV audience, they have priced everyone else out of the market. If this industry threatens to pull out of Silverstone – and motor racing in Europe – I, for one, will take them up on their bluff.'

Stewart Grand Prix, a newcomer to Formula One, has been championed by the anti-tobacco lobby as the way forward for motorsport. Jackie and Paul Stewart have both voiced disapproval of Formula One's link with tobacco. What is more, Stewart Grand Prix is in fact backed by sponsors that specifically did not want an association with cigarette money. 'If Jackie Stewart can do it, they can all do it,' believes the British Labour MP, Kevin Barron, one of the tobacco industry's most ardent critics. Paul Stewart said the decision to shun tobacco was not based on any moral objection. 'We never completely ruled out tobacco money when we were looking at Formula One. It was never a contractual issue, but our sponsors said they would prefer no tobacco sponsorship, and my father had hoped we could do without it. Ford [which supplies the team's engines] were not particularly keen, nor were Hewlett Packard. And then we got backing from the Malaysian tourist board, and by this time we were reaching the sort of budget where we would not need tobacco sponsorship.'

The UK government's decision to reverse its intention to clamp down on Formula One sponsorship left Jackie Stewart dismayed. He hoped that Stewart Grand Prix was helping Formula One into a new era, but now feels the government has undermined attempts by people inside and outside the sport to wean grand prix off tobacco. 'The image of motor sport has suffered terribly, and years of good work are in serious danger as a result,' was Stewart's view. His Formula One rivals told him it was not possible to compete at the highest level without some tobacco money; that he would be cutting his potential budget by between 30 and 50 per cent. Yet Stewart raised the £30 million he needed to compete in his first year, and has found new sponsors that will help finance his 1998 challenge. But he feels that non-tobacco sponsors are losing faith in the prospect that Formula One might change. One of the most damaging consequences could be that Stewart Grand Prix itself is forced into accepting tobacco money in order to compete. After the team lost its $5 million sponsorship from the Malaysian tourist board, Stewart gave a clear indication that he might be forced to take tobacco money. 'You cannot rule out an industry of that size ... Our Stewart Ford team have got a lot of publicity recently, and perhaps tobacco companies have seen it as an opportunity to become involved.'

Tobacco sponsorship of Formula One creates a lot of heated debate, but many of the arguments are merely academic. In reality, making a complete ban stick would be very difficult indeed. Tobacco companies have wriggled around advertising bans before, and will probably do so in the future. If ever an industry has to think about marketing itself laterally, it is tobacco. No country in the world has yet devised a ban watertight enough to stop such a resourceful business as the cigarette industry. Sometimes tobacco manufacturers just poke fun at the existing legislation (and make a mockery of the voluntary curbs suggested by Max Mosley). At the 1997 British and French Grand Prix, the Williams-Renault racecar had R.? emblazoned across its side. On the Peugeot-Jordan was written Bitten & Hisses (Jordan has a serpent's head on the nose cone). No Formula One viewer would have been left in any doubt that the decals were meant to signify Rothmans and Benson & Hedges. The cigarette company West once changed its name to East to get round a ban. Camel has used either Came 1, or just a picture of the animal. However, this sort of thing does not even come close to the subtleties which some cigarette makers use. The necessity of side-stepping restrictions over the years has inspired advertising agencies working for tobacco companies to produce some of the best creative work in the business. Today, even colours can communicate a tobacco brand. Indeed, almost any object can be used to deliver a brand message. Metonymy, the substitution of an aspect of a product for the product itself, has become a fine art in tobacco advertising. A flash of purple denotes Silk Cut; a gold cigarette box denotes Benson & Hedges; a red-and-white chevron on a trackside hoarding says Marlboro. No direct reference to the brand is needed.

Another strategy for cigarette manufacturers might be to diversify into non-tobacco products – so-called brand stretching – in order to sidestep legislation. Would the tobacco company's name on a racecar then be advertising cigarettes or another product? For example, Dunhill, once solely associated with cigarettes, now has a range of branded luxury goods. Which items would Dunhill be promoting if it sponsored a racing team? Marlboro Classics, the leisurewear brand, is now the second largest mail-order brand in the United States. In Indonesia, where tobacco advertising is restricted, Marlboro Classics is a strong brand. And in central China, which has TV restrictions and where Marlboro cigarettes are not currently available, the Classics range is seen as a forerunner to the launch of the cigarette brand. Camel, which once advertised its cigarettes through Formula One, now has a popular range of boots, belts, shirts and trousers. If Camel returned to Formula One, how could legislation be devised that would distinguish between its cigarettes and its clothes?

British American Tobacco, the world's second largest cigarette manufacturer, whose 250 brands include Lucky Strike, 555 and Kent, is not bothering to diversify into other branded goods. BAT liked Formula One so much it bought a team, Tyrrell, in partnership with racecar engineering group Reynard and Craig Pollock, Jacques Villeneuve's former manager. Rather than follow the defensive moves of other cigarette companies, BAT went on the offensive, taking tobacco's involvement in sport further than ever before. BAT, which owns 51 per cent of the team, is committed to invest around $275 million over five years. The deal has the potential to drive a coach and horses through tobacco sponsorship restrictions around the globe. The team will be called British American Racing, in a nod to the sensitivities of legislators who would take exception to the word tobacco. Still, the BAT marketing department will make sure there are few people who will not know the identity of the owners. Owning, rather than sponsoring a team, means BAT can feature different brands on their two racecars depending on the markets and laws in each country.

If a lot of this manoeuvring looks like a cynical twisting of the rules, remember that the politicians who drafted them are not averse to a little manipulation of the law. The 1997 Luxembourg Grand Prix was actually held at Germany's Nürburgring because the small Benelux country does not have a circuit. The grand prix was staged with full cigarette branding. Despite both countries having a cigarette advertising ban, the race was given a special dispensation by the German government. German grand prix races are normally held under similar rules to those in Britain: the racecars can run in tobacco colours, but not use names and logos. As well as hosting its own grand prix, Germany also hosted the European Grand Prix in 1995 and 1996. With three leading German drivers in the pack, there was huge public interest in the country in Formula One. However, for 1997 the FIA was reluctant to increase the number of races held in a country that imposed advertising restrictions. So what happens? A cosy pact is struck whereby the tobacco companies are allowed to abandon their voluntary agreement not to advertise their brands. And the German government – for one day only – lifts its threat to take legal action if the voluntary agreement is broken.

Anti-smoking groups pull at their hair in frustration at the lack of political will. In December 1997, though, it did look as though European politicians had reached an accord on tackling tobacco sponsorship. A heated and lengthy meeting of European Union ministers in Brussels ended with agreement to ban all forms of tobacco advertising in sport. Britain demanded, and got, an extension for Formula One, but at least it was felt that progress had been made. There are still issues to be resolved by ministers, but the ban should come into effect at the end of 2003. However, those 'events or activities organised at world level' (i.e. Formula One) will get an extra three years to adjust. By the end of 2006, racecars promoting tobacco companies will be banned from circuits within the European Union. There was a twist in the tail. At the 1998 Australian Grand Prix, Max Mosley said the FIA may impose a unilateral ban on tobacco sponsorship and advertising as early as 2002, not just in Europe, but for all races. His condition was that governments or the World Health Organisation came up with proof that there is a link between people taking up smoking and tobacco sponsorship of racing. It was a surprise about-turn, and potentially embarrassing for Tony Blair, who had fought hard for any open-ended exemption for Formula One. Brussels, and the WHO, think there is enough evidence to prove the link, but Mosley is not convinced. Still, Mosley's apparent willingness to concede some ground was welcomed. But was it as concessionary as has been made out? Clive Bates, director of Action on Smoking and Health, believes Mosley was trying to drive a wedge between ministers by appearing more responsible, in the hope of getting Formula One's exemption extended or the ban scrapped.

Formula One can overcome its dependency on tobacco if it wants. But the FIA and the teams reason that if they successfully extend the deadline for any ban – and such a ban is still in doubt – the more pain-free the transition will be. Formula One constructors have an insatiable thirst for money; they will consume as much as they can get for research and technology. Frugality is not a word that enters their vocabulary. On the other side are the tobacco concerns, with millions of pounds to spend on advertising, and even more to spend on court action should anyone try to stop them. There is every reason to believe that tobacco sponsorship of Formula One will continue, either overtly in Asia and South America, or covertly in Europe under different guises. Perhaps the best the anti-smoking lobby can hope for is that tobacco sponsorship will simply fade away. Governments will gradually chip away at cigarette manufacturers through higher taxes. There will be an incremental tightening of loopholes in advertising law. Legal action brought by sufferers of smoking-related illnesses will continue to bring manufacturers bad publicity. And peer pressure will probably eventually make smoking no more acceptable than spitting. By then, Formula One may have adapted to a life without the weed.

Chapter Six: FORMULA FOR TV

The Power of Television

FORMULA ONE AND television are inextricably entwined. The power of television to reach huge audiences world-wide is Formula One's lifeblood. For their part, broadcasters need sports like Formula One to fill the extra airtime on offer from terrestrial and satellite stations. Television companies are willing to pay handsomely for the rights to broadcast Formula One – because advertisers are willing to pay big bucks to reach the sport's vast audience. No other sport so regularly reaches such a large number of people in one hit. More people watch football on a Saturday afternoon, but there are never as many people watching the same football match (except in the four-yearly World Cup). Tens of millions of pounds are paid by broadcasters for the right to screen Formula One to every corner of the globe. That money is paid to Bernie Ecclestone, the man whose companies hold the licences to exploit Formula One on behalf of the governing body, the FIA. It was Ecclestone who skilfully packaged Formula One into a sport palatable for television, and whose operation brings in annual revenues of some £300 million as a result. A local company, for example ITV in Britain, will provide the on-track coverage for a race, but Ecclestone controls the distribution rights and coverage throughout the rest of the world. Now he is planning to provide his own live broadcasts via a giant mobile studio, further concentrating his power over Formula One. Multi-channel digital television and pay-per-view are about to hit racing in a big way, or so Ecclestone hopes. If he is right, he can add another $200 million revenues to Formula One's coffers.

The secret of Ecclestone's success has been to make Formula One entertaining and available. But he could not have done it, of course, without the broadcasters themselves. Television stations' investment in programming, and their willingness to 'create' a climate of showbusiness and glamour around the sport, has been instrumental in boosting Formula One's popularity. For years, the BBC's limited coverage of Formula One was all that was available to race fans, not just in the United Kingdom, but in countries which took the broadcasting feed. Now commercial broadcasters, terrestrial and satellite, have taken over *en masse*, ensuring that there is barely a country in the world that cannot receive Formula One races, either live or highlights. Germany's Kirch Groupe paid $70 million for broadcast rights for five years, while Italy's Telepui paid $200 million for ten years. The Formula One television revolution is set to continue, however, with an extension of pay-per-view and digital broadcasting. If Ecclestone's project takes off, the money currently pouring into Formula One will multiply rapidly. If it fails, Ecclestone's planned launch of his Formula One interests on the stock market will flop. From London to Lebanon, Malaysia to Sydney, the future of Formula One depends on Ecclestone's ability to expand the sport as a television spectacle.

How big is Formula One's television audience? If you believe the FIA, it is ten times the world's population! According to official figures, the cumulative audience for the 1997 championship was 50.7 billion people, a rise of 20 per cent on 1996. The statistic includes every time an item on Formula One appears on television, no matter how short. The full 1997 figures issued by the FIA were:

Viewers	1997	1996	1994[1]
Race only	5,413,890,031	5,365,472,075	5,314,955,000
Qualifying sessions	1,196,716,550	818,625,924	
Additional programmes	4,195,458,378	4,585,763,186	6,123,207,000[2]
News coverage	39,926,580,093	30,992,557,185	33,781,344,000
Total viewers	50,732,645,052	40,992,557,185	45,219,506,000

These figures are processed by the FIA from audited figures supplied to it by broadcasters which screened Formula One. The sport was available in 202 countries in 1997, compared with 150 in 1994. The figures compare with the cumulative television audience of 32 billion who watched the 1994 football World Cup in the USA. Interestingly,

[1] Regarded as the year that interest in Formula One began to soar.
[2] Includes qualifying sessions.

the audience size for the actual races has remained static, at about 350 million viewers for each of the 16 races. The real rise in television audiences is coming from people turning into increased coverage of qualifying sessions and news items on Formula One. Unfortunately, comparative figures for 1993 were not available. In any case, sponsors and advertisers who base their marketing strategies on audience ratings regard such astronomical statistic as irrelevant. At best, the figures indicate simply that there are more Formula One-related items on television. Market research agencies treat all such figures with caution. The reason is that it is unclear whether the FIA figures refer to actual or potential television viewers. Official literature on Formula One's television appeal refers only to the sport being 'broadcast to' this number of people.

Part of the problem is that, like much in Formula One, comprehensive data on television audiences is shrouded in secrecy. The bigger the audience, the more money there is to be made, so everyone has a vested interest in talking up the figures. However, Britain's *Financial Times* newspaper has had access to independent research on television audiences, and the statistics present a far more conservative picture. According to comprehensive global data compiled for one large company, which was considering sponsoring a team, the actual average audience for each race is about 60 million.[3] This breaks down as 32 million per race in Europe (or 20 per cent of the region's potential audience); 18 million (14%) in Brazil and Argentina; 2 million (14%) in Japan; 3 million (5%) in Asia, and 300,000 (0.3%) in the United States, where no grand prix is held.

Some points to bear in mind about these statistics for global television viewers: firstly, they are probably on the low side, especially for audiences in Asia (in fact, the FIA has claimed that 70 per cent of the average 350 million viewers for each grand prix are in Asia, though how they arrive at this figure is unclear); secondly, the audience size still puts other individual sporting events in the shade; and thirdly, sponsors and advertisers carry out their own market research, and all the evidence shows they like what they see – companies are queuing up to sponsor Formula One. One final point to underline, perhaps, is that interest in Formula One is rising, no matter what base figures one

---

[3] America's CART series is broadcast in 19 languages to 188 countries, generating 61 million viewers per race, according to official figures. ESPN holds exclusive world-wide television rights. Eurosport, which broadcasts CART in Europe, claims about 700,000 viewers per race.

chooses to use. The races are available in more countries, and more airtime is devoted to highlights and feature programmes. More people are attending races, and revenues from merchandising (still under-developed by most teams) are growing. Research groups, such as the reputable UK firm Sports Marketing Surveys, are recording more cover-age of the sport in newspapers and on television news (rather than sports) programmes everywhere. In Germany, for example, television audiences for Formula One rose 208 per cent between 1994 and 1996, according to SMS, largely because of interest in Michael Schumacher. In the UK audiences rose 43 per cent in five years from 1990. And, in what could be an important future trend, women viewers of Formula One in Europe rose 10 per cent between 1994 and 1996, say SMS.

The low US audience figures are something that Ecclestone is trying to address. If Formula One is ever to be a truly global series, racing will have to return to America sometime. That means building the sort of television coverage that sponsors want in advance of a US Grand Prix. In March 1998, the broadcasting rights to show Formula One in America were switched from the ESPN station to the smaller, but fast-growing cable operator Speedvision. The surprise move was not without its problems. A late announcement of the deal by Ecclestone meant that the opening race of the season, the Australian Grand Prix, was not available to most viewers. Initially, US audience figures for Formula One will be lower. By the end of 1998, Speedvision forecasts that it will be linked up to only 20 million homes, compared with ESPN's current 60 million subscribers. There might be fewer viewers in the short term, but Ecclestone calculates that US audiences will grow faster now that Speedvision is devoting more time to the sport. The station screens the qualifying sessions, and there is far more pre- and post-race analysis. Speedvision said it was committed to broadcasting the post-race cel-ebrations and drivers' press conference, something US viewers had not seen for years, and would show replays on Monday nights. There will also be repeats on the Fox Sports Network. However, there are still question marks over the coverage. Speedvision (like ESPN before them) will not be sending commentators to all the races because 'it is not economically feasible'.

As Europe is Formula One's spiritual and economic heartland, audi-ences are naturally larger here. Elsewhere in the world, the popularity of Formula One is growing, even in areas that still remain largely untapped by the teams and sponsors. Asian countries will be the first beneficiaries of Formula One's expansion into new regions. Malaysia is expected to have its own grand prix in 1999, and China and South Korea are likely to follow. The Malaysian race circuit being built is promised to be one of the best in the world, with technological innovations that include high-technology fibre-optic communications. The Chinese are particularly keen on motorsport, and car clubs are springing up all over the country, despite the fact that many members do not drive. The cumulative television audience in China for the 1996 Formula One season was 200 million people. China's circuit, the Zhuhai International, has already hosted motor races sanctioned by the FIA, and the race is on to find drivers who may one day compete in Formula One. Mitsubishi, the Japanese car company, is part of a project to find and train racing drivers. As the company pointed out: 'Given the size of the population, there must be a new Ayrton Senna among them somewhere.' Whichever Asian country gets the first grand prix, it will stimulate further TV interest throughout the region, and push up the price of the broadcast rights that Ecclestone sells. Everywhere, so-called emerging nations want a grand prix. Lebanon, the small Middle East country of 3.1 million people, still trying to shake off the effects of a savage civil war, is well down the road in preparing to stage a leg of the series. A purpose-built circuit is in the pipeline, but in the meantime the entrepreneur behind the project, Dr Khaled Taki, hopes to stage a Monaco-style street race. Beirut, which is trying to rebuild it reputation as the French Riviera of the Middle East, holds Formula Three races, but is negotiating with the FIA about safety and conditions in order to bring the 6.7km road circuit up to Formula One standards. Dr Taki told the FIA that the event would attract some 250,00 spectators and generate revenues of $600 million. A group called the Pan Arab Formula Corporation has been set up to help raise the $50 million needed to stage a race early next century.

There are more countries wanting to host a Formula One grand prix than can be accommodated in the calendar, and Lebanon will have to take its place behind several other hopefuls. But the reason why Formula One's organisers are so interested is that a Lebanese grand prix would expose the whole Middle East to the sport. The potential for television revenues and sponsorship from Arab companies is huge. Despite the underdeveloped satellite television network in the Middle East, there has been a boom in interest in sporting events, from golf to horse racing. Although there are no official figures for television audiences for Formula One, anecdotal evidence suggests that the sport is riding a wave of enthusiasm. In the Middle East, as elsewhere,

Formula One fans tend to be young and upwardly mobile, and have disposable income. As with music, there seems to be something universal about Formula One. The motor car has a universal theme. And the fact that Formula One is a non-participatory sport (apart from two dozen drivers) means the audience is put on a level playing field. There is no them-and-us division between those who 'play' and those who do not. The showbusiness of Formula One, meanwhile, is something everyone can understand. Television has brought all these strands of Formula One together under one roof and offered it to the world.

Television has arguably shaped Formula One more than any other sport. Every sport has had to accommodate the power of television in some way or another. But in Formula One's case television has shaped not only the rules and regulations, but the very nature of the activity. Compulsory pit-stops for refuelling and tyre changes, an unnecessary and sometimes unsafe practice, were introduced to increase television excitement (pit-stops matter little to the paying audience, because they cannot see anything). Racetrack corners have been re-designed to slow the cars down: to improve safety, says the governing body; in a cynical attempt to make it easier for the television viewer to read the carefully positioned advertising billboards, say the critics. Even the traditional laurel wreath that used to garland the winning driver has disappeared, because it masked the sponsors' logos. Now all the drivers wear branded baseballs caps. The FIA has even considered splitting each race into two races of 45 minutes to maximise the entertainment value, the idea being to double one of the more exciting moments of the race – the start. One problem with this is that races often have to be re-started, which could throw broadcasters' schedules into turmoil.

For Formula One's purists – and they are a passionate and vocal group – the 1990s have seen a diminution of the sport they love. Formula One has been compromised by the power of television and big business, they claim. 'That's a load of bollocks' is the uncompromising response of Murray Walker to suggestions that television has damaged Formula One. Walker, one of the UK's most celebrated television commentators, adds: 'There are people who say you do not need to have tyre stops because it is perfectly possible to make a set of tyres that last the whole race. But if they stopped tyre stops, the racing would be no more exciting, and in my opinion it would be far *less* exciting. Formula One needs vast amounts of money to keep it going. Therefore it needs sponsorship. And therefore you have got to make the thing interesting to the public.'

Understanding what drives broadcasters to screen Formula One is central to an understanding of why the sport has developed the way it has. The BBC was among the first broadcasters to take Formula One seriously, and its coverage secured grand prix a place in the psyche of many nations. It is therefore worth looking at how the BBC developed its Formula One coverage and the controversial way it lost the broadcasting rights to the sport. Murray Walker, whose high-octane commentating style both delights and infuriates in equal measure, himself played a big role in raising the profile of the sport. Now in his seventies, he has seen television coverage move from grainy highlights footage in the 1950s to the technology driven outside broadcasts of today. 'Television's role has been absolutely massive,' explains Walker. 'The British public started to get really interested in Formula One in 1976, the year James Hunt won the world championship. Before that, the BBC used to show races from time to time, maybe the British and Monaco Grand Prix live, and highlights from a couple of others. But never the whole series. Back then, the public used to get is Formula One information from the newspapers, not television. The stories did not even appear on the sports pages, they used to appear in the editorial pages. It all began to change when James got a hold on the public.'

In 1978 the BBC made a policy decision to cover the whole grand prix series, though still not all the races would be screened live. 'The drill was that I would go out and watch the practice sessions, return home on the Saturday and go into the television studio to watch the actual race on Eurovision, as it was then called. I did the commentary live, but the BBC put out edited highlights for most of the races. I think we were pulling the wool over the public's eyes in those days. No one actually told them I was not broadcasting live from the trackside.' The level of public interest in Formula One did not justify the huge cost of sending a hole production crew to the circuits. So the BBC used the host countries' pictures. This presented its own problems. Many races were not covered live because the quality of broadcasts were not good. Walker said: 'In those early days the BBC did not think the production standards of most of the countries, particularly in places like Brazil, were high enough to cover the whole race. It was not just money or lack of air time that stopped the BBC from covering all the races. This was the 1960s and 1970s, and sometimes it was just not practical for producers.'

For many sports producers, it was a Hollywood film that provided the answer to some of the technical and cinematic problems they faced.

John Frankenheimer's 1966 *Grand Prix* is not only the best film ever made about motor racing, it was for years the template used to bring Formula One to the small screen. Frankenheimer, a former BBC producer, followed the European grand prix calendar for 1966. Frankenheimer and the film's stars, James Garner and Yves Montand, relied heavily on technical advice from drivers like Graham Hill, Jack Brabham, Jochen Rindt and Bruce McLaren. After seeing rough footage of the Monaco race, a sceptical Enzo Ferrari offered Frankenheimer the full co-operation of his organisation. The camera technology used for the film was the latest available, enabling Frankenheimer to get some stunning on-board shots. The film won three Oscars, and helped persuade broadcasting bosses in Europe and America that motor racing could make attractive television if only more resources were devoted to it.

During the late 1970s and '80s the popularity of Formula One seemed to grow faster than the BBC's ability to keep up with it. Certainly that was the feeling inside the sport. The BBCs highlights package on a Sunday evening, with the occasional live race, was far less than the sport's governing authorities thought it was worth. By the mid-1970s commercial sponsorship was playing a big part in the sport, and there was a feeling that the public service BBC, which banned advertising, was only grudgingly prepared to satisfy the public appetite for Formula One. The BBC had only just come through the now infamous Durex condom row. The contraceptive manufacturer had become a sponsor of the Surtees grand prix team. Durex wanted to bring the product out from under the counter, and saw Formula One as a way of winning greater public acceptability. BBC bosses, however, were enraged that it would mean broadcasting the name Durex into the nation's living-rooms. The corporation actually withdrew from covering the British Grand Prix at Brands Hatch in 1976, the year James Hunt was challenging for the championship. Without television advertising, there was no point in Durex continuing the sponsorship, and the promotion, which was intended to carry a socially responsible message, was pulled. The BBC, however, redeemed itself for the last race of the season, which would decide whether Hunt or Niki Lauda won the championship. Using new satellite technology, the corporation broadcast the race world-wide. The technology was a success, and if it proved one thing, it was that there was a strong appetite among television viewers for more.

Thankfully, after the Durex incident, a more mature attitude prevailed, and also a more professional one, over the following years.

Jonathan Martin, a producer and ardent motor racing fan, became head of BBC sport and set about ensuring that Formula One was given more coverage by the corporation. He brought in Murray Walker, who had cut his teeth on motorcycle commentary, as a full-time replacement for Raymond Baxter, who went on to become one of Britain's most familiar faces as front-man of the popular science series *Tomorrow's World*. Martin took a real interest, said Murray Walker, making it a personal challenge to improve the depth of the BBC's grand prix coverage. Martin worked closely with Bernie Ecclestone and the Formula One Constructors' Association to improve the output. An important move was to start taking the corporation's Outside Broadcast Unit to some races to maintain the quality of the coverage. Even so, not every race was broadcast live. Fans who were able to turned to the pan-European satellite channel Eurosport, whose depth of coverage was greater than the BBC's. 'We take the helmets off the drivers,' said Eurosport's publicity machine, with comprehensive feature and interview material. Even when Nigel Mansell was chasing the world championship in 1992, only the European races were guaranteed to be live on BBC. Also the corporation had an irritating habit of ending transmission as soon as the chequered flag fell. Despite the limitations, however, the BBC and Murray Walker became synonymous with Formula One. The BBC used to play an atmospheric Fleetwood Mac number during the opening and closing credits. Not everyone had heard of Fleetwood Mac, but everyone certainly recognised the music as that 'Formula One theme'.

On the morning of 13 December 1995, Jonathan Martin took a telephone call from Bernie Ecclestone. He thought it would be just another routine discussion about the corporation's coverage. Martin always enjoyed a chance to swap views about his favourite sport with Formula One's most powerful individual. As it turned out, Martin recalled later, the conversation was among the worst ten minutes of his life. Ecclestone, in characteristic style, came straight to the point. He told Martin that a couple of executives from Independent Television, the BBC's main rival, had been to his Knightsbridge office. They had offered him a five-year deal to start broadcasting Formula One. Ecclestone did not say how much ITV's offer was, only that Martin would not be able to match it. The announcement that Formula One was moving to ITV was made at a press conference just one hour after the two men ended their telephone conversation. Ecclestone had the deal stitched up before he even telephoned Martin.

The BBC was outraged, immediately firing off a press release saying that it had not been given enough time to respond. All this public indignation, however, was a token gesture, an attempt to retrieve something from an embarrassing situation. Martin, who described ITV's price as 'hugely in excess of what we were paying', knew it was a lost cause. ITV had agreed to pay around £65 million for the broadcasting rights for five years, whereas the BBC had been paying barely a tenth of that. Ecclestone was well aware that the value of broadcasting rights to sports events was soaring, and once the BBC contract came up for renewal he took advantage of the new environment. Not just in Britain, but throughout the world, contracts to broadcast football, rugby, cricket and boxing had been changing hands for massive sums. The day before the BBC lost Formula One, the American network, NBC, announced it had landed the rights to the next six Olympics for a staggering $2.3 billion.

Surprisingly, journalists at the BBC did not see the wind of change blowing their way. Despite the leaky nature of the media world, outside of Ecclestone's clique of confidants and the ITV negotiators the plans remained secret until the last moment. BBC staff were shocked at the ruthless way in which Ecclestone had handled the corporation, which, after all, had been working with him for almost 15 years. Murray Walker's interpretation of this 'kick in the crutch' was that ITV had pressed Ecclestone not to contact the BBC until the very last minute. ITV, which itself had lost valuable sports contracts to satellite television, wanted to make a big splash with the Formula One announcement. Walker said: 'What Bernie did to the BBC was hard, you could say. But, in mitigation, Bernie would say that he was sworn to secrecy by ITV.' The news was especially tough for Martin, who had nurtured Formula One coverage since becoming head of BBC sport in 1981, and who regarded himself as an ally of Ecclestone's.

Murray Walker, then aged 70, thought that was the end of his commentating days. As close to the sport as anyone, he had heard no whisper of ITV's interest. 'I had just got into my car after doing an after-lunch speech at the National Motor Museum at Beaulieu. I switched on the four o'clock news, and there it was. It was complete bolt from the blue. As far as the BBC were concerned, they were negotiating for a renewal of the contract. Then Bernie phoned Jonathan Martin to tell him the news. When Jonathan picked himself up off the floor – because Formula One was his life – he said: "Gosh, Bernie, it would have been nice to have been able to put in a competitive bid." And Bernie said:

"Unless you have been cheating me all these years, Jonathan, there is no way that you could possibly pay what they are paying, so there was no point in talking to you about it." '

The switch to ITV was not the end of Murray Walker's career. After 18 years working on Formula One full-time with BBC, Walker joined the ITV commentary team on a two-year contract. He believes the BBC was doing an excellent job covering the sport, but felt there was always a feeling within the sports department that they should be doing more. This was especially true in the early 1990s. As in the mid-1970s, when James Hunt captured the British imagination, the 1990s witnessed another burst of enthusiasm for Formula One, though for very different reasons. As Ecclestone himself was to acknowledge, the televised death of Ayrton Senna in 1994 brought new interest to the sport. In fact, 1994 was to be a momentous year for Formula One, with other unrelated accidents (including the death of driver Roland Ratzenburger, a fact often forgotten in all the talk about Senna), and allegations of cheating. Then came the 1995 racetrack rivalry between the British driver Damon Hill and the German Michael Schumacher. Even non-fans in both countries were captured by this nationalistic duel for the championship. Media attention poured down on Formula One. Finally and belatedly, the BBC decided to show every race live.

Tony Jardine, the BBC's former pit-lane reporter who also joined the ITV team, believes the corporation should have learned from Eurosport, whose feature-led presentations have been copied by ITV. 'The BBC's coverage was not good in the last three years or so,' said Jardine. 'Formula One was crying out to have at least one other preview show. In the 1990s, grand prix racing had been popularised and scandalised, and was getting viewers who had simply not been interested before. There was great disappointment inside BBC sport at how conservative we were being.' The BBC made little effort to explore the personalities and issues behind Formula One; to set the scene. Analysis was minimal. If an engine blew up, the viewer rarely found out why. For years Jim Reside, a senior producer, and others broadcasting the sport, had pressed for the BBC to find time in the schedules for a magazine-style programme, but the controller could not be persuaded. Until, that is, it was too late. One of the great ironies is that 48 hours before the announcement of the transfer to ITV, the BBC's Formula One team got its long-awaited permission for a preview programme. Jardine recalls: 'I got a fax from the office asking if I would like to go and do features for a grand prix magazine programme. It was exactly what we needed;

what we had been pressing for.' The BBC's 1996 coverage was comprehensive and probably the best they had ever done. But it was too late.

The loss of Formula One has been extremely damaging to the broadcaster's reputation. If the BBC had devoted more time, ITV might never have risked the challenge in the first place. No one at the BBC appeared unduly worried that the broadcasting rights might be taken away, said Jardine, despite the recognition that they should have provided a better service. 'In my opinion there was no feeling within the Beeb that they would lose the rights. After all, we thought, where would it go? At that time we were getting audience figures for some races of 7.5 million and 8.2 million viewers – some really big hits. And we could point to what the BBC had done for the sport in the past.' The famous BBC arrogance – we do it best and we do it our way – seems to have led to a complacent belief that Formula One would never leave 'Auntie Beeb'. Jonathan Martin may have been too close to the sport to see the threat from commercial television coming up behind him. He had been heard on more than occasion to say that Ecclestone was a friend who would not end a 20-year partnership with the BBC. A mistake. For Ecclestone, business is business and friendship is friendship: he does not confuse the two.

If the BBC recognised any threat at all, it was from BSkyB, the satellite broadcaster 40 per cent owned by Rupert Murdoch's News Corporation. At the time ITV was not showing a lot of big sports. It had no real infrastructure, no real sports department to speak of. ITV bought in sport, and shipped it out to the regional network of stations. Although ITV had covered Formula 3000 in the past, it had never before tackled anything as complicated as a global Formula One series. 'So,' explains Tony Jardine, 'when it was actually ITV, and not someone like BSkyB, which challenged the BBC for Formula One, it was something of a stunner. I could not believe it.' History shows the BBC should have been more alert. ITV has a history of taking over sporting events that were first built up by the BBC. In the 1970s, after Olga Korbut, the child gymnast from Russia, became a celebrity in Britain, ITV took BBC's gymnastics contract. In 1984, when interest in runners Sebastion Coe and Steve Ovett was at its height, ITV took domestic athletics. And after Torvill and Dean brought a new audience and attention to ice skating, ITV bought the rights to that too.

Why did ITV want with Formula One? The simple answer is that it wanted to rebuild audience figures which had been haemorrhaging to other channels. When viewers move on, so do advertisers. ITV had been losing out in the competitive world of broadcasting rights. Most of top-level football had gone to BSkyB, as had boxing. Horse racing too, had gone to other channels. Faced with the loss of lucrative advertising revenue, it should, then, have been no surprise that a demoralised ITV would hit back with something big. In the end the network struck a double blow. Two weeks before the announcement of its Formula One coup, ITV broke the news that it had secured rights to live coverage of football's FA Cup Final from 1998. The decision to bid for Formula One's broadcasting rights was made in September 1995, at a regular meeting of ITV's Sports Management Group. Here representatives from ITV's big three shareholders – Granada, Carlton and United News & Media – get together with network executives. Andrew Chowns, ITV's controller of legal and business affairs, cannot remember who first floated the idea of bidding for Formula One rights. He just recalls instant agreement that this was the blockbuster sporting event that ITV needed to regain its credibility.

Chowns began working with Eileen Gallagher, managing director of London Weekend Television, on a proposal to put to Ecclestone. Their idea was to turn Formula One coverage into a personality led and analytical event, with a promise to broadcast every race live over the next five years. There would be a magazine-style preview programme based around each practice session, with attempts to broaden the appeal beyond the motorsport aficionado. More would be done to boost the profile of British drivers other than Damon Hill. On race days, coverage would start 30 minutes before the start, with interviews from the track and pre-race analysis. Chowns promised that ITV would 'plug' coverage of the races during advertising breaks throughout the week. The ITV deal meant more money for FOCA, but also the sort of higher profile that sponsors wanted for the sport. Previously, the BBC's coverage had focused almost exclusively on the big four teams: Ferrari, Williams, McLaren and Benetton. ITV promised to broaden the coverage. Ecclestone liked what he heard.

Chowns, a lawyer and negotiator used to a bit of tough talking, recalls Ecclestone's frank way of doing business. 'I telephoned him to introduce myself and let him know of our proposals. His reaction was: "If you have got something to say, come to my office and say it." He is a disarmingly direct person. In the movies and on TV you always see people doing these deals in a direct way. Most of the time it is never like that. But it was with him; it was, "Come and tell me what you

want, and I'll give you the answer." ' Chowns had two more meetings
with Ecclestone to define the proposals, and the whole deal was completed within four months. It was a remarkably short negotiation time,
given the size of the contract, said Chowns. But then this is the
benefit of dealing with a single, all-powerful individual like Ecclestone.
'Normally I am dealing with committees and various levels of authority,' Chowns recalls. 'With Formula One it is just Bernie Ecclestone.
Full stop.'

ITV, although still the UK's largest advertising vehicle, urgently
needed to arrest its audience decline. In Formula One, the network
now had a potent weapon in its armoury. The profile of a typical
Formula One audience, young and high-spending, was just the type of
viewer ITV had been losing. Just how bad things had become for ITV
was revealed in figures from the British Audience Research Board which
showed that the network's share of commercial viewing among young
men – where the majority of advertisers focus their marketing – had
slipped below 50 per cent. ITV was desperately bullish after winning
the Formula One contract, trumpeting in its sales literature that 83 per
cent of ABC1 men of between 16 and 34 viewed at least one race during
the 1996 season. Fifty per cent watched four or more races. This is the
sort of volume and quality of viewer that big advertisers – tele-
communications companies, car makers, financial services – want.
Sunday afternoon is regarded as dead time for advertisers. Now they
had a vehicle that was receiving audience figures of 5–6 million people.
What is more, these are in effect new viewers in advertising terms;
people coming from a non-commercial channel to a commercial one.
You cannot achieve that sort of conversion with other big sports,
football for instance, because so much football is already shown on
commercial channels, such as BSkyB. Chowns explained: 'There are
not that many opportunities to convert a non-commercial audience
into a commercial audience in one stroke.' It is unlikely that ITV has
'lifted' the BBC's audience profile entirely, and it is too early to say
whether the network's money has been well spent. What sometimes
happens when sport transfers from the BBC to ITV is that it dilutes
the profile. A lot of new viewers to ITV will not be ABC1 men. That
said, according to early research from advertising agency M&C Saatchi
there has been no substantial diminution of the 'quality' of the audience. ITV is getting around 40 per cent of its target ABC1 audience in
the UK, only marginally down on the BBC.

The weak point in ITV's coverage has been the introduction of commercial breaks. It did not help, in the war of words following ITV's 'takeover', that there were persistent rumours in the trade press that the network had promised not to run commercials. Other rumours were put around that ITV was planning to show advertisements using a split-screen technique. Chowns said there was never a possibility of not running advertisements. After all, that was the reason for buying the broadcasting rights in the first place. The split-screen idea was shown to focus groups, but Independent Television Commission guidelines rule out such a technique. The ITC says television cannot show continuous action alongside a commercial (even though sponsors' logos on racecars are already at the heart of the action). ITV's big concern was how best to fit adverts into a two-hour event that has no natural breaks.

One of Ecclestone's concerns was whether ITV could resist the temptation to sell large numbers of high-priced advertisements. In some countries, race fans barely get to see a whole lap without interruptions. Advertising breaks are commonplace during races shown in France and on Eurosport, and in Germany some interruptions can last up to five minutes. Whichever way ITV placed the adverts, it was expecting a full post-bag of criticism. As part of the damage limitation exercise, ITV set up focus groups with an assortment of die-hard fans and occasional viewers to watch footage interspersed with advertisements. The proposals for commercial breaks came down to two options: ten one-minute breaks or five two-minute breaks. Alongside this went research to find the most-viewer friendly way of projecting a sponsor message either side of the commercials – the so-called 'bumper break' slot, which was bought by Texaco for £12 million over three years. The focus groups found the ten one-minute breaks far too bitty. And it was decided that the bumper breaks would be two-second bursts each.

As ITV expected, the post-bag from fans was less than complimentary. Luckily for ITV it was not until mid-season that any important on-track action was missed. That helped make the breaks more tolerable, and commercials now seem to have been accepted. For Murray Walker, advertising breaks are just a fact of life if fans want better coverage. He said: 'With the exception that the action is interrupted, which nobody likes if you can help it, the fans are getting an incomparably better deal from ITV. I am not an ITV staff employee, and I am honestly not biased on this, but with ITV the fans get more time, they get many more background stories and a much longer run-in to the race. And there is post-race analysis. If the BBC had not lost

it to ITV, they would have eventually lost it to BSkyB. Had they lost it
to Sky, in my opinion, the production standards would not have been
anything like as good, and they would still have got commercials. With
ITV the fans still get their Formula One free. The only action that has
been missed – and sod's law meant it was one of the most exciting
events – was when Damon Hill passed Michael Schumacher in the
1997 Hungarian Grand Prix. If I had been watching it at home I would
have been bloody irritated. It is unfortunate, but that's just the name
of the game. ITV want to recoup their money, and the money comes
from advertising.'

On top of the £65 million ITV is paying to Ecclestone for the broadcasting rights, it also has to finance the production costs. It awarded a
£6 million production contract to MACh1, a company made up of
Chrysalis Sport, an independent operation, and United News & Media,
an ITV shareholder. Although several ex-BBC staff moved over to
MACh1, Andrew Chowns said the company was chosen because it
offered a completely fresh approach. Neil Duncanson, MACh1's executive producer, was deliberately planning a culture shock for Formula
One fans. Out went the famous, if tired, Fleetwood Mac music that for
years had introduced the BBC's coverage, to be replaced by a tune from
a more modern star, Jamiroquai. There would be no cosy anchorman
back in the London studio. Everything was done from the trackside,
which meant building a dedicated outside broadcast truck and studio
costing more than £1 million. About 35 staff go to each race, compared
with eight when the BBC was producing Formula One, admittedly on
a far smaller budget. The 1997 British Grand Prix at Silverstone, when
ITV was the host broadcaster for the rest of the world, was the network's
single biggest outside production event. With 206 staff and 50 cameras,
it cost more than £750,000, and ITV had to rely heavily on manpower
and equipment borrowed from the BBC.

ITV's Formula One audience figures have been running on average
at about 300,000 fewer viewers per race than the last year of the BBC's
coverage, in 1996. Ratings in 1997 varied between 3.2 million for the
Spanish Grand Prix and 6.8 million for the Brazilian Grand Prix. Murray
Walker puts it down to the Damon Hill factor: the fact that the former
world champion and national hero is no longer racing with a competitive team. Walker said: 'For the first three races of 1997 we got
much higher audience figures than the BBC for the same races in 1996.
And then it went down, not a lot, but down nevertheless. In 1996
Damon Hill had the British public by the throat, and in 1997 he didn't.

I guarantee you that if Damon had done as well as he did in 1996, we would have another two million viewers.' What really matters to ITV, though, is not beating the BBC, but making profitable use of the advertising dead-time on a Sunday afternoon. 'Ratings are double, treble, quadruple what we used to get in the same slot,' according to Andrew Chowns. 'That is what matters; making use of the airtime in the best way possible.'

There are critics who dislike Formula One on commercial television, executives at the BBC among them, no doubt. The fear is that commercial stations have a Reader's Digest attitude to sporting events: as long as people pay for the books, who cares whether they are read? will ITV jettison Formula One as soon as it has fulfilled its commercial purpose in bringing in advertising revenue, as happened with gymnastics, snooker and skating? Such views are high on principle and low on reality – irrelevant, even, in the modern era of Formula One under Ecclestone. Formula One is a business, or rather a commodity, to be bought and sold to the highest bidder. Ecclestone is just as likely to switch contracts when the time comes as ITV is to dump Formula One. He is negotiating and re-negotiating contracts all over the world to ensure that Formula One reaches the biggest audiences, and brings in the biggest fee. The thing about Formula One at the moment is that Bernie Ecclestone holds all the aces. All the time grand prix interest is growing, he will have broadcasters knocking at his door, willing to play their part in his great plan to expand Formula One in each country of the world. And, as we will see next, Ecclestone's Formula One television revolution is not over. Multi-channel digital technology and pay-per-view herald the possibility of a new era in the way race fans enjoy their sport. Ecclestone will control this, as well.

The Future is Digital?

'BAKERSVILLE', IT HAS been christened. An imposing steel-clad mono-lithic hangar that travels to each grand prix. Bakersville is Bernie Ecclestone's mobile television studio. It is so-called because it is run by Eddy Baker, manager of FOCA TV, and a former mechanic at Brabham when Ecclestone was in charge of the team. Inside Bakersville is the digital future of Formula One as a television sport – at least this is what Ecclestone would have us believe. Indeed, Ecclestone is so convinced of this that when all the technology is fully up and running he will have invested some £50 million of his own money in the project. Ecclestone says it will cost him £20–30 million a year to run. 'It's my money,' he said. 'Nobody takes any risks except me.' Bakersville requires two Boeing cargo planes and a fleet of trucks to transport 200 tons of equipment around the Formula One circus. The complex provides Formula One coverage to FOCA's digital broadcasting clients – those media companies that are offering fans their sport on a pay-per-view basis. Bakersville dominates the paddock at every race meeting, a message to the world's media that this is the way forward for Formula One television. Paul Stewart, managing director of Stewart Grant Prix, says that every time he sees it, he thinks: 'It does not have to be in the paddock. It could be five miles away. But it is there as a symbol that Bernie means business. And that is part of the genius of Bernie Ecclestone. He understands marketing and he is always looking to the future.'

FOCA TV has been broadcasting for several years, mainly doing pit-lane interviews and providing the in-car footage. From the 1996 season FOCA provided a complete package, with up to 30 cameras set up at each race, independent of the host country's own broadcaster. It was to be another year before plans for the flotation were revealed, but already

Ecclestone was setting up a state-of-the-art demonstration of his Formula One television revolution. Inside Bakersville are about 120 people – the size of three grand prix teams – operating a bank of computer and television screens in front of which sit the commentary teams for each country that takes the feeds. These people are separated from the regular television commentators, who traditionally use booths opposite the pits. The complex has its own power supply and air-conditioning. It is totally independent. Bakersville is transported around Europe in 16 trucks carrying containers which are slotted together to form a huge building. For grand prix further afield, moving Bakersville is such a logistical headache that it determines the shape of the Formula One calendar. The Brazilian and Argentinian Grands Prix now have to be separated by a free weekend, rather than run on consecutive weekends as used to the case.

New television technology is opening up a world of possibilities for sports and their sponsors, though it also carries inherent dangers. A broadcasting war has been raging among media empires trying to secure programmes for their new satellite and digital stations. Companies have placed television rights to top sporting events at the forefront this battle. The result is that the value of these rights has soared, especially for Formula One. Top-level sport has generally been available to a European audience on free television, but pay-per-view (PPV) deals have opened a new and lucrative revenue stream for broadcasters. Kirch Group paid Ecclestone $70 million under a five-year PPV deal for Formula One broadcasting rights for Germany, Switzerland and Austria. Italy's Telepui bought the rights for the next ten years for $200 million, and Canal Plus has the rights for France and Spain. Rupert Murdoch has been looking closely at Formula One, and analysts say it cannot be long before his BSkyB starts buying up rights. The success of Ecclestone's plans to float Formula One is based on the value of these and future broadcasting deals. The forecasts are that Formula One Holdings could earn more than £600 million from digital by the year 2003. But what does the viewer get out of it?

With digital technology it is possible to transmit more than one channel over the same band width normally used by a traditional analogue channel. Viewers use a hand-held remote control device to switch between different parts of the action on the tack and in the pits, or to view data that is normally available only to the commentators. DFI and Canal Plus offer six channels: Channel 1 is the main signal showing traditional track, on-board and pit action. The commentators face a wall of six screens, and can invite people to go to another channel is there is, say, an interview with Damon Hill. Alternatively the viewers can surf through channels themselves. Channel 2 monitors the battle between the leading cars; 3 focuses on the rest of the field; 4 is for the in-car cameras, and is constantly switching between drivers; 5 has interviews and highlights, with regular repeats; and 6 concentrates on the data, such as speeds and pit-stop times. It is not just that digital technology offers a wider range of images and information. The broadcasts come in a higher-quality picture, with CD-quality sound and reduced risk of interference. The signal is received via a satellite dish and decoder. What makes Formula One attractive to broadcasters is that it is more suited to digital programming than many other sports. With Formula One, there is a variety of things going on simultaneously on the track. Compare that with, to take an extreme example, boxing. There is, however, a drawback. Even though digital offers a better service, viewers must be persuaded to pay for something they can often get free.

In Germany, where digital Formula One broadcasts are already available, the decoding box was in 1997 selling at around 890 D-Marks (£330). In addition there was a monthly subscription fee of 40 D-Marks. In France, Canal Plus viewers can pay 88Fr per race (about £10), or subscribe for the whole championship at a discount. The German service provider is DF1, which also has PPV news, films and other sports. But Formula One racing was seen as DF1's flagship event. It was also important for Ecclestone, and his Formula One flotation plans; he wanted to prove that digital could succeed. He had high hopes. In Germany, television audiences for Formula One rose 208 per cent from 1994 to 1996. If digital was going to work anywhere in Europe, Germany was the likely place. However, it has not been a success. Subscribers failed to sign up in the numbers anticipated, largely because DF1 failed to get on the all-important German cable television network. About 16 million German households are linked up to cable, and it was crucial that DF1 should gain access to the network. Six months after being launched, and with around 20,000 subscribers, there was speculation that DF1 was close to folding. Telepui's experience with pay-per-view has been better, with about 90,000 homes connected by the end of 1997. About 18,000 homes have subscribed to Formula One, compared with 60,000 subscriptions for football. Telepui estimates that it needs 500,000 subscribers to digital to break even.

These are early days for what is a long-term investment, so no one yet knows how it will turn out. Ecclestone says he could make a profit if just 10 per cent of Formula One viewers signed up, though financial analysts who have considered his stock market flotation forecasts believe this figure is too low. Talk to Formula One executives, and many seem to have faith in the project simply because they have faith in Ecclestone's judgement. However, there are still plenty of sceptics, and one of them is Murray Walker, a man who knows a thing or two about what interests the television viewer. 'There is no doubt that the actual digital coverage is incomparably better than even the ITV viewer receives, because digital gets enormous resources thrown at it. But I'm not convinced that for Formula One a lot of people will want to jockey around five or six different channels. My belief is that most people want to watch the race pictures that are selected for them by a producer, and have a commentator tell them what is happening. I think you'd have to be a died-in-the-wool anorak to want to flick around all the channels rather than just watch a race.'

Digital technology, and the whole broadcasting revolution, also offer new opportunities in the way advertisers and sponsors reach their target. At its simplest, companies could sponsor the various digital channels. At its most complex, digital will change the relationship between viewer and sponsors. Technology already exists to enable broadcasts to segment their audiences on behalf of sponsors. FOCA TV will be able to control and edit pictures as they see fit, so advertisers and sponsors that do not need global coverage will be able to target individual countries. For example, broadcasts will be able to super-impose advertisements on to blank billboards dotted around a circuit. When winning drivers stand on the podium after a race, 'virtual' ads could be placed behind them, tailored for particular countries or markets. During an ice hockey game, Canadian viewers saw an ad for a tyre company in the centre of the rink, while Swedish viewers saw one for Ikea. 'Painting' adverts on to moving targets, like racecars, is a little more difficult, but the technology will be available eventually. It will be possible to show the same cars, but carrying different sponsors' names in different parts of the world. One possibility is that it could be a way around government bans of tobacco sponsorship. Those countries without tobacco bans would receive broadcasts showing the advertising. Those that have imposed a ban would not. A more practical benefit for Bernie Ecclestone and the teams is that they would have more space on racecars and billboards to sell.

None of this is much use to sponsors, however, if Formula One is marginalised on pay-TV stations that no one watches. Sponsors are very wary of digital. Indeed, they are wary about the whole shift of sporting events from general access channels to exclusive cable and satellite channels. Public access television has been the shop window for Formula One, and sponsors have invested millions of pounds on long-term strategies on that basis. If Formula One fans turn into digital channel-hoppers, it will fragment the single large monolithic audience they are trying to target. Barrie Gill of CSS International, gave a cautious warning: 'Formula One should not be deluded by technology. Every sport could have its own channel, though this brings dangers. Sport is about inspiration and participation, and if the ordinary citizen does not have access to it except on digital, then the sport will suffer. Sport's authorities will have to decide between guaranteed income and future interest in the sport. Mass audiences are essential for a healthy sport.' Ecclestone has to be careful not to divide the very fan base that has enabled him to build his empire.

Chapter Seven: MOTORS AND RACING

Introduction

DOES FORMULA ONE have any practical relevance for the motorist any more, or is it purely about entertainment? Once upon a time there was a clear link between racecar engineering and the vehicles you could buy in the showroom. Manufacturing giants like Renault or Mercedes-Benz entered their own teams in races to demonstrate the superiority of their technology – technology that was then installed into their road cars. On a smaller scale, Colin Chapman, founder of Lotus, like Germany's Ferdinand Porsche, developed racing and road cars in parallel, using the same technology in both. As the economics of motorsport engineering changed, so did the connection between road cars and racing cars. The big motor companies pulled out of direct involvement in Formula One, becoming suppliers rather than competitors. Also, manufacturers out-sourced more research and development, which reduced their need to test-bed new ideas on motor racing. At the same time, a network of specialist subcontractors emerged in Britain to service the needs of racing world-wide. From rallying to IndyCars, competitors may need the sponsorship money of motor corporations, but for their technology they turn to highly skilled niche firms in Britain. All these changes have obscured the link between racing and production cars. However, there are still substantial technical benefits being passed on from racing cars to road vehicles. It is just that, these days, those benefits are not so obvious. The next two sections explore the industrial side of Formula One, looking first at the technical spin-offs for the major motor companies, and then at the micro level, with an assessment of the motorsport industry in Britain. The first part shows why motorists can still thank racing for the reliability and comfort they enjoy, the second at how Britain's motorsport industry continues to help push back the boundaries of vehicle technology.

Racing Improves the Breed

EVEN AFTER 100 YEARS of motoring, and in the face of clear evidence that the internal combustion engine has played a large part in causing damage to the health and the environment, the car's fascination for countless hundreds of millions of people remains undimmed. In Formula One, that fascination with both machinery and driving ability is taken to an extreme. The engine has assumed a mystique of its own. Enzo Ferrari turned them into something to be idolised; the low growl of a Ferrari engine is unmistakable to anyone with a passing interest in Formula One. It was the British owner-entrepreneur racers of the 1960s, as we have seen, who rejected the brute force of large engines, in favour of the subtler techniques of aerodynamics and chassis design. But this did nothing to reduce the allure of engine power for motorsport fans. Why? Because engines remain one of Formula One's last links with the everyday road cars people drive. It is this connection that motor manufacturers trade on when they sponsor Formula One constructors. Performance demonstrates the superiority of equipment, and it sells cars. Motor racing has contributed much to the development of production cars, but nowhere more than in the area of engine development. This section looks at the transfer in technology between racing and production vehicles, not just in engine development, though, but also in componentry and tyre technology. Just as there are few original thoughts, there are few original engineering breakthroughs. Most are adaptations and advances on previous developments. For many years, grand prix racing has been a bridge between aerospace technology and road cars, stealing from the former and giving to the latter. Now, however, the technological spin-offs are getting harder to see. There is a danger that restrictions on Formula One technology imposed by the sport's rule body, the FIA, and unlimited restrictions on road car technology, may make racing less relevant to the road user.

Tobacco companies are commonly held to be Formula One's biggest bankrollers. In actual fact, cigarette makers vie with engine manufacturers for the title of grand prix's most benevolent backers. As detailed in an earlier chapter, tobacco companies' directly and indirectly spend around $350 million a year in total on their Formula One programmes. Car manufacturers too would not get much change from $350 million for a season in Formula One. In addition to the supply of free engines and back-up resources to the top teams,[1] there are additional marketing and hospitality costs. A large part of the funding for the pre-season launch of a racecar might be covered by the engine supplier. McLaren's extravagant launch of its 1997 vehicle was estimated to have cost Mercedes $1.5 million. The German car company's Formula One budget is about $60 million a year. Ford is thought to spend more, and Peugeot slightly less, on their own grand prix projects. Renault, the French car maker which formed a hugely successful partnership with the Williams team, spent a minimum of $500 million between 1989 and 1997 on its Formula One programme. Motor manufacturers justify such costs with two slogans: *Racing improves the breed* and *Win on Sunday, sell on Monday*. The first adage refers to the trickle-down effect of racecar technology into road cars; the second, to a marketing belief that racetrack triumphs will boost forecourt sales. Grand prix racing has certainly been critical for test-bedding automotive technology in the past. But now that modern racecars have more to do with aircraft than motoring, are there any tangible benefits to be had for the car buyer? There is a perfectly reasonable school of thought which argues that the last Formula One innovation to reach road cars was the development of the baby seat and harness. Nor can today's car makers point to a clear link between winning in Formula One and showroom sales. The connection was easier to make at the birth of racing some 100 or so years ago. When, for example, Renault won the 1906 grand prix at Le Mans, the car's technological supremacy enthused a nation. Between 1906 and 1907 production at Renault's Billancourt factory nearly doubled from 1,600 cars to more than 3,000, and by 1908 it reached 4,600. Although Renault has pulled out of

---

[1] There are three types of engine deal: 1) Works deal, in which teams get engines and back-up in return for branding on the racecar and other endorsements. 2) Pay deal, which can cost a team $10–16 million a season. 3) Build your own engine. Only Ferrari does this.

Some engine suppliers do not make their F1 engines, but simply brand them. For instance, the Mercedes engine supplied to McLaren is built by Ilmor Engineering, in Britain.

Formula One, the enthusiasm of other engine suppliers is not dimmed. BMW, Mercedes, Honda, Porsche, Audi – and manufacturers from emerging countries like South Korea and Malaysia – have all either recently joined Formula One, will do so in the future, or have thought very hard about the possibility. Grand prix racing remains as attractive to the globe's major car companies as ever.

Today's 200mph Formula One car is the end product of 100 years of research and development. To put it crudely: strip away all the computers and other hi-tech gadgetry, and the essence of what is left of the car was conceived just after the turn of the century – a multi-cylinder internal combustion engine, a driver sitting between the front and rear wheels, operating a gearbox link to the rear wheels, and a chassis mounted on springs on four corners. What has followed in motor racing has basically been refinements by constructors and engine suppliers. But, as motor engineers and car buyers might exclaim – what refinements! In the 1950s disc brakes made the transition from racing when Jaguar (whose racecars used an aerospace design adapted by Dunlop) put them on its road cars. In the following decade, fuel injection used in the Climax V8 Formula One engine began to be utilised in the mainstream car market. (Injection, in fact, was first developed in 1907, and was used by Bosch and Mercedes-Benz in the 1950s.) Today, fuel injection systems are seen as crucial in bringing down emissions and improving energy efficiency in cars. The 1970s saw the importance of aerodynamics and balance in Formula One, with the results of experiments in chassis design and engine position being used to improve the shape and comfort of road cars. Knowledge of airflow over and under the car became a black art in Formula One, but it was not long before sports car companies like Porsche were putting aerofoil wings on their road vehicles. In the 1980s, lighter but tougher composites and alloys were developed to increase racecar speed, but were soon taken up by the rest of the motor industry; and, for the first time, mainstream car producers really started to give serious thought to the aerodynamic work that racecar designers had been doing for the previous 15 years. By building on these designers' work in high-speed handling, cornering and grip, car manufactures learned important lessons abut fuel efficiency and braking.

As for the 1990s, the most important transfer in technology has been in electronics. Formula One cars are packed with gadgetry, and fully wired up to technicians in the pit-lane who monitor every aspect of performance. There was a time in the early 1990s when racecars were so crammed with on-board computer systems that the drivers seemed to have turned into mere automatons. Rule changes by the FIA now restrict the use of driver aids, as part of the attempt to restore levels of both driving skill and entertainment in Formula One. With racecars constrained in the use of new systems, it may not be long before a standard road car is as 'smart' as any Formula One vehicle. Traction control, active suspension and electronic throttle control are already available on top-of-the range cars, Ferraris included. There are still benefits that have yet to filter down to road cars, notably in the wider use of thermoplatics-based composite components to improve weight, safety, and wear and tear. The more restrictions there are on Formula One technology, however, the fewer opportunities for technology transfer there will be.

John Wood, director of the Motor Industry Research Association, believes Formula One will still improve the quality of production cars. It is just that the benefits will not be as clearly identifiable. He explained: 'I think the analogy is more like the space race. NASA did not set out to design a better saucepan (Teflon), but that was a result. And this is how Formula One spin-offs will come in the future; not in a single definable thing like a disc brake, but in the technology that is probably developed incidentally. It may not be the thing that is developed for the racing that is important, it may be the technique that is developed in order to make the thing for racing cars. Formula One these days is very much about moving the whole art forward. And out of that you get techniques that are applicable to a wider arena.' For example, Ford's racing engines were produced by the British engineering company Vickers, the defence and car company that owned Rolls-Royce until 1997. Cosworth developed a revolutionary casting process to enable racing engineers to cast water and oil lines into the engine block, rather than machine them in later. Money, time and reliability were improved. Ford now uses the process in its production engine factory in Canada.

Ferrari, the only Formula One team that makes its own engine and chassis, has been incorporating racing technology into its road cars since the company began in 1947. In 1990s there has been the F50, as close to a street-legal Formula One Ferrari as you can get, complete with carbon-filter monocoque and a $500 million price tag. Then came the F550, with most of its engine technology, including enlarged valves, ram air induction, titanium connecting rods and lighter crankshaft, taken from the F50 and Formula One racers. One of Ferrari's latest road car developments, and one that may well trickle down to standard production cars quickly, is the F1-style gearbox on the F355. Developed by Ferrari and Italian sub-contractor Magneti Marelli, Selespeed is an electro-hydraulic gear and clutch command. Similar systems have been used by every Formula One constructor for many years, but transferring this technology to road cars has taken time , owing to its cost and complexity. Under the system, drivers shift gears sequentially up or down, as on a motorcycle, using a paddle mounted behind the steering wheel. Buttons on the steering wheel may also be used. The system dramatically speeds up gear-shifting, stops gear 'crunch' when manually changing gears, and protects against the over-revving that damages engines. It also means that drivers can keep their hands on the steering wheel. The gearbox is now used on 70 per cent of orders for the F355, and Ferrari says all its cars will eventually use the system; meanwhile the company's owner, Fiat, is experimenting on its volume production cars. If it takes off in road cars, the system could be the single most significant technology to come out of Formula One for many years.

In the meantime, however, Ferarri's road cars, and McLaren's racing-derived MF1, are something of an exception, as remote to motorists as Formula One itself. But mainstream manufacturers, too, are also deriving technology benefits from their Formula One involvement that may be more relevant to car buyers. In 1996, when Ford's vice-president of Advanced Vehicle Technology, Neil Ressler, confirmed at the US motor show in Detroit that the company was to supply engines to the new Stewart Grand Prix team, he made another, less publicised comment. This was that Ford was setting up a Motorsport Technology Department (MTD). Ford had decided that it wanted a specific team dedicated to transferring motorsport technology into mainstream products. Essentially, Stewart Grand Prix would form the experimental laboratory for new ideas coming out of the MTD. Around 50 engineers, experts in areas from material science to computing, work on what Ford likes to call the three P's: products, processes and people.

Products: the rapid development of new components, which are then exposed to Formula One testing. Such things as new lightweight starter motors, valve lifters and vibration dampers are all being tested at Stewart Grand Prix for eventual inclusion in Ford's volume vehicles. The team is also experimenting for the 1998 season with a radical new carbon-fibre gearbox. Before teaming up with Stewart Grand Prix, Ford had been linked with Benetton Formula, which proved a useful testing ground. One challenge facing Ford motorsport technology boffins was how to utilise more widely in productions models its engine control system, the EEC-V. Computers now control almost every function of an engine, and the EEC-V is capable of 1.7 million commands each second. Ironically, the first Ford engine control system used in Formula One was a modified version of a production system, the EEC-IV. It was installed in the engines supplied to the Benetton race team, where it was refined and upgraded over several seasons. Engineers installed the EEC-V in the high-performance Taurus SHO engine. The technical challenge was to keep the power of the high-revving SHO engine under control before it hit the 'redline'. In past experience the engine had bust the redline before the control system could kick in. Lessons learned from refining the EEC-V in Formula One and IndyCar racing provided the solution.

Processes: the rigours of motorsport mean that design, manufacturing and testing all have to be done at breakneck speed, but in a controlled environment. Lessons learned can be extremely useful for organising the main manufacturing operation. For example, each racing driver, each circuit, each different weather condition requires the engine to be set up differently to get the maximum out of the racecars. In the old days, the recalibration of EEC was done via modem links from the racetrack to the computer back at the car company's engine plant. PCSs – Portable Calibration Systems – have been developed to do the work these days, speeding up the process considerably and cutting down on costs. PCSs are now invaluable for engineers calibrating road vehicles in tests in far-flung places and varying climates. Another advance was the snappily named Flash Erasable Electrically Programmable Read Only Memory chip – Flash EEPROM for short. First used with Benetton in Formula One, these chips speed up recalibration of the EEC computer. The spin-off for the road car user is that engineers in dealerships can recalibrate an engine's emissions, or make driving adjustments, without having to replace the whole EEC system. Of course not every Ford car has such technology. 'We could put these systems in passenger cars today,' says Ford. 'The EEC-V controller has the capacity. It just comes down to cost and demand.' Experience shows, however, that the dissemination of new technologies throughout production car manufacturing is only a matter of time.

People: racing is being used to 'hot-house' the best young engineers.

They learn about meeting deadlines, data-analysis, and turning theory into practice, all under the pressure of a Formula One or IndyCar timetable. Engineering for extreme conditions will feed down the production line. Quantifying the monetary value of putting engineers through racing programmes is not possible. Ford only knows that at the end of these stints, be it one season or several, it gets engineers who can think on their feet and make decisions while working under competitive, stressful conditions. Ford views racing as one of its best fitness programmes. Martin Whittaker, head of Ford Motorsport in Europe, believes that bringing engineers through race programmes must be cost-effective because the learning curve is so much faster. 'If you have got a problem with a piece of engine, you can't write a few memos and hold a committee meeting. You have to deal with it immediately. The race is on Sunday. You have to be ready to compete. Problem-solving becomes a here and now issue for racecar engineers, not a matter for next month. The wrong decision means you don't race.' These engineers take news skills, new attitudes and new ways of working back to production engineering. In what ways might it help? Engineers, by working in a tight-knit environment alongside the team's own engineers, get to see the racecar evolve from start to finish. It gives a better understanding of manufacturing a product as a whole. The knowledge and demands of racecar engineering – the efficient utilisation of weight and space, tolerances and safety, and so on – stay with engineers throughout their careers. At least, that is the theory.

The above principles of products, processes and people apply, in one shape or form, to all the engine suppliers currently involved in top motorsport. However, there is another important area of technology transfer which has not so far been mentioned – the use of Formula One by 'second-division' car makers as a fast-track to acquire knowledge they would otherwise have to wait many years to develop. The governments and companies of South Korea and Malaysia, for example, are impatient to get their hands on the latest advanced manufacturing technology. In aerospace, motoring and computing, these countries have been buying the expertise that they cannot wait to develop organically. A lot has been said about Formula One's gravitation to the East because its tobacco companies want to take the sport into their most important markets. That is only part of the story. China and Indonesia, Malaysia and Korea view success at Formula One as a sort of industrial virility symbol. That is why they are falling over themselves to stage a leg of the grand prix season in their countries. It cannot be too many years before motor manufacturers such as Daewoo (which bought one of the Britain's premier motor research centres) or Proton (which bought the famous Lotus sports car company) begin supplying engines to Formula One or IndyCar teams. Ten of millions of pounds of fresh funds may soon be pouring into top motorsport thanks to Asian countries' willingness to show the world the technological strides they have made over the past few years.

The Malaysian government's sponsorship of Stewart Grand Prix (*Visit Malaysia*, read the decal) was about more than just attracting tourists. 'The deal will spur our automobile industry to greater heights,' said prime minister Dr Mahathir Mohamad, in his usual triumphant tones. Malaysian engineers are working with Stewart Grand Prix – 'and through this knowledge, we can design and develop our own car engines,' said the prime minister. Petronas, the Malaysian state oil company, signed a five-year sponsorship deal with the Sauber team. The agreement will help raise Petronas's profile, but more important for Mahathir is the valuable data analysis that oil companies get from testing products in Formula One. In the 1980s Mahathir had a 'Look East' policy, which meant looking to Japanese companies for technology transfer. The move into Formula One, and the acquisition of Lotus (a specialist in composite technology), reflected official frustration with the slow pace of technology transfer from Mitsubishi, the Japanese company that was in partnership with Proton. If they join Formula One as engine suppliers or constructors, Malaysian or Korean car companies would, in effect, be doing no more than what Honda did before them. The Japanese company saw Formula One as a fast-track to the technical knowledge it needed to make an assault on the luxury car market then dominated by American and European manufacturers. The strategy worked.

Honda first entered Formula One in the early 1960s to gain technical and marketing support for the company's diversification from motor-cycle to car manufacturing. Honda established its own grand prix team, and made its début in the German Grand Prix of 1964. Honda's early designs were based on motorcycle technology, and the engines and chassis were grossly overweight. The company formed a partnership with John Surtees, who had won both the motorcycle and motor racing world championships. It gave Honda a British base and access to more up-to-date technology. The team came fourth in the 1967 constructors' championship, and won two races in 1968. Overall, however, Honda's cars were more an embarrassment than a showcase, and that year the company decided to pack it in and return home. Besides, a change in corporate strategy at Honda's Tokyo headquarters led to the company's withdrawal at the end of the 1968 season. The United States government had introduced expensive new controls on car safety and pollution. Honda decided to put money directly into refining its production cars for what was – and still is – the world's biggest volume car market.

Honda reappeared on the Formula One scene in the 1980s. The experiment in the 1960s had done little to improve Honda's image or its technical abilities, but there were two reasons for returning to grand prix. Firstly, Formula One technologies were taking a quantum leap forward in engineer and chassis design; secondly, the company wanted to establish itself quickly in the booming European road car market. Japan's domestic car market was saturated, and export-led growth was the only route to expansion. This time, though, Honda was not interested informing its own team. The company's technicians urgently wanted to get to grips with the latest engine management systems, which merge fuel injection, ignition and electronics into an integrated powerplant. Honda did not need to run a team to acquire this knowledge; it was enough to be an engine supplier, leaving the chassis design to specialist firms. Honda initially formed a partnership with Spirit Grand Prix, but the team failed to live up to the Japanese company's big ambitions. In 1984 Honda became the exclusive V6 engine supplier to Williams Grand Prix Engineering. To cope with the weight on the engine, Williams had to produce a lighter chassis with a completely new layout. The engine suffered from poor fuel consumption and piston failure, but research and development took Honda engines into new areas of expertise. The company was notorious for the secrecy with which it guarded its technical data and specifications. Even engineers from Williams GPE working alongside Honda personnel could be frustrated by the lack of information they were getting. Yet, by 1987, the Japanese company had built the most powerful and reliable Formula One engine of the time. Unfortunately for the Williams team, Honda took that engine elsewhere, to McLaren, for the next season.

Fuel injection was first developed for aircraft engines, though the technology was used on an experimental basis in motor racing in the early 1950s. At that time, the systems were however, far too complex for use in mainstream production cars. Honda entered Formula One, the second time, with its turbocharged 163 engine in 1983. The engine included a fuel injection system that it was testing for introduction into Honda's production cars. Between 1985 and 1988 new regulations, including lower fuel allowances, were introduced by the sport's governing body with the intention of reducing the power of supercharged engines and making normally aspirated engines more competitive. Honda's response was to develop a far more efficient fuel injection system, which was used in its 1988 Formula One engine for McLaren, the 168. Using advances in microprocessor technology for fuel injection made by Bosch and Hitachi, Honda took the development several steps further. Despite the more restrictive FIA regulations, the 168 engine gained a 13 per cent improvement in fuel economy. The engine also measured precisely the amount of fuel needed to race, which meant that the car did not have to carry 'safety' fuel to avoid running out of petrol before the finish. In 1988 the two Honda-McLaren cars, driven by Ayrton Senna and Alain Prost, qualified either first or second twelve times, finished one and two ten times, and won 15 of the 16 races that season. A remarkable record that many pundits believe will never be beaten.

All this was great publicity for Honda, an ideal build-up to the launch of the company's showpiece Acura NSX mid-engined sports car. Which, of course, was the whole idea. Honda, better known for its economy models, stunned the motoring press with its challenger to Ferrari, Porsche or Chevrolet Corvette. The two-seater NSX used the race-derived engine from Formula One, technology which gradually filtered down to Honda's mainstream models. In 1990, more than 1,500 of the first year' shipment of 3,000 cars to the US were pre-sold. The public perception of Honda Corporation shifted overnight. Honda now stood for quality, not just 'economy and comfort', and in the boardrooms of US rivals and the corridors of power, concern was fuelled about the onward march of Japanese technology.

Honda had a 'spend what it takes' philosophy to racing at this time, helped no doubt by the strength of the Japanese economy and the power of the yen. By 1990 the company's Formula One budget was running at about $100 million a year. When Formula One's rule-making body announced that from 1989 turbocharged engines would be outlawed, manufacturers and teams scrambled to find the best alternative. Would it be twelve cylinders, or ten, or eight? While other teams could only afford to invest in one configuration each and hoped it would be the best, Honda had the budget to develop three engines to discover which had the most potential (it was ten). At one point Honda had 150 engineers working exclusively on Formula One at its research centre at Wako, Japan. Outwardly, it looked like wastefulness. But John Wood, a director at the Motor Industry Research Assocaition, Britain's leading vehicle R&D centre, could see a clear connection between these projects and Honda's road cars. 'Honda had scores of people working on various Formula One engine projects. But these engineers were never kept on the racing programme for ever. Honda moved them around. It might have developed engines for Formula One that, in the end, were never used. But Honda still acquired a variety of technologies. This expertise was ploughed back into the mainstream along with the engineers. It was not long before it started showing up in their road cars. We could see the changes when we stripped down the cars. Honda recognised the value of competition.' Honda's president, Nobuhiko Kawamoto, was himself a Formula One mechanic in the 1960s.

The Japanese economic recession led to Honda withdrawing from Formula One in 1992. Executives in Tokyo felt they could no longer justify the costs while the road car division struggled financially. The company said that Formula One was becoming too remote from everyday motoring, and to profligate in an era when the Western world was becoming concerned about cars and the environment. A more plausible explanation, however might have been that Honda had simply milked Formula One for all it was worth, and now was the right time to make its exit. At the same time Honda was also putting down warnings about the high costs of competing, lest its rivals were thinking of an assault on Formula One. The cynical version is looking more plausible. In recent years profitability has improved at Honda, thanks to sales of its sports utility models and a company-wide restructuring. Now the company looks set to return to Formula One before the year 2000. The company had, in any case, kept open the Formula One door through its sister company Mugen, which supplied engines to the Jordan team. What could stand in the way of Honda's return is the need to sustain its growing share of sales in the American road car market. Honda is strongly committed to the CART Indy world series, which is becoming popular outside American and beginning to challenge Formula One for audiences.

Honda won the CART championship in 1996, and sales of road cars were boosted as a result. For Honda to compete in two championships, CART and Formula One, at the same time might be prohibitively expensive. Honda keeps the cost of competing in CART a secret, but probably the company makes a loss on its CART expenditure, while recouping money on the marketing and publicity. The going rate to an engine supplier for an assault on Formula One is $60 million a year, and even higher in the early years to get the project off the ground.

Honda's return, for a third time, has less to do with technology, and more with the marketing potential of Formula One. The allure of winning on Sunday in order to sell on Monday has grown along with Formula One's international stature. It is probable that Honda will re-enter Formula One with its own team, either making both engine and an all-new chassis, or buying an existing constructor. Either way, it would be a significant change in attitude and intention towards Formula One. In the 1980s, when Honda was interested in technology transfer, building the chassis seemed a side issue. The two are not easily separated, of course, where Formula One is concerned. But the balance would seem to have shifted in favour of the publicity potential of Formula One's global popularity. The FIA's restrictions on Formula One technology means there is less and less to be gained from test-bedding new ideas in grand prix. Motor manufacturers have their own large testing facilities which are more than sufficient, and increasingly they out-source specialist technological work. No matter. Formula One in the late 1990s offers global marketing platform like no other. A Honda grand prix team would merely be a promotion vehicle in the battle for sales with the likes of General Motors, Toyota and Volkswagen.

Renault, the French car manufacturer, played the publicity card to perfection. The company's partnership with Williams GPE (Renault also supplied Benetton) was among the most successful engine supply deals ever in Formula One. The combined might of Renault's engine power and the design expertise of the Williams team overpowered rivals. The partnership won the constructors' title five times between 1992 and 1997. The year Renault did not win with Williams, 1995, it won with Benetton instead: making six titles in a row, and equalling Honda's record between 1986 and 1991. Renault may have learned a lot about vehicle technology in the 1970s and 1980s. The company effectively stamped turbocharged engine technology on Formula One after launching its RS01 engine at the 1977 British Grand Prix. But in the 1990s Renault's involvement has been about stamping an image on what was a stagnating state-owned enterprise. Nigel Geach, who as director of Sport Marketing Surveys monitors the shifting sands of successful sponsorship, believes the public perception of Renault has been transformed in the last decade because of Formula One. 'A Renault used to be a standard, boring French car. Increasingly, they are being seen as racy cars that people aspire to, precisely because of the change in image following success in Formula One. Renault is obviously producing better-engineered cars as well. But if you need to construct an image in order to sell those better-engineered cars, then Formula One has worked wonders for Renault. Similarly, in touring cars, Volvo changed its image radically. They used to be boring old Swedish cars. Now there is something flashy about them.'

Renault has shown little evidence of direct technical benefit from Formula One for its production car design, except in electronics. A Formula One engine was put into a prototype, the Initiale, but that seemed to be all. Renault's Formula One engineering budget of $60 million a year, plus 150 highly skilled designers and technicians, has really been part of a marketing drive for the company. Renault's Jean-Jacques de la Rivière explains: 'In technology terms, today's Formula One has more to do with the aircraft industry than cars. A racing engine is built to go 300 kilometres. The best Formula One engine is the one that breaks down at the finish, because racing is about being on the limit. I think most people would want their car to go further than 300 kilometres! Sure, I exaggerate to make a point. Lessons can be learned for production cars. But maybe those lessons are so remote it would be cheaper to experiment in the factory, not go through the expense of Formula One.'

As a marketing venture, though, de la Rivière is adamant that Formula One has proved ideal. Despite spending $60 million a year on its Formula One programme, plus that sum again on support marketing, Renault still regarded grand prix racing as value for money compared with other forms of advertising. Yet, at the end of 1997 Formula One season, Renault pulled out of Formula One. The car company cannot pinpoint exactly when, but during 1996 it started to feel it was getting diminishing returns from its investment. Renault had been such a success that it was no longer a surprise when Williams won. Damon Hill's engine broke down a couple of times during races. So, for want of anything new to say, the press was starting to write 'beginning of the end' stories. Also, Renault was undergoing a corporate restructuring pending the sale of the government's remaining stake. All divisions, including Renault Sport, were going through efficiency programmes. A feeling was growing within the company that the time was right to withdraw, while Renault engines were still at the top. Renault Sport's president Patrick Faure felt there was nothing more to be gained once the production division had solved its image problem. 'Formula One has been very good for the image of the company. The image of Renault was not very good before. Now our research tells us that our image is excellent all around the world.'

Renault's withdrawal probably saved Formula One from a severe engine supply shortage. It was not healthy for competition to have such a dominant force taking all the prizes. Peugeot, Renault's French rival, and Yamaha might both have pulled out, and it is unlikely that other engine suppliers would be lining up to enter the sport if Renault was still involved. Peugeot desperately wanted to emulate its French rival, but instead suffered a series of engine failures in front of hundreds of millions of television viewers during the 1995 season as a supplier to Jordan. The 1996 championship was marginally better, though still not as good as Peugeot hoped. How Jacques Calvet, chairman of Peugeot-Citroën, must have rued the day he changed his mind about Formula One. In 1992 he had been far from enthusiastic about the sport: 'I would prefer to find a championship which is closer to ordinary cars than grand prix racing. We like to accept challenges which improve our road cars – like rallying and sports cars.' What did change Calvet's mind was seeing the massive global and positive publicity Renault was getting from its Formula One programme. With Renault on its way out of the sport, Peugeot decided to sign a three-year engine supply deal – from 1998 to 2000 – with the Prost team.

As soon as Renault heard that Peugeot was staying in Formula One, the company suddenly decided to make its engines available through other sources. Formula One has an allure that makes it difficult to break the link completely. And with one of its key European rivals planning to continue its involvement, it made sense for Renault to keep the door open in case it ever wishes to return. Renault sold the licence to its V10 engine to Mecachrome, a French aeronautics company, which hires the powerplant and its technicians to constructors for about $16 million a season. Williams and Benetton, both used to receiving Renault engines free, now bought them. At least they were able to recoup some of the cost by selling the vacant advertising space on their cars. Torn between giving up a valuable marketing vehicle and risking its reputation by continuing with Formula One, Renault thought it could get the best of both worlds. If the Mecachrome engines under-perform, then Renault has put distance between itself and failure. If they triumph, then the spin-doctors in Renault's publicity department will be able to ensure that its name gets about. Renault's problem was that once out of Formula One, it is a struggle to get back

in. As Patrick Faure explained: 'Formula One has become so technical
that, if you withdraw, it takes such a long time to return to a high
level. It could take Renault two, three or four years to return to the
level achieved before you stopped.'

In all this jostling for position, one should not lose sight of the fact
that the whole idea is to sell more production cars. However, try as
you might to find data proving that a successful Formula One season
directly leads to a rise in forecourt sales, the conclusive evidence is just
not there. Engine suppliers know what the costs are, but measuring the
returns is a different matter. It is a feeling, not a science. That is because
modern Formula One has become a far subtler marketing tool. Even
Ferrari knows that a bad season in racing will not necessarily affect
sales of its road cars. Formula One for car manufacturers is today about
creating an image, building a positive consumer attitude towards the
car. Peugeot does not expect car buyers to rush to the showrooms on
Monday morning after it wins its first grand prix (a Peugeot engine has
still to win a race). 'We get feedback from marketing surveys which
tell us how consumers view Peugeot,' said company spokesman Jean-
Claude Lefèbvre. 'We know that if there is a good feeling, then that is
good for sales. But, I agree, it is not possible to say that because Peugeot
did well in a race then it means we sold X amount of cars. I think 20
or 30 years ago it would have been easier. But back then racing cars and
road cars had more in common. The marketing has changed along with
the technology.'

For German luxury car manufacturers BMW and Mercedes, technology transfer does not come into the equation. They are engaged in
a marketing battle over new models, new designs, and brand advertising, and Formula One has become part of this. BMW announced in
1997 that it would supply engines to the Williams team from the year
2000, in a five-year deal that would cost the manufacturer between $80
million and $100 million a year. 'It is time to emphasise our brand
values,' said Bernd Pischetsreider, BMW's chief executive, when he
unveiled the plan. 'BMW must bring out its face more than in the
past.' Why? Because Mercedes, whose engines powered McLaren to a
storming 1998 season, is basking in world-wide publicity generated by
its Formula One involvement. BMW needs to catch up. Audiences for
Formula One are soaring in some of BMW's and Mercedes' key markets,
not least in their backyard. The number of television viewers watching
Formula One in Germany rose 208 per cent between 1994 and 1996 on
the back of interest in drivers Michael Schumacher and Heinz Harold

Frentzen. Mercedes' return to grand prix racing in 1997 is interwoven with the company's commitments to other motorsports. Some events, like the International Touring Championship, are used to showcase particular models, in this case the Mercedes C-class. Formula One, said the company's motorsport chief Norber Haug, is about consolidating Mercedes' global position, not about putting a sign on the side of a McLaren which says 'Buy Mercedes'. 'Formula One is about Mercedes' overall image,' said Haug. 'It is about strategic marketing and, importantly, communicating with younger people. The motorsport projects, including Formula One, are about communicating with customers.' Not a word here about technology transfer. For Mercedes, Formula One is part of a global promotional package designed to create the right impression.

Being involved in engine supplies means being involved at the sharp end of Formula One. Before leaving the subject of technology transfer, however, it is worth mentioning a less glamorous part of the business – the tyre and oil companies which back Formula One. Ever since racing moved to enclosed circuits, which gave advertisers a captive audience, the motor industry's allied trades have been big sponsors of motorsport. However, as with engine manufacturers, promotion is not the only reason behind decisions to spend tens of millions of pounds on sponsoring Formula One or IndyCars. Factored into the equation is always the question of whether there are any technical spin-offs to be had. And in the case of tyre development in particular, the spin-offs for road tyres have been significant. Tyre technology is undervalued compared with engine and chassis design, and deserves more recognition that it gets. Motor manufacturers put huge resources into ensuring their cars are fitted with suitable tyres and the reason is simple: a good set of tyres will flatter the ride and handling of the average road car. Much of the research data that has contributed to this 'flattery' comes directly from competing in motor sport. Modern tyres are made of complex composites. Carbon fibres, Kevlar, glass, steel, nylon and cotton are among the materials bonded together by rubber. The way these materials are bound together can vary considerably, depending on the weather, the load and the conditions under which they have to perform. The rigours of Formula One and IndyCar racing have proved ideal testing grounds for the likes of Goodyear and Firestone. For example, a Formula One car is capable of 0–100mph in four seconds, and can brake to a standstill in under six, with the rubber reaching temperatures of 120°C.

About 80 per cent of tyre development takes place in the laboratory, most of the work being in computer stimulation. But the crucial last 20 per cent – to decide whether the product actually works – has to take place on a test track. Developing race tyres requires far more precision than production tyres, the latter being turned out in their tens of thousands by a highly automated process. Racing rubber involves more individual attention and analysis. Tyres used in racing are returned to the manufacturer for investigation, and the results passed to the passenger car tyre team. Goodyear's Eagle and Aqua road tyres are based directly on rain tread patterns used for racing. Features to have filtered down from racing to road tyres include low-profile sidewalls, wide treads and contoured treads, heat-resistant compounds and stronger fabrics. Lightweight tyres, which run cooler and last longer, are another development from racing. Since the 1970s tyres have lost 20 per cent of their weight and last on average 67 per cent longer.

For as long as there has been motor racing, there have been engineers trying to get more out of the rubber under their cars. In the early days of racing, appalling road surfaces, often made of melted tar and stone, took their toll on the wheels. Prior to 1906, mechanics would cut off the rubber with a knife, replacing it with a new inner tube and outer casing. However, at the 1906 grand prix in France, held at the historic racing town of Le Mans for the first time, Renault used a new system devised by Michelin. This was a detachable, fully inflated tyre which was bolted on by eight nuts. It cut substantially the time needed to change to a fresh set of tyres, and gave Renault a victory by 32 minutes. Renault's win was strongly contested, however. Objectors said the company had won because the tyre was a technological aid, and not because of the superiority of its driver and engine. It was one of the earliest rows over 'driver aids', a subject which periodically blows up around grand prix racing to this day.

The next major leaps in tyre technology did not come until after the Second World War. In the 1950s technology used in wartime aircraft tyres began to filter down into motorsport thanks to developments at Pirelli. During the 1960s tyres became wider. As the power of engines grew, larger tyres were the only way the wheels could maintain enough traction. Dunlop began investing heavily in special compounds, and made a big name for itself on the back of Formula One. Competition from Goodyear, which entered Formula One in the mid-1960s, inten-sified technological development. The biggest advance was the intro-

MOTORS AND RACING   241

duction of 'slicks', treadless tyres whose greater contact patch meant greater grip (except in the rain). Rubber technology became so important that racecars were being refined around tyres, as designers realised that factors such as aerodynamics and grip were just as vital as engine power. Along with improving technology, however, went higher research costs. First Dunlop pulled out, and then, in 1984, Michelin stunned Formula One when it to quit the sport. This left Goodyear and Pirelli to battle it out.

From 1992 to 1996, Goodyear was the sole supplier of tyres to Formula One teams. Having the field to itself was a mixed blessing, however. Goodyear could publicise its position as market leader in Formula One, but the media rarely bothered to cover the company because winning on Goodyear tyres was a formality. What interest the motoring press had in tyre compounds, constructions and tread patterns centred on other forms of motorsport. There was a feeling among the teams that Goodyear's monopoly had made it complacent. For Luca di Montezemolo, president of Ferrari, Goodyear needed to be shaken up because it had 'fallen asleep'. Even Goodyear admitted that more competition would not be a disadvantage. Racing against oneself was not good for competitive engineering. Michelin, the French tyre company, has long harboured ambitions to return to Formula One. But it was the Japanese tyre maker, Bridgestone, which ignited the competition.

Bridgestone, which owns the Firestone brand in America, began supplying tyres to the Arrows and Prost Formula One teams from 1997. It added a fresh dimension to grand prix racing, because tyre differences *do* matter. Tyres have rightly been called Formula One's secret weapon. The difference between qualifying on a good set of tyres and a worn set can be ten places on the starting grid. The battle between Goodyear and Bridgestone became an important sideshow to the main event. Bridgestone regarded its Formula One début in 1997 as something of a test season. Goodyear-shod cars were lapping more than a second faster than Bridgestone. But then, Goodyear was supplying the best teams. For Bridgestone, the big battle would come in 1998. Suddenly, the media were writing about a 'tyre war'. It was all good publicity, and fuelled the real battle between Goodyear and Bridgestone – the one for a larger slice of the world-wide market for tyres. With Bridgestone the No. 1 supplier in Asia and Goodyear No. 1 in North America (while Michelin was market leader in Europe), Formula One became part of a global strategy to extend their reach.

In response to the challenge from Bridgestone, Goodyear stepped up the service it was providing to the teams at each race. A group of Goodyear technicians was allocated to each team, where previously they would have worked with two, sometimes three teams. The reason is straightforward: with increased competition, response times and testing have become more critical. There is simply no time to service more than one team. As soon as the cars return to the pits, in a race of in qualifying, the tyres are immediately tested for temperature and wear, to discover which compounds work best. The data is transmitted straight back to Goodyear's headquarters at Akron, Ohio. Developments in Formula One tyre technology have been pushed to the limit – sometimes over it. Softer compounds mean more grip and faster lap times, but they degrade faster. Goodyear was taken to task because several tyres blistered under the intense heat of racing. Tyre manufacturers supply two types of tyre for each grand prix, and teams choose which to use in qualifying and the race. If, as happened with Goodyear, one set of tyres was too soft, the teams have no alternative but to use the harder compound. This happened to Michael Schumacher at the 1997 Belgian Grand Prix, and the German left the company is no doubt about his displeasure. Goodyear admits that in its quest to push back the boundaries, it my have made some mistakes. But, in its defence, the company points out that better balancing of the cars by the teams, and more care by the drivers, could have improved the situation.

Goodyear's racing manager, Cal Lint, acknowledges that competition from Bridgestone had an important galvanising effect on his race team, though it has also pushed up the costs of competing. 'We have reached the stage where small changes in tyre technology are expensive,' he said. 'We are getting 99 per cent out of a tyre, but getting that last one per cent can be very costly. When there is no competition, you do not tend to choose the most expensive route. Now there is competition, costs will be going up.' That said, Lint is in no doubt that the battle with Bridgestone has had a massive effect in raising the company's public profile, and in contributing to improvements in road tyres. 'It has not just meant more investment in technology. Competition improves turnaround times at the factory, it means more quality testing and more work on the computers to sort out what's good and what's not. It just raises the standard all round.' All positive stuff, as far as Goodyear was concerned. It came as a rude surprise, therefore, when Goodyear's chief executive, Sam Gibara, told Formula One teams late in 1997 that the 1998 season would be the company's last in Formula One.

Apart from a brief absence in 1980–1, when Goodyear grew tired of the political in-fighting that was damaging Formula One's reputation, the company has been a supplier for 33 years, making it the sport's longest-serving sponsor. Much was written about how Goodyear was stunned to see how really good the Bridgestone tyres were. Others said that Goodyear had baulked at the rising costs. True, Formula One is expensive. Period. When it had a monopoly, Goodyear supplied around 700 tyres to each grand prix weekend. Some teams got their rubber free. Others had to pay upwards of $650 per tyre. What has really annoyed Goodyear's bosses is the introduction of compulsory use of grooved tyres, a new regulation designed (but failing) to slow lap times. According to Goodyear: 'The things we learn from racing are passed down the line to road tyres. We are interested in developing tyres that advance technology to a higher level of performance in terms of grip and traction. We learn from being at the edge of technology. Getting us to supply tyres that are designed to slow racecars does not fit with out engineering programme.' Unless it could test on the edge, Goodyear could see no technological mileage in remaining a Formula One supplier. All that was left for Goodyear were the marketing possibilities, and the company had already exploited those for all they were worth. In the end, Gibara made a straight business decision: costs vs. publicity vs. technology transfer. He could see no benefit in continuing.

Before leaving this chapter, a few words about the companies that oil the wheels of Formula One. The petrol giants that supply Formula One with fuel and lubricants spend millions of pounds – around $15 million a year in the case of Texaco – on direct team sponsorship. But these companies, also, can lay claim to some small technological benefits from their involvement. Until 1957, racing cars ran on chemical fuels, not petrol. Although the oil companies sponsored Formula One, they could not claim any direct relevance between the fuels used in racecars and those at the petrol pump. The switch to more standard fuel immediately sparked more investment in sponsorship and research and development. British Petroleum became one of the biggest sponsors among the petrol companies. The company used to pay Rob Walker's Cooper team £10,000 a year, a sizeable sum in the late 1950s and early '60s. The team's driver, the legendary Stirling Moss, was paid by Shell, which saved Walker from paying him a salary. While the switch from chemical fuels generated more funds for the sport, it did give a sinister new twist to racing. Petrol was more inflammable, and the sight of a racing car exploding into a ball of flames after an accident became an all too familiar one at grand prix meetings. It is difficult to comprehend today, but questions of safety and medical facilities at circuits did not became a major issue until the late 1960s. And it took at least another decade for the racing authorities really to get to grips with the petrol hazard. The imposition of new design rules, the positioning of the petrol tank, developments in advanced materials, and the introduction of cut-off valves to stem leaks after an accident, have all helped to contain the problem.

The fuel used in racing cars today is strictly controlled by the FIA. For a start, the fuel must include compounds used in petrol for road cars, mixed in similar concentrations. FIA officials test each team's fuel before a race. Using sophisticated scientific equipment, they measure its precise colour and density. Then, throughout the race weekend, the FIA takes random samples which are matched with the original 'finger print'. Regulating fuel is one of the ways the FIA seeks to maintain a level playing field for the constructors. It means the scope to experiment with new fuels is limited. Research into lubricants is a different matter, and is where Formula One can be most valuable to the oil majors. In 1988, Shell, already a sponsor of McLaren, teamed up with Honda, the team's engine supplied. The McLaren link brought the two other companies together in a partnership that lasted several years. Honda engineers and Shell's lubricant scientists worked closely on developing low-viscosity oils to reduce the power losses that come from friction. The new formulae were tried and tested in the McLaren racing cars, and eventually found their way on to the market. The research was sparked by the FIA, which in 1988 imposed new regulations that started a quest for greater fuel economy. Thinner oil means lower friction, and therefore improved economy. The result was Shell's Helix lubricant brand, available world-wide. Shell now sponsors Ferrari in a deal that allows the race team's technical staff to work alongside the oil company's R&D department.

One of the oil industry's famous marketing campaigns was for Mobil 1, a synthetic oil derived from the company's racetrack research in the 1970s. Backed by a multi-million-pound advertising campaign, Mobil 1 was made number one at the forecourt. Today, Mobil is a technical sponsor of McLaren. Mobil takes a mini laboratory to each race to monitor the performance of its products. Samples are taken throughout the race weekend, and just a few minutes' analysis can detect possible problems with the engine's performance. The analysis is carried out by Mobil technicians, not McLaren's, and is all part of the sponsorship package agreed with the team. For Formula One, Mobil blends enough oil for about three races at a time. That way, if the batches are substandard, they can be discarded without huge cost. But also, as the oil is constantly refined, Mobil gets to test variations throughout the year. Admittedly, these processes could be carried out without the need to go through the rigours of Formula One – but racing provides an element of urgency that would otherwise be absent. As the company explained: 'Formula One provides extreme conditions under which to test our products. Our mobile test laboratory is there to help the teams, but also for us to translate findings back to people developing road car products. It is a process that never stops. We are always working on the next product idea. It might take up to 18 months to introduce a new product, from development to the high street. In Formula One, when we have to introduce a new oil, from development to the track, it takes about two weeks.'

Until about the 1970s, there was a clear relationship between motor racing and the motor manufacturers' R&D work, of which it was an extension. Renault, Mercedes, Ferrari and Fiat had dominated racing and dictated the pace of technological progress. Since the 1970s and '80s, the relationship has become more complex. For example, motor manufacturers took ignition technology from Formula One and used it in road cars. But that ignition technology, which might once have been developed by the manufacturers themselves, was developed by specialist engineers who were dependent on advances made outside motoring, in the electronics industry. Also, by the 1980s sponsorship had entered the equation in a big way. The practical economic exploitation of racecar technology no longer mattered when $50 million could buy unrivalled global television coverage. Marketing has become as important as technology transfer for engine manufacturers and allied trades. Probably more so. That said, this chapter has shown that there are still spin-offs to be had. The process may not be as simple as before, when manufacturers could 'lift' technology straight into their road cars. The breakthroughs today are more incremental, but they are there to been seen in electronics and composites. And, of course, more than ever the human dimension is playing a bigger role. A spell as a racecar engineer breeds a more skilled and knowledgeable production car technician.

Made in Britain

BRITAIN HAS BEEN the technical centre of excellence for world motorsport for some 30 years. Its future dominance cannot be guaranteed, but there are currently no signs of it being challenged. Depending on which study one chooses to believe, there are between 20,000 and 50,000 people working in motorsport in the UK. The combined business is worth anything between £1.3 billion and £2 billion. The roots of Britain's pre-eminence lay in the motor clubs of the 1950s and '60s, where racecar engineers such as John Cooper, Colin Chapman, Eric Broadley and the Cosworth two – Keith Duckworth and Mike Costin – cut their teeth. But there were also economic changes at work in the European motor industry that paved the way for the emergence of UK Formula One constructors. Out of these developments came the cottage industry of racecare specialists dubbed Grand Prix Valley, the hub of which is Silverstone racing circuit, one of several disused Second World War airfields which became home to burgeoning racing clubs and related business.

The importance of 'the Valley' may not always be appreciated by the politicians and the wider public, but it remains one of the few industrial sectors in which Britain reigns supreme. The engineers and the products that come out of Grand Prix Valley feed into a chain that spreads throughout the world. Jackie Stewart, former driver and now team owner, explained: 'If you are a top-line designer you come to the United Kingdom. If you want to build a racecar, you come to the United Kingdom. The skills and the technology fan out into the motor industry at large. If you go to Porsche or Mercedes-Benz, or to companies in France and the United States, you will find British-trained designers at work. Britain is the capital, the sharp end, but nobody outside motorsport seems to know this. We have not done a good job projecting the variety and vitality of motorsport engineering. I hope that will change as Formula One continues to grow.' Two examples that illustrate the skill and diversity of Britain's motor industry expertise: the vehicle that enabled Richard Noble to break the land speed record, *Thrust SSC*, was built by G-Force Precision Engineering, a West Sussex company better known in motorsport as a maker of racecars for America's IndyCar series; and at the opposite extreme: when German car maker Audi wanted to build exact replicas of its historic pre-war Auto Union V16 racing cars, it handed the job to British specialists Crosthwaite and Gardner.

Eight of the 12 teams that began the 1997 Formula One championship were based in the UK. And until 1997 even the blood-red Ferraris, a symbol of Italian identity, were designed and developed near Guildford, Surrey, and shipped to Maranello to have their engines fitted. The work has now been taken in-house, but the most prestigious team in racing still relies heavily on British expertise. Apart from some important motorsport suppliers in Italy – Bremebo for brake discs and callipers, Magnetti Marelli for electronics, and Dallara for IndyCar chassis – there is little competition to the UK firms. McLaren's Ron Dennis believes that Britain's self-sufficiency in motorsport engineering and technology – what the economists might call its 'critical mass' – means it would be many years before another country could threaten its dominance. 'With no time or financial pressures the Germans could probably mount a challenge,' Dennis said. 'But it would cost twice as much as it does in Britain.' Within two hours' drive, at the most, Formula One teams can get anything designed or built. Keeping up with Britain simply is not possible for most countries. It is a case of: if you can't bet them, join them.

'Made in Britain' runs through most racing cars like 'Brighton' through a stick of rock. The Ford engines that power Stewart Grand Prix are made by Cosworth. In July 1998, Ford bought the racing engines division of Cosworth, and the rest of the operation was sold to Volkswagen's Audi subsidiary. The engines in McLaren racecars carry the name of Mercedes, but are made by Ilmor Engineering. Judd Engine Developments manufacturers the Yamaha engines supplied to Arrows. Hewland engineering dominates the world market for racing gearboxes. Van Diemen is the largest manufacturer of racing car chassis in the world. Lola is one of several British companies pre-eminent in composites. If teams want engine data analysis they will probably go to Pi Research. And if they want cockpit safety harnesses, car jacks or electric tyre warmers, they also come to Britain. It is the same with other forms of motorsport. The Japanese cars Subaru Imprezas have dominated the World Rally Championship, but only after they were turned into race winners by Dave Richards' company Prodrive. Where does film star Paul Newman buy cars for his Haas team? – in Britain, as do all the teams involved in America's IndyCar racing. Penske, a name synonymous with the Indy 500, moved its operation from America to Dorset so it could keep up with technological developments in the UK. Reynard, the world's biggest racecar constructor, is a household name on the American racing scene, but is based on an industrial estate in Oxfordshire. Many of the specialist firms do not just serve racing, but transfer their technology into general products for the motor industry. AP Racing has a virtual monopoly on carbon clutches, and has supplied parts to every championship-winning Formula One constructor since 1968. Its parent company is one of the UK's large motor component suppliers.

This is a long list, but it only begins to scrape the surface of the breadth of expertise. There are hundreds of smaller specialist firms run by skilled craftsmen, turning out high-precision parts in small quantities. The motorsport sector has a high rate of business failures, but also a high rate of start-ups. Only in tyres does Britain not have a presence. The structure of the motorsport industry makes surviving outside Britain that much more difficult. Ferrari's team boss, Jean Todt, has often decried the lack of suitable engineers to be found in Italy. And for the Sauber Formula One team based in Switzerland, the problems are even greater. For a start, said team boss Peter Sauber, the costs are much higher. It is important, he believes, to have teams competing in Formula One that are not located in Britain. 'After all, this is a world championship, not a British championship. It is just that in Britain you have a large reservoir of people to choose from. In Switzerland, you have to teach them yourself.'

Trying to estimate the economic value of all this enterprise is not easy. It is even more difficult trying to narrow it down to just Formula One's contribution. The first problem is that the vast majority of the firms supply other forms of motorsport and specialist car companies. Secondly, a number of the companies double as contractors to the aerospace or defence industries. It is complicated because, although people refer to a 'UK motorsport industry', it is not actually an industry at all. Motor racing is really a market, supplied by a diverse collection of businesses which also supply several other markets. The engineering input that goes into producing a Formula One car is very different to that of a rally vehicle or kart, but they could well be supplied by the same companies. Or take McLaren's factory at Woking, more a microcosm of an aerospace factory than a car plant. The company has diversified so much that it is probably pointless trying to put a value on how much the Formula One operation injects into the local economy. TAG Electronics, part of McLaren International, supplies electronic components to several Formula One teams. But it also has a customer base of 60 other companies. Rather than put a value on the Formula One sector, all that one can really do is try to assess the size of UK motorsport interests in total. Even then it is important to remember that, as we are dealing with hundreds of businesses – sometimes one-man businesses – it is only possible to generalise.

The president of the FIA, Max Mosley, estimated that 5,000 people are directly employed in Formula One in the UK, but this number is based largely on anecdotal evidence. It is a figure that others who have studied the sector agree on, though they are quick to underline that they cannot be sure. In 1996 the Institute of Public Policy Research published the results of the first comprehensive attempt to assess the size of the motorsport sector as a whole. Total turnover was put at a maximum of £2 billion, with 44 per cent of output going for export. The IPPR identified 633 companies exploiting a link with racecar engineering, including the 12 major players at that time. These 12, whose accounting information is more readily available from Companies House, were estimated to have a turnover of £500 million (making an average turnover of £33 million). The remaining 621 companies were calculated to have a turnover of between £1 billion and £1.5 billion. (Of the 12, Ferrari has since taken its design in-house and Simtek and Pacific have folded. Stewart Grand Prix began competing in 1997.) The turnover of Reynard (£15 m) and Lola (£12m), both major motorsport companies, was included among the 621 firms. The IPPR put the number of employees working in motorsport engineering at between 25,000 and 30,000.

Another set of figures, this time from the Royal Automobile Club, put the total number of people working in motorsport in 1997 at 50,000, a figure which includes racing schools, circuit management, retail and publishing. According to the 1997 *Autosport Directory* there are more than 3,300 companies, clubs and other organisations involved in motor racing. A third study, published in 1998 by two academics, Nick Henry and Steven Pinch, estimated that the sector employed 30,000 and was worth £1.3 billion. Though small when compared with other sectors, the Valley should not be dismissed lightly, said the authors. They called it 'a superior model of industrial organisation, which holds important lessons for the rest of British industry ... Motor Sport Valley is a knowledge pool, a centre of world class excellence, which is on a constant learning trajectory. To be outside the Valley is to risk your position within the knowledge community.'

Whatever the figures, all agree that the number of people employed in motorsport, and its value to the economy, are growing. This is due mainly to the continuing growth of Formula One, though rallying is also big business in Britain. Since the IPPR report, Ford has boosted business at its long-time partner Cosworth through an engine deal with Stewart Grand Prix. Cosworth also makes Ford's IndyCar engines, where business is also growing. Mercedes has increased its workload to Ilmor Engineering; McLaren continues to expand its racing technology operations; and BMW has moved its touring car team from Germany to the UK. As BMW's chairman, Bernd Pischetsrider, explained at the time: 'The UK offers us the infrastructure, component suppliers, skills and flexible overtime we need to be successful in touring car sport.' It is also probable that car makers from Malaysia or South Korea will enter Formula One and seek a presence in the UK. Proton, the Malaysian manufacturer, bought Lotus in 1997 in order to get its hands on the company's engineering expertise.

British excellence in motorsport design and technology does not by itself explain he dominance. Grand Prix Valley grew out of Britain's aerospace and motor industries. But if these two industries were all that it took to build a motorsport industry, then America too would have developed a similar sector. Rather, Britain's success has much to do with the way its engineers and designers work, and the economic circumstances leading to the decline of the UK aerospace and motor industries. By the 1960s and 1970s many engineers found working within declining organisations frustrating. The result, believes Andrew Walmsley, managing director of Cosworth Engineering, was that many engineers just got fed up and left. 'They found the environment restrictive, but their skills found their way into specialist engineering and motorsport. This environment was more exciting, more stimulating.' Racecar engineering requires a totally different organisational set-up from that of larger companies. What motor racing needed was small, rapid-response companies – just the sort being set up by engineers energised after being set loose from the confines of larger companies.

Mass-production engineering is all about churning out the same products with minimal variation, whereas Formula One requires uniqueness and innovation. Take engine design, the closest Formula One comes to mass production, as an example. Although Britain has Ilmor and Cosworth, the latter producing the best Formula One engine of its day, it is Honda, Renault and Mercedes that have build the best engines of recent years. Britain's engine manufacturing is one of the few areas of Formula One technology where it has not kept its superiority. Perhaps the reason is that building an engine is a known quantity, where a lot of money and resources are needed. But in aerodynamics and chassis design, where British talent excelled, engineers need plenty of room for flair and innovation. Colin Chapman often said about his designs: 'I don't know why, but I think it will work.' His gut feeling about an idea was very often correct.

The success of UK Formula One constructors came because they put their emphasis on speed, efficiency and flexibility. In comparison, engine building requires long lead times and so was left to larger manufacturers. Bernie Ecclestone got it exactly right when he said that Formula One was a commando operation, not a battalion operation. 'We make decisions quickly and we can change direction easily. Management is in a single pair of hands.' In modern Formula One, the most successful teams have been the small, highly motivated units of the sort epitomised by Williams Grand Prix Engineering. Frank Williams explained: 'We have a flexible management structure. Patrick [Patrick head, technical director] can go down to the shop floor and get something done immediately. We work fast; change direction quickly. This situation is not unique to Formula One. But I think the attitudes and the way we work, is particularly true of the motorsport industry.' It is no coincidence that as McLaren grew, it lost its focus and ability to react quickly. In such an aggressively competitive environment as Formula One, it is difficult to maintain control unless you are 100 per cent committed. At McLaren, Ron Dennis's problem was that he perhaps tried to spread himself too thinly. In the last couple of years he refocused the team, bringing in other managers to share the load. Only then did Mclaren get back to its winning ways.

The quick-response demands of Formula One are as true for the suppliers as they are for the constructors. Take Active Sensors, a small company in the south of England set up by two brothers, Chris and Peter Smith, in 1994. The company makes sensors that Formula One technicians use to monitor a car's performance. Within two years of the company's formation they were supplying the majority of the teams. How did they grab the market so quickly? Chris Smith is in no doubt that it is because of the speed at which they could respond to an order. 'We can design a sensor, build it and get it to the customer before our multinational competitors have prepared a quotation,' he said. Formula One is often described as a form of warfare conducted every two weeks. The best companies will be the ones that strike first and hard – but they need the suppliers to provide the materials of war just as fast. One reason the 'grandee' teams on the Continent – Renault, Alfa Romeo, Ferrari – struggled to keep up with Formula One's élite was because their size made them too inflexible for modern Formula One. The Ferrari team is to this day desperately trying to overcome the rigidities and the politics of being part of a larger organisation. The manufacturers' teams were simply too inflexible, said Bob Tyrrell, commercial director of the legendary Tyrrell team. 'They were not in it to live, like we are.'

It is the nature of Formula One that its participants and suppliers are involved in performance-critical activities, using advances in technology to achieve fractional increases in lap times. The turnaround times for new innovations have to be extremely fast. One reason why motorsport engineers enjoy the job is that new ideas can be tried and tested within weeks, even days. In larger industries, new ideas can take many months to come to fruition. Consequently, a company like Williams Grand Prix Engineering or McLaren International will contain some of the best motor industry specialists around. Innovation is the life blood of many of these companies, but that means the average amount of money spent on research and development is high, at between 15 and 20 per cent of turnover. Frank Williams believes that a motorsport business must be constantly inventing and reinventing itself. 'We are always working on something new, something original. That is how we try and stay ahead.' Ideas and expertise spread quickly throughout motorsport engineering because of collaborative projects and job mobility. British Aerospace recognised this in 1997 when it signed a five-year-joint-venture agreement with Mclaren to work on aerodynamic and simulator projects. But what could a giant like BAe want from a company like McLaren? BAe's chief executive, Sir Dick Evans, said: 'They have ways of working that we can learn from.'

The intense rivalry between motorsport firms helps contain costs and raise engineering standards. In sectors that are regarded as 'niche' markets, competition is usually limited. Not so in motorsport, where competition is fierce. Every link in the supply chain is under enormous pressure to meet quality standards and improvements. The teams and engine manufacturers at the top of the production pyramid are ruthless with the firms that supply their components. After each Formula One race, the cars are stripped and the parts examined, and redesigned if necessary. If the racing teams are not happy with the quality of the component, finding an alternative supplier is not normally too difficult. Motorsport firms are always dividing, with staff leaving to establish their own operations, such as the two founders of Ilmor Engineering who left Cosworth to set up a rival engine company. It means there are always new companies emerging in competition and piling on the pressure to improve quality and performance. The fact that motor racing, for many engineers, is both a hobby and a business goes a long way to explain why there are so many owner-entrepreneurs involved in the motor industry. (Interestingly, according to the IPPR report on the motorsport sector, 55 per cent of respondents said 'home' was the location of their business.) A distinctive feature of the sector is the large number of collective and collaborative projects. This helps disseminate ideas and gossip, and leads to what has been called a 'community of knowledge'; it also makes it difficult for suppliers and teams to protect their know-how from leaking to other firms. It is one reason, perhaps, why Formula One can sometimes appear absurdly secret. If an innovation can remain secret for just a couple of months, it could earn a few championship points before the competition has the chance to catch up.

Compared with orthodox business economics it all sounds a little chaotic. In other industrial sectors, such a fragmented collection of operations would normally be prone to takeovers and rationalisation, but there is no sign of it happening in motorsport. It is possible that things like takeovers, diversification, or floating on the stock market, just seem like distractions to businessmen involved in something so aggressively competitive as motorsport. The dictator-style management needed to operate in motorsport means there is simply no time to take one's eye off the ball. The loss of a technological lead in such a competitive environment can be swift. In an era of what the economists call 'globalisation', it is rare to see such a high concentration of specialist firms, working efficiently and in harmony side by side. Italy has its cluster of knitwear and ceramics companies, and Germany its group of machine tool specialists in Baden-Württemberg. Another comparison is with California's Silicon Valley. Britain's

Formula One's owner-entrepreneurs started out as members of a racing club network; and 1970s California likewise had its grouping of computer associations that brought together whizzkids such as Microsoft's Bill Gates, Apple's Steve Jobs, and a selection of other software experts to swap information about their technical interests. Like the British engineers, these ambitious young computer visionaries had to be self-motivated and self-reliant. Neither group could rely on the finance of large corporations. They had to find cheap solutions to their own problems.

The claim that the Valley's future was endangered by a ban on tobacco sponsorship and Bernie Ecclestone's threat to take Formula One eastwards was dealt with earlier in this book. As we saw, the threat has been much overplayed. The motorsport industry is economically and culturally rooted in Britain, and will be difficult to dislodge. Even if Ecclestone carried out his threat to dispense with a number of European grands prix and stage them in Asia, there is no reason to think that subcontractors in the Valley would follow. Formula One plays only a part in the work of many of these firms, which serve other racing and engineering interests. However, since Grand Prix Valley has been compared to California's Silicon Valley, it is worth making one further point. Silicon Valley is starting to see the break-up of its network of specialists. For example, many software programming companies have moved out of California. And it is worth remembering that Britain's motorsport component sector emerged at the expense of the Italians and French. So, though changes in Formula One might not cause the demise of the Valley, it does not therefore mean that such networks of specialist firms will always be a feature of the industrial landscape. Britain's motorsport industry could be a showcase for the UK's skill base, but domestically its success has gone largely unrecognised outside racing. Perhaps, because it is a small sector compared with other industries, the Valley's importance is not given consideration. But, as this chapter has shown, the sector plays an important part at the bottom of the supply chain. Maybe the biggest threat to Grand Prix Valley is if it is taken for granted or, worse, ignored.

Chapter Eight: FAST MONEY

The Drivers

RACING DRIVERS ARE as much a part of the business as any other aspect of Formula One. Not that there was any reason – or likelihood – that commercialism should have left them untouched. Money has made Formula One drivers more remote from the fans who support them, but that has not dimmed public adulation. Team bosses regard winning the constructors' title as the pinnacle of Formula One. Not so the fans. Unlike some other forms of motorsport, it is the drivers who are the focus for national attention, not the racecar. It is the racing driver who wins at Monaco; but the sports car that wins at Le Mans. Hill versus Schumacher, Schumacher versus Villeneuve: these contests provide the human drama that helps explain the huge growth in interest in the sport. What goes into making a modern racing driver is as complex and money-orientated as any engine or chassis design. And the drivers can cost just as much. A team lower down Formula One's pecking order will have to survive a season on around $20 million. That is $5 million less than Michael Schumacher is paid by Ferrari, and that does not include his earnings from personal sponsorship and business interests. Driving ability and salary are no longer the only considerations for a team principal looking to fill a driving seat. Personality and nationality are now crucial elements of the package. Is the driver sponsor-friendly? Does he come across well on television? Does he fit in with the corporate strategy of the engine supplier? Will he be good for the team's commercial interests? Some drivers are paid a salary, some make their money out of performance bonuses, others actually pay the teams to let them drive. Excluding Schumacher, salaries have actually fallen in the late 1990s, though there is still enough money being made for drivers to afford a coterie of advisers. Many drivers could not function without a manager, a media adviser and a fitness trainer, along with a private jet and flat in Monaco. The top drivers are cocooned in a lifestyle designed to help relieve the stress of making decisions. 'I don't buy clothes,' quipped Ferrari driver Eddie Irvine a couple of years ago, 'I wear Cerruti.' Now that Ferrari has switched its official clothing supplier, Irvine has changed the cut of his suit to Tommy Hilfiger.

The driver with the fattest wallet is Michael Schumacher. When he joined Ferrari in 1996, aged 26, he became the highest paid driver of all time, on a three-year contract worth a total of $75 million. Schumacher: the best Formula One driver currently racing; Ferrari: the richest team. They were made for each other, thought Gianni Agnelli, head of Fiat, Ferrari's parent company. With a combination of Schumacher's talent and Ferrari's resources, the team was hoping for its first title since 1983. There was a lot at stake. Ferrari earns substantial sums from merchandising (the company estimated that if Schumacher had won the championship in 1997 it would have sold $50 million of merchandise) and a share of income from television broadcasting revenues. But racing is also Ferrari's publicity machine, as there is no advertising budget as such. Racetrack success enhances the appeal of the production cars, where investment in new models has poured in. Furthermore, Italian financial analysts believe Fiat has pencilled in a stock market flotation for Ferrari, using an eventual Formula One championship title (for it is seen as only a matter of time) as a marketing launch pad for the listing. With Schumacher's contract coming to an end in 1999, Ferrari hoped to have won the constructors' and drivers' titles by now. Arguably, Ferrari needs the German driver more than he needs them, so it is likely to dig deeper into its reserves in order to keep up the fight. The German newspaper *Bild* set the hares running when it reported that Agnelli had agreed to pay $80–90 million to keep Schumacher for another three years, and in addition had offered him a lifetime job as Ferrari's roving ambassador. The strategy was to stop Schumacher decamping to McLaren, whose German engine supplier, Mercedes, and German title sponsor, West cigarettes, would be delighted to get their countryman behind the wheel. The story rang true, even though Ferrari publicly denied it. Now that Formula One is big business, even Schumacher was regarded as a mere cog in the wheel of competing international enterprises.

Being the best at his job has turned Michael Schumacher into a rich man. *Forbes* magazine, which published an authoritative annual list of the world's wealthiest sportsmen, placed Schumacher fourth for 1997 with earnings of $35 million. On top of his $25 million annual salary, Schumacher made an estimated $10 million from endorsements. Not bad for a driver who last won the Formula One drivers' championship in 1995. Schumacher actually dropped one place in the *Forbes* listing from 1996. He is now behind Michael Jordan, the basketball player, whose earnings totalled $78.3 million, and boxers Evander Holyfield ($54.3 million) and Oscar de la Hoya ($38 million). Schumacher was one place above Mike Tyson, whose salary from boxing was put at $27 million (there were no endorsements – hardly surprising, given his prison record). Schumacher has endorsements from Omega watches, Nike sportswear and Dekra, a German vehicle pollution control company. And there is also the Schumacher Collection: more than 50 products bearing his name, including toy cars, jackets, a champagne brand, and *eau de toilette* fragrance 'for men who go to the limit every day'. What the *Forbes* figure does not include, however, is profits from Schumacher's private businesses and investments. He has a share of a karting club in Germany, and guest public appearances – at a fee between $75,000 and $100,000 a day – are also lucrative sources of additional income. Michael Schumacher is a one-man company, whose main turnover comes from racing cars.

Schumacher's business interests mean he is constantly on the move, even during the winter 'break'. Asked what he was going to do during one close season, he reeled off a list which included: a motor show visit, several sponsors' days, kart races, charity functions, a meeting with German politicians, and much else besides. Schumacher was told from the outset that if he was going to be *numero uno* in Formula One – and rich – fulfilling such commitments would be an essential part of the job. For, while Schumacher has got to the top because of his undeniable talent, another reason for his success is that he has been expertly managed by those looking after his affairs. His manager Willi Weber and, in the early days, Jochen Neerpasch, former head of Mercedes' sports division, have guided him around many of Formula One's pitfalls. Both men, steeped in motor racing unlike a number of other managers, knew what was required. Weber was careful not to push Schumacher into sponsorship agreements and driver contracts before he was ready. The manager said that he always knew Schumacher had the talent to make it to the top, so there was no need to rush into deals.

There have been plenty of brilliant drivers who never made it to the top. There is, after all, only room for one champion at a time, and the figures explain how tough it is. Only 15 drivers have won the world championship since 1970. Only six teams have won the constructors' title since that date. No wonder Ayrton Senna once called Formula One the sport of broken dreams. Not everyone gets the right drive at the right time. But Weber and Neerpasch ensured that Schumacher did. Michael Schumacher got his big break thanks to Mercedes. In 1989, along with two other drivers later to compete in Formula One, Heinz-Harald Frentzen and Karl Wendlinger, Schumacher was plucked from Formula Three by Neerpasch to drive for Mercedes in sports cars. In what was a closely guarded secret, Mercedes was planning a return to Formula One with its own team after a 35-year absence, and was grooming the three Germans in preparation. The drivers were given the best of everything – cars and crew. It was a unique scheme. But when Mercedes chief executive, Edzard Reuter, abandoned the plan to enter a team in Formula One, Schumacher's career might have slid off the track. Weber and Neerpasch found Schumacher a brief slot at Jordan in 1991, but he was then snatched away by Benetton.

Many drivers have blamed bad luck for not getting on in Formula One. Schumacher seemed to have been blessed with only good fortune. Compare him to Frentzen, for example, who struggled to get into Formula One after Mercedes changed its plans. Frentzen had driven in Formula 3000 for Eddie Jordan, but it was Schumacher who first got a break in Formula One – from Eddie Jordan. The drive was made possible because Jordan's Belgian driver, Bertrand Gachot, was imprisoned for assaulting a London taxi driver with CS gas after a traffic altercation at Hyde Park Corner. Another stroke of good fortune. Camel cigarettes had sponsored Frentzen in Formula 3000, but it was Schumacher that the tobacco company's money helped steer to Benetton. Even in his private life Schumacher gets the breaks. Frentzen's girlfriend of four years, Corinna, switched to Schumacher, and they were married. The careers of several drivers have stalled because of crashes, but Schumacher's has luckily been free of serious accidents. State of mind is very important in Formula One, and when you are used to winning at everything, your confidence soars. Success breeds success, as the saying goes. This is why sponsors are willing to pay large sums of money to be associated with Schumacher, and why fans try to identify with him by buying his, and Ferrari's, merchandise.

Can this adulation and expense be justified by the results? Ferrari, as one would expect, does not doubt that it is getting a good deal. If Schumacher is a couple of seconds faster than the next driver, that adds up to 30 seconds over a season. How many millions of pounds would it cost to engineer that sort of performance into the engine and chassis? Many, perhaps tens, of millions. But it runs deeper than the fact that Schumacher is the fastest driver. It is what he, as an individual, does for the team that makes him so valuable. Schumacher is credited by those around him with an ability to motivate his engineers and mechanics. While some drivers need to be lifted and comforted by the team, Schumacher does not. Another example of his supreme confidence. Engineers who have worked with Schumacher testify to his ability to impart crucial information about how a car is working. Building a racecar is now more of a science than ever. So, drivers like Schumacher (or Alain Prost and Ayrton Senna), who can relay factual details about the car's performance can give a team the edge.

The awe in which Schumacher is held made it all the more sensational, therefore, that he was involved in what became known as 'the Villeneuve Incident'. The script went like this: it was the last race of the 1997 season, one of the most finely balanced of the decade. All Jacques Villeneuve had to do to win the championship was stay ahead of Schumacher. On lap 48, Villeneuve made a dramatic overtaking move on the inside right. Schumacher twitched his steering wheel to the right – as seen on the in-car camera – and the Ferrari's front wheel rammed into Villeneuve's car. There was a sting in the tale. It was Schumacher who spun off, but Villeneuve went on to finish third and win the title. Schumacher described the collision as an unfortunate and instinctive reaction. Opinion, though, tended to agree with Damon Hill when he said that a drivers' instinct is normally to turn away from danger. That Hill had suffered a similarly crucial accident at the hands of Schumacher in 1995 made the public's condemnation all the louder. If observers gave Schumacher the benefit of the doubt on that first occasion, they certainly did not on the second. For many Formula One commentators a suspension and a large fine seemed the only possible punishment. After all, bans and suspensions are common practice in nearly every major sport. Yet, what followed simply served to illustrate how important Schumacher was to Formula One.

The problem facing the FIA's World Motor Sports Council was: how does it reprimand the sport's single most important competitor without damaging the sport itself? Jackie Stewart spoke for many when he said before the council meeting: 'Michael Schumacher in my mind is the best and most talented driver in the world. But if he is seen to behave in a manner that may not be correct, then a lot of the other drivers in all the other formulae are seeing an example which they believe they can follow. I think that's very dangerous for our sport.' The council ruled that Schumacher's second place in the 1997 championship should be taken away from him (and that he take part in a road safety campaign). Hardly much of a sanction for a man for whom winning is all that matters. It was evident from the media backlash that they felt business had got in the way of sporting principles. The banker Nicky Samengo-Turner, who advises the motorsport industry, believes that the financial consequences of a ban would have reverberated around the sport. 'Formula One was desperately trying to keep its nose clean. With the flotation coming up, with Ecclestone's concern about image and the eyes of the financial community on Formula One, I think everyone could have done without this. But can you seriously deprive Formula One of its top driver? Millions upon millions of pounds have been put into Ferrari because of this man. You cannot just take Schumacher away.'

Michael Schumacher's significance to the business of Formula One is illustrated by the actions of two Ferrari sponsors. When Schumacher signed his Ferrari deal, the size of the salary drew gasps from several quarters. AGIP, the Italian state-owned oil company and a sponsor of Ferrari, was one of them. AGIP's Umberto Esposito described the price inflation of Formula One sponsorship as 'crazy'. He said: 'We are not willing to go down that road. When one reads about the size of Schumacher's salary one has to ask whether it makes sense.' The company's deal with Ferrari was not renewed. But there is never a shortage of sponsors where Michael Schumacher is concerned. AGIP's place was taken by Shell, the Anglo-Dutch oil group, whose money helped pay a large, but undisclosed, chunk of the driver's $25 million salary. Part of Shell's calculation was the power of Schumacher's popularity to improve its profile in Europe, but specifically in Germany. Shell's image in Germany, Europe's biggest car market, has been left in tatters after a high-profile environmental campaign against the company. Germany had been the centre of a Europe-wide protest against Shell's plan to sink the Brent Spar North Sea oil storage installation in the Atlantic Ocean. 'Green' campaigners wanted Shell to dismantle the platform onshore. It did not matter that Greenpeace eventually conceded that sinking the installation was, after all, the most environmentally friendly solution. It was too late. Shell's reputation was damaged, and the company needed a high-profile promotional drive that would accentuate the positive.

Jacques Villeneuve, the former IndyCar racer and 1997 Formula One champion, is another driver whose financial future is being carefully crafted. Like Schumacher before him, Villeneuve has been held back from major sponsorships, in readiness for the right deal (whenever that might be), though it is worth noting that his team, Williams, allows only limited personal sponsorships. With his youth, looks, talent, and fame in America, Villeneuve has the potential to earn big money from endorsements. Add to this the fact that he is the son of the famous Gilles Villeneuve, and Jacques appears to be a brilliant marketing opportunity just waiting to be exploited. But the driver's manager, Craig Pollock, has been biding his time, letting Villeneuve build up some credit before the big deals come rolling in. These may well come in 1999. Pollock, the BAT tobacco company, and racecar builder Reynard are partners in a new Formula One team, and it is likely that Villeneuve will join them as driver. Such a move was being played down by the Villeneuve camp, which is only natural given that he drives for another team with different tobacco sponsorship. All the signs point to a move, however, especially as Players Limited, a division of BAT, was the main sponsor of Team Green, Villeneuve's IndyCar team.

Craig Pollock, Villeneuve's former sports instructor at his boarding school, did not commit the driver to any long-term personal sponsorships while racing in America, so as not to inhibit a switch to Formula One. This move has given Villeneuve an international profile that he would not have got had he remained in America. While in Formula One, Villeneuve has been building a reputation for being a maverick. He is the only senior driver who is not a member of the Grand Prix Drivers' Association, believing that the group's acceptance of recent FIA rule changes is wrong. Villeneuve is always talking about driving on 'the edge'; he says he is not scared of dying. Whether his image is contrived or natural, Villeneuve is now Formula One's bad boy, and some sponsors will pay good money to use this persona as a marketing tool. Nike, for example, will trade off sportsmens' rebel image, though they had already signed up Michael Schumacher, another driver who sails close to the wind. A lack of personal sponsorships has not hindered Villeneuve's earnings too much. He arrived in Europe already a millionaire from his American racing. Villeneuve's 1996 salary from Williams was reported to be $5 million, rising to $6 million in 1997. His earnings from merchandising and appearances were thought to be no more than $1 million, though his value will have shot up considerably after winning the world championship. The size of Villeneuve's salary from Williams in 1998 is also unclear. However, it has been suggested that Villeneuve was paid an additional $5 million. Under his contract, the money was due if Williams changed its engine supplier. Renault left Formula One at the end of 1997, but Williams then began buying the same engines from Mecachrome, a long-time partner of the French car manufacturer. The issue Villeneuve's camp and Williams had to resolve was whether this constituted a change in supplier.

Born in April 1971, Jacques Villeneuve was 11 years old when his father Gilles Villeneuve, the brilliant Formula One driver, was killed during practice for the 1982 Belgian Grand Prix. Villeneuve junior was born in Canada, schooled in Switzerland, and toured with his father – so he was constantly on the move. He raced in Formula Three in Italy and Japan, and when the Formula One establishment would not take his abilities seriously, began racing in North American Formula Atlantic. In 1995, aged just 24, Villeneuve became the youngest winner of the Indy 500, and went on to take the CART series championship. Villeneuve came to Formula One with the Bernie Ecclestone seal of approval. Ecclestone was keen to get this new act into his circus, hoping – correctly, as it turned out – that Villeneuve would help raise Formula One's profile in North America and Canada. Exactly how influential a role Ecclestone played in Villeneuve's decision to go Williams remains a secret known to just a few people. But go he did, enlivening Formula One the way he had Indy racing. Runner-up in his first season, 1996, Villeneuve took the Formula One world driver's title a year later.

However, by the middle of that award-winning 1997 season, it had started to look as if things were going wrong for Villeneuve. Trailing in the championship, and censured by the FIA for criticisms he made about rule changes, he appeared to be sliding off the track, literally and metaphorically. At the time, it was difficult to grasp why. But on reflection, part of the problem may have been that business was getting in the way of his sport. There were tensions in the Williams team over pay negotiations, and the speculation over his joining the BAT-Reynard-Pollock deal must have been a distraction. Also, sentiment was starting to turn against Formula One's golden boy. There was a feeling that Villeneuve had become too precious, too self-important. It was not any one incident in particular, just an accumulation of small issues: his refusal to co-operate – and attempts to stop others co-operating – with the author of an unauthorised biography; the signing of an exclusive photographic contract with a picture agency; and stories about his refusing to sign autographs in case they were sold for commercial gain. Maybe it was the advisers looking after Villeneuve's financial interests, rather than the driver himself, who were to blame. Either way, for those people looking to blame Formula One's ills on commercialism, it was more ammunition.

It was after the Formula One drivers' world championship was established in 1950 that grand prix racers became more widely known outside the world of motorsport. Stirling Moss, Juan Manuel Fangio and Mike Hawthorn were among the leading drivers who were paid retainers by the motor manufacturers, and oil and tyre companies. They received a small amount of appearance money, and occasionally funding from wealthy enthusiasts like Tony Vandervell, who ran the successful 1950s British team, Vanwall. At this time, though, there was probably more money to be made in sports car racing with Aston Martin or Jaguar than Formula One. The financial circumstances of drivers changed thanks to television and sponsorship, and the gradual reorganisation of Formula One. Even so, when more money started flowing into Formula One, the drivers were still the last to benefit, after the team bosses and circuit owners.

It was Jackie Stewart, three-times world champion, who pioneered the era of the businessman-driver. He helped make Formula One fashionable, and became the role model for a rising generation of stars in all racing formulae. By the time Stewart retired in 1973, he was commanding a salary of around £200,000, and was worth £5 million, it was reported at the time. Stewart took the view that if the wind of commercialism was blowing through the sport, the men who risked their lives every race should benefit from it. A watershed in drivers' perception of their job was the death of Jim Clark, at Hockenheim in 1968. Chris Amon, then driving for Ferrari, later spoke of how he felt on hearing of Clark's death. 'If it could happen to him, what chance did the rest of us have? I think we all felt that. It seemed like we'd lost our leader.' Stewart took over Clark's mantle as the public face of Formula One, but he brought with him a completely different attitude to his role as leader of the pack. Guy Edwards remembers: 'Clark was not really interested in the business side of the sport. Stewart, though, was a different animal. If Jim Clark hid his light under a bushel, Jackie made sure that he was centre stage, and maximised his earning potential with the same professionalism he applied to his driving.' In 1969 Jackie Stewart signed up Mark McCormack's International Management

Group to look after his interests, a radical move for a racing driver. Stewart's affairs were promoted and protected by Martin Sorrell, who went on to become the multimillionaire head of the world-wide advertising group WPP. Stewart was not completely motivated by money. He mounted a successful, and at the time controversial, campaign to improve safety. Stewart's demands for better conditions were viewed by sections of Formula One as, to put it bluntly, somewhat wimpish. But a crash, leaving him upside down and drenched in petrol among picnic debris at the trackside, convinced Stewart that something had to be done. When racetrack owners dragged their feet over his calls to provide circuit ambulances, Stewart employed his own doctor. In the end, though, Stewart and other drivers brought about long-overdue changes to the lives and conditions of racing drivers. Today's racers can be grateful to Stewart for improving their pay, and they can also thank him for helping them to live long enough to spend it.

Now, a game of idle speculation: how much better a driver is Michael Schumacher than the great 1950s hero Juan-Manuel Fangio? Is he 640 times better? Or, take Stirling Moss, said to be the best driver never to have won the world championships: is Schumacher 485 times better? This is assuming that Schumacher *is* better. It is impossible to know, of course. Yet, if you compare their salaries, this is how Schumacher is valued in relation to his Formula One forerunners. In the mid-1950s, the *maestro* Fangio earned about £25,000 ($37,500). Moss, in 1961, was Formula One's highest-paid driver, earning £33,000 ($49,500). Moss's salary is worth about £180,000 in 1998. Although Schumacher's £16 million-a-year basic salary is an exception, it brings into the sharp focus the rise in earnings over the past 40 years. Formula One drivers, like people generally, prefer to keep their finances to themselves. Even so, the motorsport press corps can usually be relied upon to find out somehow. Most senior drivers average a basic retainer of $4–6 million. Eddie Irvine at Ferrari was on about $5 million for 1997, but the team agreed to take up its option on him for 1998 at a reduced rate, thought to be $3 million. Heinz-Harald Frentzen at Williams is paid about $6 million. And Damon Hill was thought to have received $6.3 million for his 1997 drive at Arrows, down from the $7.5 million he got a year earlier at Williams. It was estimated that in 1997, the year after Hill won the world championship, he earned between $2.25 million and $3.25 million from endorsements (notably Adidas, and television adverts for the Pizza Hut food chain) and other activities. He was allowed space on overalls and helmets for personal sponsorship. Hill tries to keep personal appearances to a minimum, as he finds them time-consuming and prefers to spend as much time as possible with his family at their large home on the outskirts of Dublin. At the other end of the scale (excluding pay-drivers, for the moment) are new drivers like Jan Magnussen, who joined Stewart Grand Prix in 1997, and was paid about £500,000.

Salaries in Formula One have steadily fallen since the beginning of the 1990s. The top of the driver salary market was the late 1980s and early 1990s, when Nelson Piquet, Ayrton Senna, Alain Prost and Nigel Mansell could command around $12 million for their services (Formula One folklore has it that Senna was paid a $23 million retainer by McLaren). With the exception of Michael Schumacher, the pendulum has swung back in favour of the teams, and it is now a buyers' market. There are more good drivers than seats available. One reason is the cut in the number of teams racing in Formula One. In 1989 there were 20 teams, and in 1998 there were 11. Pay-drivers, some of whom race because of the money they bring rather than on merit, further reduce the number of seats available. Team bosses, Frank Williams for example, have dug their heels in over pay, while at the same time a number of talented new drivers, prepared to race for less, have emerged on to the scene. This was brought home to Benetton in 1997, as its financial situation worsened. Why pay 20 per cent of the team's budget – about $12 million – to Jean Alesi or Gerhard Berger, when it could get rising stars Giancarlo Fisichella and Alexander Wurz for around $4 million between them?

Despite the fall in salaries, the star status of Formula One drivers means there is now more money to be made from endorsements and private sponsorship. However, not all constructors are keen on too much personal sponsorship, which can distract from a driver's commitment to the team and clash with its own commercial interests. Ron Dennis, at McLaren, believes in 100 per cent commitment to the team. This sounds like typical management-speak, but in Formula One there is clear logic behind such a glib phrase, for there is no room for distractions. McLaren spends millions of pounds trying to shave fractions off lap times. Yet, as Dennis said, 'A fit and focused driver could achieve that for nothing.' Some drivers, too, are less inclined to go for the money. Former driver and now television commentator Martin Brundle regarded the endless cycle of securing private deals, and the demands it made on his time, as not worth the hassle. Brundle thinks a driver can worry too much about his bank balance and not enough about the car he is driving. It is a danger Michael Schumacher should be aware of, he believes.

There is another group of drivers concerned to strike lucrative sponsorships, though for different reasons. Few new drivers get a start in Formula One without having money from personal sponsors to offer the constructors. Every team owner wants the best drivers, but not all can afford them. If the team cannot find sufficient corporate sponsorship, then often the only way the owner will be able to field a team is by taking drivers who offer to pay for their seat. Pay-drivers – so-called rent-a-drivers – are a much ridiculed breed because all too often they bring with them a big cheque but little talent. While it is easy to be dismissive of pay-drivers, though it is worth remembering that even the best got their breaks thanks to backing from someone else. Michael Schumacher was placed in Formula One by Mercedes-Benz and a £250,000 purse. Niki Lauda bought himself into Formula Two, then Formula One, through a bank loan. Marlboro and Elf have been behind many of the best Formula One drivers, including René Arnoux, Alain Prost and Michele Alboreto. These drivers were placed in teams well down the grid and then nurtured up through the ranks as they gained in experience. Even before the rise of serious commercial sponsorship, drivers relied on benefactors. Guy Edwards, a former Formula One driver, who won a Queens Gallantry Medal for helping to pull Niki Lauda from his burning car in 1976, recalls that drivers have always had to tout themselves around. 'The old sources of money were the only sources, and if you wanted a drive in England you'd better spend some time at the Steering Wheel Club in London making yourself busy with wealthy private entrants and team owners.'

Rubens Barrichello, who took about $6.5 million to Stewart Grand Prix in 1997, has proved particularly adept at getting personal sponsorship. For such drivers, however, planning and targeting the sponsors, and then meeting their demands, can be very time-consuming. It is something of a myth that, when not racing, drivers are living an exotic lifestyle of sun, sea and sex. They are very often sorting out sponsorship deals, especially during the winter break. Barrichello raised more than £4 million from drinks Pepsi and Corona, and from Davene cosmetics. The companies trade off Barrichello's fame in his home country, Brazil, and he must return home regularly to make personal appearances for his sponsors. Even minor drivers can attract huge sums in personal sponsorship. Ukyo Katayama, largely unknown in Europe and South America, was a celebrity in his home country, Japan. He was sponsored by Mild Seven, a cigarette brand owned by Japan Tobacco, which reputedly backed his drives for Minardi with $7 million a year. In return, Minardi paid Katayama's salary of around £450,000. Without the money, Minardi would have struggled to compete.

Team owner Tom Walkinshaw's solution to the conundrum of balancing costs and benefits was to bring the biggest pay-driver of all time to Arrows. Pedro Diniz, another Brazilian driver, was contributing up to $12 million a year for his drives. Diniz's arrival at Arrows in 1997 helped pay for development of the team's ill-starred cars, and offset the $6.3 million salary paid to fellow team driver Damon Hill. Diniz's very wealthy father is the owner of a successful Brazilian supermarket chain, Pao de Acucar, whose shops sell vast quantities of dairy products supplied by the Italian food group, Parmalat. The Italian company contributes a large chunk of Diniz's sponsorship money, and in effect, manages Diniz's career, negotiating with the team and looking after his interests. Parmalat could just as well take sponsorship on the side of a racecar, except that by reaching its audience via the 'personal' route the company feels it has more control over its marketing strategy. Life as a pay-driver can be tough. Diniz is the butt of jokes about his playboy image and is criticised about his abilities as a driver. He may yet prove the cynics wrong, however. After all, having kept pace with teammate Damon Hill for much of the 1997 season, Diniz could be more than just a fat cheque. The problem is that, once a driver gets a reputation for being a 'money-bags', the first question any team will ask him will always be: how much can you offer us?

Pay-driving is a sensitive issue in Formula One. In no other major sport does someone buy the right to compete at the highest level. It means that the two dozen or so drivers competing in each race are not necessarily the best in the world. Drivers with questionable talent, such as Giovanni Lavaggi and Taki Inoue, take the seats that could be given to genuine young talent. All Formula One drivers have to qualify for the FIA's Superlicence, which is supposed to maintain standards. But the gulf between the talent at the top of the grid and at the back suggests that there are loopholes in the Superlicence procedure. Many people in Formula One would like to see the practice of rent-a-drivers stopped, if only for safety reasons. However, the balance between cash and competition is weighted in favour of cash. Pay-drivers are now a firmly established part of business of Formula One, and are here for the foreseeable future.

The annual round of musical chairs involving drivers looking for seats is always one of Formula One's intriguing events. The months of August and September usually see half a dozen senior racers jostling for a big seat and a fat salary. The paddock is awash with rumour and speculation: who's in, who's out; is there a future superstar coming up from the lower formulae? has anyone been tempted from IndyCars? was that story in the media a plant in order to raise a smokescreen? Jackie Stewart may have been the first 'professional' driver, but today's machinations make his negotiations look quaint. A handshake was enough to secure a deal with team owner Ken Tyrrell; there was no need for a contract. Now, drivers and their managers will play the field looking for the best deal, after which the terms of any agreement will be recorded in minute detail in a contract. Eddie Jordan believes driver choice makes up only a quarter of the package needed to compete, along with engine, chassis, and tyre choice. But recruitment is enormously complicated nevertheless. Sponsors and engine suppliers now have a far bigger say in finding the right driver. At the Prost team, the nearest modern Formula One comes to a national entrant, having at least one French driver is obligatory – the constructor's French sponsors include Peugeot, Canal Plus, Alcatel, Gauloises and Total. Finally, to complicate the process of driver recruitment even further, there is Bernie Ecclestone: mediating, power-broking, and with an eye on the big picture to ensure that the interest of Formula One – and his interests – are protected.

Eddie Jordan knows all about the problems of trying to find the right driver. Jordan always had an eye for talent. In Formula Three and Formula 3000, he gave drives to Jean Alesi, Johnny Herbert and Martin Brundle. In 1991, the year Jordan's team moved up into Formula One, he thought he had secured the services of a graduate from the lower divisions, a driver called Michael Schumacher. It took one race for the rest of the paddock to realise that Jordan had a future star on his hands. Schumacher was taken from under Jordan's nose by Benetton chief Flavio Briatore in acrimonious circumstances. Six years later Jordan and Briatore were to cross swords again over another driver, Giancarlo Fisichella. Trading in racing drivers can be a profitable business for teams. Fisichella, under a ten-year agreement with Benetton (the subject of a separate dispute because Fisichella regarded it as unfairly restrictive), was on loan to Jordan Grand Prix for 1997 and 1998, or so Eddie Jordan thought. After Fisichella distinguished himself in the 1997 season, Briatore wanted him back for 1998, claiming he had a right to buy back the driver before a certain date. As is so often the case with such disputes, this one turned on the fine print of the contract. A High Court in London ruled in favour of Briatore. Jordan, though, got £1.25 million compensation for the loss. Such issues just complicate the already difficult job of driver-hunting. 'You have got to choose two drivers,' explained Eddie Jordan. 'Do you want a quick driver or an experienced one? Do you have the budget to pay for two drivers, or someone who brings money with them? You have to ask yourself whether this year you are going to put more money into development rather into the drivers, or vice versa. And you never really know if you have made the right choice until the driver actually gets out there and competes. The balance has to be right, but you never know whether you've made the right choice until they are on board. And it all depends who is available on the market in the first place.'

Damon Hill, world drivers' champion for Williams in 1996, ended up at Jordan Grand Prix in 1998 after a disappointing year with Arrows in between. At the end of the 1997 season, Hill was on the market along with four other established drivers, Gerhard Berger, Jean Alesi, David Coultard and Mika Hakkinen. The best seats on offer were to be found at McLaren, Benetton, Jordan and Prost. So, how does this game of three-dimensional chess work? That season, McLaren's Ron Dennis held all the aces. Clearly the best team of those with seats available, McLaren was also being tipped as the team to beat in 1998. It meant that Dennis would always have the upper hand in any negotiations. Coultard and Hakkinen both wanted to stay at McLaren, but Mercedes, the team's engine supplier, was understood to have wanted to find a seat for Hill simply on the basis that a former world champion has a higher profile. McLaren's Ron Dennis and Hill discussed a deal involving a fixed-fee plus a performance bonus: about $2 million a year and $1 million per win to a maximum of four. It remains unclear how much money Hill was looking for, but the deal was never agreed. In 1996, in return for staying at Williams for the 1997 season, it was widely reported that Hill wanted up to $13 million, almost double what he was getting. Hill was effectively sacked by Williams in 1996. Although the rumours had been around for weeks, Hill said he was not officially notified until the end of August, by which time a number of the best driving seats were taken. He took a drive at Arrows for 1997, on a salary of around $6.3 million. (When Hill joined Williams as a test driver in 1991 he earned around $30,000. His salary went up to about $150,000 for his first season as a racer, rising to about $1.5 million in 1995.)

A year later Hill again looked as though he had misread the market.

He turned down McLaren's offer because it 'did not accord with what I had been led to believe from our prior negotiations, and as I did not consider that it demonstrated a serious commitment to me as a driver from McLaren-Mercedes.' McLaren's view is slightly different – that there were no negotiations, only a straight take-it-or-leave-it offer. (Ron Dennis is not a man to go in for protracted negotiations. He once tossed a coin to settle a $1 million difference in pay negotiations with Ayrton Senna. Dennis lost.) Also, Dennis wanted to keep something in reserve in case Michael Schumacher came back on to the market at the end of 1998. He would love to have the German in his team, as would Mercedes and West. They could certainly afford it. Hill also discussed a two-year deal with Sauber worth $20 million in total, but the offer was withdrawn because the driver wanted too long to consider it. The former world champion, however, was going to stick it out until he got what he felt he was worth. Hill told Britain's *Independent* newspaper: '[Formula One] is a huge sport, with a huge audience, and it is all about money ... Nobody would be offering me money if I was not good. Sponsors want to be associated with Michael Schumacher and Damon Hill.'

By the beginning of September 1997, Hill's choice of team lay between Jordan, Prost and Arrows. He had come near to signing for Jordan the previous year, but was dissuaded by differences over the length of the contract (Hill wanted to be tied in for only one year) and doubts about how the team might perform. More crucially, Jordan could not pay the sort of salary Hill was asking. Twelve months on, however, Jordan was in a different position. It had signed a new Mugen-Honda engine deal, and Benson & Hedges had committed itself to further sponsorship. Honda may have preferred departing Benetton driver Jean Alesi, because he has a Japanese wife, which would have helped with promotional activities in Japan. However, Honda was not supplying the engines free, so its bargaining power was reduced. B&H were keen to get a high-profile British driver to the team. It is also possible that Bernie Ecclestone played a role. Formula One television audiences in the UK fell in 1997, which was blamed by ITV on the fact that interest in Damon Hill had waned because he was in a poorly performing team, Arrows. Ecclestone would have been far happier to have the former world champion driving in a competitive car. Ecclestone had said that he would 'do what he could' to help Damon Hill find a drive, but emphasised that he only had influence, not control. To him, probably, McLaren would have been ideal, but Ecclestone's leverage over Ron

Dennis at McLaren would not have been strong because the two were in dispute over the Concorde Agreement.

Negotiations with Jordan, Prost and Arrows continued in parallel until Damon Hill signed for Eddie Jordan on 16 September. It seems likely that Benson & Hedges put up the extra money to tempt Hill to join the team, though the cigarette company's British parent, Gallahers, does not publicly discuss the terms. However, *Autosport*, the authoritative UK racing magazine, reported that Hill was being paid £5 million for a one-year contract, with an option for a second year. News of the deal did not go down at all well at Prost, because team principle Alain Prost thought he had secured Hill's services. Prost said he felt let down, that he had regarded Hill as a friend. 'I now view him in a different light,' said the Frenchman, who was left to sign up the relative newcomer Jarno Trulli to drive alongside Olivier Panis.

As the life of a professional racing driver becomes more complex, so they find more need for a clique of advisers to do the negotiating, guide them around the pitfalls, and get them the best deal. There are legal associates, PR managers and sports agencies. But the most important advisers in modern Formula One are the managers, and their power rises commensurately with the importance of their driver. The king of them all, therefore, is Willi Weber, a former hotelier and Formula Three team owner who has managed Michael Schumacher since the driver's days in minor German club racing, and who now also handles his brother Ralf. Weber charges a reputed 20 per cent to look after Michael Schumacher. Given that Weber's current contract with the driver has run from 1989 (and ends in 1999), there seems little doubt that Schumacher has helped turn him into a millionaire several times over. Weber has wet-nursed Schumacher through his career, even to the extent of sorting out his dietary requirements and moulding him for television appearances. The manager has built his reputation and wealth by devoting all his time to his clients. Weber sees his role as simple: to take the pressure off Schumacher's shoulders so that he can focus on driving. That means taking total control of the driver's affairs. Weber is a big wheel in the Formula One paddock, and makes it his duty to know all the important people. He once explained his role to *Car* magazine: 'I am the eyes and ears for Michael and Ralf. I have to know everything that's going on – and that means being trusted, listening and learning every day, everywhere.'

There are three types of manager. First there are men like Weber and former driver Keke Rosberg, who handles Mika Hakkinen. These two have racing in their blood. The second group includes Michael Breen, Damon Hill's manager and a lawyer, and Craig Pollock. These managers are on the inside, but still regarded as outsiders by the establishment because they have not grown up with motor racing. The third group are those managers who come touting young drivers with big cheques from personal sponsors. Managers are not necessarily popular with everyone in the pit-lane. Frank Williams dislikes dealing with them, preferring to negotiate directly with drivers. It has been said of Frank Williams that if a driver asks for a $4 million salary, he will give him $5 million. But if the manager asks for $4 million on the driver's behalf, Williams' counter-offer will be $3 million. Williams once banned International Management Group's Tim Wright, who used to handle David Coultard, from his garage. There had been a bitter row over why Coultard's car had crashed during a race, and subsequent leaks to the media.

At the turn of the decade, Alain Prost and Ayrton Senna used to look after their own negotiations, as did Gerhard Berger in more recent years. They used lawyers to draw up the paperwork, but drivers could save themselves 15 per cent or more in fees by negotiating themselves. The reason more drivers do not handle their own deals now is that contracts have of necessity become far more complex. The advice these days is to get everything detailed in the contract: from how much of the overalls may be used for personal sponsorship, to whether a scooter will be made available for use at the racetrack; from the number of pit-passes for the family, to guarantees that the driver will be allowed full testing facilities.[1] When Jackie Stewart first drove for Ken Tyrrell, he never had a contract. A handshake was sufficient. When Stirling Moss used to race for Rob Walker they had a verbal agreement to share the starting and prize money. Moss got 60 per cent and Walker 40 per cent. Once again, the rise in commercial sponsorship is largely to 'blame', though Stewart can perfectly well understand why. With so much money at stake, he says, no one wants to leave anything to trust or chance. The terms of contracts will vary enormously. At Jordan Grand Prix the norm for a newcomer is a two-year contract, with an option for a third year, explained the team's financial controller Richard O'Driscoll. At the end of each season, the driver will have a month in which

---

[1] Johnny Herbert, the British driver, did not have anything about testing written into his Benetton contract, and subsequently missed out badly as the team concentrated more and more resources on his teammate, Michael Schumacher.

he can buy himself out of the contract for a sum agreed when the contract was signed. That sum can range from $4 million to $8 million. Locking a driver into the right contract can be very lucrative. Jean Alesi was bought out of his Formula 3000 contract to join Tyrrell in Formula One. Later, Eddie Irvine bought himself out of Jordan Grand Prix to join Ferrari.

The expansion of the business of Formula One has brought a new set of pressures for the drivers. They are highly privileged, and their life-styles make them the envy of countless millions. So, there is under-standably little sympathy for them over the increased burdens of com-peting in Formula One. Even so, the financial pressures that now permeate every layer of the sport affect the drivers as much as the teams and sponsors. Drivers are now tools in the global strategies of major corporations. For the young and commercially naïve, Formula One is a difficult place to survive. Murray Walker, the television com-mentator, believes that concern with money has taken the fun out of the sport. 'It is all terribly serious these days,' Walker said. 'While I am not against people being serious, I think Formula One has become so money-orientated that it is very difficult for them to have any fun and relaxation. They are either racing the cars, testing the cars, or with the sponsors.' The image of Formula One is being carefully crafted off the track. Everything has to be well polished – including the drivers. Teams are presented as fast, efficient, hi-tech enterprises. The drivers are sold to the public as clean-living young athletes who drink mineral water and wear designer suits. Jacques Villeneuve, with his 'grunge' look and bad-boy image, stands out like a beacon from this crowd. Villeneuve, though, simply proves the rule.

It is difficult to imagine Villeneuve fitting in at Stewart Grand Prix or McLaren. To work for Jackie Stewart you have to follow his fatherly advice, be respectful to the sponsors, and put up with him straightening your tie. Jan Magnussen, a driver at Stewart Grand Prix, was asked not to wear his normal jeans and T-shirt in front of sponsors. And Paul Stewart, the team's joint owner, admits that he would probably have to 'have words' with Villeneuve if he were driving for the team. Even at Paul Stewart Racing, his Formula Three team, presentation was important. David Coultard, now a world championship challenger with McLaren, was put through public speaking classes, and given lessons on dress sense. For Jan Magnussen, who had a reputation for spending more time in the pub than in the gym, Formula One was a culture shock. A brilliant Formula Three driver, Magnussen seemed to freeze when faced with the challenges of Formula One, both on and off the track. Drivers never experience anything like the hot-house atmosphere of Formula One until they become part of it. Magnussen did not take to the lifestyle nor the demands, and in June 1998, after several disappointing races, he was replaced by Jos Verstappen. Paul Stewart makes no apologies for making his drivers conform to a professional image. 'We are a commercial enterprise,' he said. 'We have a right to ask for a certain standard, for the sponsors and for the appearance of the team. If that means getting a driver some tutoring in public speaking, then so be it. I don't care what they wear at home. But if they are meeting our partners – not just the drivers, but other employees as well – then jeans and T-shirts are not appropriate.'

Image has to be worked at, but can pay big dividends. McLaren, which has a German engine supplier, Mercedes, and German title sponsor, West cigarettes, does not have a German driver. The team and its sponsors have, however, concentrated on promoting Finnish driver Mika Hakkinen in Germany. In 1997 a survey in the German magazine *Automotive und Sport* found that Hakkinen was second only to Michael Schumacher in terms of media exposure. And this in a country which has also produced Heinz-Harald Frentzen and Ralf Schumacher, in addition to his brother Michael. Hakkinen's team boss, Ron Dennis, had reason to be pleased. 'We worked very hard to establish Mika. But the drivers have to work with us, not pull in another direction. We do not have arrogance in our drivers. A driver does not get out of a car having suffered engine failure and rant and rave. He understands he is part of a team, and he should feel privileged that so much money and effort is going into putting a grand prix car at his disposal in order that he can achieve his goals. If that car fails him, he has to understand that we suffer as much pain as he does. Showing his own disappointment in anything but a positive way is counter-productive to all the things that we, and the people who support us, are trying to achieve.'

While the mental stresses have increased, the physical demands have also intensified. For a sport that spends hundreds of millions of pounds on the mechanical set-up of the cars, teams have been lax in their approach to the wellbeing of their drivers. Modern drivers are fit, and emphasis on gym work has been essential for many years, but only recently have teams begun serious physiological research into what happens to a driver during races. Mike Hawthorn, who in 1958 became Britain's first Formula One drivers' champion, smoked, liked a drink, and was rejected for National Service on health grounds. A driver who was out of shape would not be tolerated now. It is the Ron Dennis philosophy again: in the search to shave seconds off lap times, everything helps, and that means having fit drivers. Today's racing driver will usually be between 5ft 6in and 5ft 10in tall, and under 11 stone. Designers like a small driver, so that the cockpit does not have to take up too much room. He is super-fit, with neck muscles capable of withstanding G-forces that would make other people squeal, and with a tuned body capable of coping with cockpit temperatures of 40°C during two hours of racing. The heartbeat will reach around 180bpm (against 40–50 in a steady state) for prolonged periods. Two hours a day in the gym is regarded as the minimum for top drivers. Diet is strictly controlled: the usual athlete's meals of pasta, fruit and vegetables, and no alcohol. McLaren's physiological analysis is aimed at discovering which parts of the body are susceptible to stresses, and then working to alleviate them. Jerry Powell, the team trainer, analyses a variety of things, from the strength of finger joints to reaction times. One thing that has been discovered is the severe impact that racing has on the lower back. Even such a common exercise as running was therefore deemed to do more harm than good, because it too leads to pressure on the back.

With so much money, so much luxury, it is easy to lose sight of the *sport* in Formula One. Amid all the technology, blue-chip sponsorship, broadcasting deals and the planned flotation, it is the drivers who keep the human interest in Formula One alive. All the time a driver can get an above-average performance out of an average car, there will be sport in Formula One. There is an argument here, perhaps, for the teams to spend more time nurturing young drivers, helping them to acclimatise to the pressure-cooker atmosphere of Formula One. Mercedes-Benz has a rising star on its books, Nick Heidfeld, a former German Formula Three champion. He has spent time at McLaren to learn the ropes, and is likely to make the step up to Formula One. Also, Jochen Neerpasch, who helped Schumacher into Formula One, has several teenage drivers on his books. But very little is done by the teams themselves to help new drivers until they come knocking on the door with personal sponsorship. With more money coming into Formula One, it should be possible to devise a more formal scheme to bring on new talent. It does not seem unreasonable to suggest that teams could 'apprentice' half a dozen drivers. Or maybe Formula One could subsidise the lower formulae, helping to put up-and-coming drivers through a sort of training system. Nicky Samengo-Turner (a corporate financier and adviser on motorsport deals) believes the flotation of Formula One could be the impetus to standardise the promotion of drivers from lower divisions. He explained: 'A flotation, creating a public company out of Formula One, will alter the mind-set of the people who run the sport. Shareholders will want consistency, and more of a show to keep viewers interested. Every aspect will be touched, including driving. There will be pressure to increase the quality of drivers because it will make more of a spectacle. I'm not saying that is a bad thing; just that somehow the quality of the driving will have to be addressed. You don't increase TV ratings fielding 24 drivers – 20 of whom have no hope of winning races.'

Conclusions

Where Now?

FORMULA ONE HAS been an outstanding, if unusual, business success story. No enterprise is dependent on just one man, but it is safe to say that without Bernie Ecclestone the conditions that allowed the sport to grow so fast would not have been created. The Ecclestone revolution is not over, though. If he takes Formula One public with a stock market flotation, it is likely to change the very nature of the activity. Indeed, there must be a concern that in the drive to satisfy shareholders' desire for higher dividends each year through TV earnings and sponsorship, it will kill what remains of the sport completely. All that will be left is theatre; everything else stage-managed to ensure the money keeps rolling in – just like all-in wrestling. Fans have already had a taste of this type of scenario. The opening race of the 1998 season, in Australia, was a contrived finish, with race leader David Coultard slowing to allow his McLaren teammate, Mika Hakkinen, to win. And in the last race of the 1997 season, Williams's Jacques Villeneuve deliberately let the two McLaren drivers pass him (conversations detailing the collusion were secretly recorded and made public). The only beneficiaries of such blatant incidents can be McLaren and its sponsors. It was certainly bad PR for Formula One as a sport. As Damon Hill said in a newspaper interview afterwards, drivers are 'caught in this bloody sponsorship and PR bloody soufflé, and it's running everything.' Bernie Ecclestone will certainly not want to kill his 'golden goose', though he cannot necessarily control what the teams do. However, the biggest threat to Formula One may not come from inside his empire, but from the outside. America's open-wheel racing formula, the CART Indy series, is expanding beyond its borders.

Ecclestone would dearly love to see Formula One return to America, though he is making more headway in Asia. Although Formula One is broadcast in 202 countries, it cannot strictly be called a 'global' sport. There is no grand prix in Africa, though South African president Nelson Mandela met Ecclestone in the summer of 1998 to discuss hosting a race, nor the Middle East. Every year rumours circulate about a return to the US, but Formula One has not visited the country since 1991. In 1982, three Formula One races were held there, plus another in Canada, but growing dissatisfaction among the drivers and teams about the quality of the circuits caused the American races to be taken off the calendar. Watkins Glen, a road circuit in New York, staged Formula One between 1961 until 1980. In the 1980s Long Beach played host with a circuit running along the harbour front and through Millionaires Row. Even with its plastic palm trees, however, Long Beach never came close to the atmosphere of Monaco. There followed some dismal races held in the car-park of Caesar's Palace Hotel, Las Vegas, and then in Detroit, Dallas and Phoenix. At Dallas, in 1984, the track actually crumbled in the heat.

A problem with trying to win back interest from American motor-sport fans is that the US already has established formulae, IndyCar and Nascar stock cars, the latter being the most popular. US fans find their existing series accessible, and enjoy being able to mingle with drivers and teams. Formula One, on the other hand, still carries an elitist tag in America. Ecclestone will no doubt eventually succeed in putting the US back on the calendar somehow, simply because the potential revenues could dwarf those from any other country. But it is going to be a struggle. Without a larger audience base, sponsors will show little interest. Another hurdle facing Ecclestone in America is the difficulty of finding a suitable racing circuit. Existing racetracks, designed for the brute force of IndyCar engines, would have to be modified for Formula One, and many circuit owners may not be prepared to spend the money. There was a proposal to construct a purpose-built circuit at Brandy Station, Virginia. But the chosen area just happened to be the site of the largest cavalry battle in US history, and after three years of legal wrangles, preservationists managed to get the plan overturned. The most intriguing prospect of recent years was a plan to stage a Formula One street race at Disney World, in Florida. Ecclestone held talks with Disney's motor sports division (the company already hosts Indy and Nascar events) but the talks were a non-starter. Disney's racing executive, Michael Waggoner, said it all fell apart because of money. 'Walt Disney wanted a large cut. Bernie wanted a large cut. You know how it is, we just could not agree on the figures.' Ecclestone had talked to casino millionaire Steve Wynn about building a circuit in Las Vegas, but they could not agree on the length of contract. A promoter called Ralph Sanchez, who runs the Homestead Circuit, near Miami, wanted to hold a Formula One race. Sanchez's argument is that the millions of European and South American tourists in Miami would guarantee a huge crowd, even if US interest was small. However, according to some accounts, Ecclestone was not impressed with the facilities.

Another reason why Formula One must go to America is that it needs to fight the CART Indy series in its own backyard, winning over its sponsors and its fans. The CART programme is beginning to expand out of its traditional heartlands, and has held races in Canada, Australia, Brazil and Japan. The FIA is so worried that it has rewritten its rulebook so that Formula One teams cannot compete in other single-seater events – that is, IndyCar races – without permission. If CART expands seriously outside America, especially in Asia and Europe, it will be competing with Formula One for sponsors, television time and spectators. CART is shown in 188 countries, generating around 61 million viewers per race, according to figures from the organisers. The audience profile is much the same as for Formula One – predominantly males under 40 with disposable income – and thus attractive to sponsors and advertisers. Andrew Craig, chief executive of CART, denies that he wants to turn his sport into a global brand like Formula One. Nevertheless, he hopes to hold a race in Europe around the turn of the century. Germany is tipped as the first European country to stage CART. The series is now screened live on the European satellite channel Eurosport, which gets about 600,000 viewers per race. Britain's Channel 5 is also showing CART, and the BBC is planning a documentary, all of which suggests growing UK interest. The introduction of more overseas drivers to CART, following in the footsteps of Britons Nigel Mansell and Mark Blundell, will also raise interest in Europe.

Andrew Craig believes there is room for both series to exist side by side. Yet, as the two have broadly similar standards and entertainment value, there will inevitably be a clash over which event is the best and provides most benefit to sponsors. (Not that this does not generate passionate debate already. But it will intensify, and become an important financial consideration.) Like Formula One, CART's need to expand is driven by its sponsors' desire to promote their global brands. A growth in the number of television channels world-wide should ensure that the public appetite for both series is met. A challenge facing both events, however, might be a shortage of engine suppliers. Ford, Mugen-

Honda and Mercedes supply both series, though that could change if global expansion continues to increase the costs of competing. Renault pulled out of Formula One in 1997 amid suggestions that it wanted to fund an entry into CART to support a marketing push for its road cars in America. Also, CART is in a better position to cope with tighter restrictions on tobacco sponsorship. Just five of the 28 cars racing in CART have cigarette sponsors, whereas there are six (soon to be seven) tobacco companies sponsoring Formula One's 11 teams.

Ecclestone will also have to fight CART in Asia, though at the moment Formula One seems to be ahead of its US rival. Formula One is generally regarded as a purer form of racing than CART, with an emphasis on technology as much as entertainment. That has made Formula One very attractive to governments in emerging nations in Asia. It means that these countries can use the sport as a symbol of cultural and economic advance, as well as an aid to technology transfer for those companies that get involved. In Malaysia, as we have seen, the prime minister himself, Dr Mahathir Mohamad, is behind his country's plan to stage a leg of the Formula One series, probably in the year 1999 or 2000. Malaysia is already building a 5.6km racetrack, costing $60 million and expected to be one of the finest in the world, in readiness to stage a grand prix. There is a lot of rivalry between Malaysia, Singapore, Indonesia and Thailand, all of whom are anxious to raise their profile in the world. According to Dr Mahathir: 'Some people thought that Malaysia was a country in Africa, while others only knew that it was a country near the island of Singapore.' A showcase event like Formula One is seen as a way to change that perception. Even the tourist board admitted that more would probably be written about Malaysia during the three days of a race meeting by the 650 or so journalists likely to attend than in the whole of the rest of the year.

What could dent Formula One's plans to tap new markets in the Far East is the economic crisis that has been destabilising Asia's 'tiger' economies since 1997. Japan holds a warning for those who think Formula One's future lies in the Far East. In late 1980s, on the back of Japan's property boom, wealthy individuals poured millions of pounds into the sport, setting up their own teams and sponsoring others. Japanese fans became some of the most passionate in the world, and drivers were treated like pop stars. Huge investments were made in circuits. Then property prices fell, the stock market crashed, and sponsors pulled out. A Japanese Formula One team with a British-sounding name, Leyton House, folded soon after its boss was arrested for fraud. Other familiar Japanese teams, such as Footwork and Espo, also disappeared from the grid. The Autopolis, a massive new circuit, collapsed under the weight of bank debts. Japanese drivers lost their Formula One seats, and in 1992 Honda pulled out. The bubble had burst. Japan remains on the Formula One calendar, and there has been more interest from the country's sponsors in recent years as the economy climbed out of recession. (Now that Japan is once again the edge of more economic woe, it will be interesting to see how this impacts on Formula One in the next couple of years.) Cigarette company Mild Seven became a sponsor of Benetton; PIAA, an industrial group, backs Tyrrell; and Honda has said it may return to Formula One with its own team.

Perhaps the lesson to learn from Japan, and from Malaysia and Korea, is that Formula One will go where the money is, following the ebb and flow of economic success and decline. The sport is flexible enough to move around the globe. This is to Formula One's benefit, though there are also inherent dangers. Formula One, like people, needs to keep roots somewhere. The core of the sport is located in Europe and, because of this, Formula One will continue to thrive in Europe no matter what the economic ups and downs on other continents. Bernie Ecclestone, however, has warned that the number of European grand prix will be cut if Formula One is banned from taking tobacco sponsorship. That old saying about cutting off one's nose to spite one's face seems appropriate. Rip out the heart of Formula One and it will die. Andrew Craig, who runs CART in America, has taken this concern on board. Despite his plans to expand overseas, Craig has stressed time and again that CART must never lose its US focus. If CART's overseas expansion were to implode, and the series needed to retrench, it would have somewhere to retrench to.

One hundred years on from those rickety vehicles that raced across the French countryside, it is little short of astonishing that just 11 different racecars and 22 drivers can now create such international interest. Whether it be governments wanting to use racing for marketing purposes, or 'anoraks' just fascinated by statistics and trivia, Formula One has the power to reach several strata of society and economy at the same time. It has become a metaphor for globalisation, technology, modernity, commercial success and popular culture. This book has explored how and why Formula One became such a huge success. So, in a bid to claw back some balance, I will end on a note of caution. For, despite the remarkable achievements of Bernie Ecclestone and those around him, there is a lot wrong with Formula One. The power that the sport confers on those who control it is one cause for concern. This manifested itself in 1997, when Ecclestone and Max Mosley saw fit to challenge and threaten governments over the tobacco issue. Sometimes this power borders on arrogance, as when the FIA felt it had a right to question the Italian judicial system's right to bring manslaughter charges against Frank Williams and five others over the death of Ayrton Senna. Also, Formula One is too secretive for its own good (it is not even known how prize money is distributed among the teams) and is rigidly controlled by a narrow group of people who are reluctant to let new entrants into the inner circle. Plans to float Formula One got bogged down in a morass of legal red tape, and the financial community has grown suspicious. Revelations about Ecclestone's secret £1 million donation to the British Labour Party, and his subsequent refusal to attend a House of Commons hearing to clarify the situation (though he did send the hearing's chairman a long letter, as we saw in Chapter 2) made it look as if Formula One had something to hide. Money is power in Formula One and too often that has overridden the interests of the fans and the entertainment. Perhaps the last word should go to Jackie Stewart, so often the conscience of Formula One. He seemed to sum up the concerns when he told his friend Murray Walker: 'This sport of ours has become a giant. Its future prosperity is in our hands. If we are anything less than totally responsible we could lose it. The bigger it becomes, the larger the target it is. We have to keep our own house in order.'

And Finally

FORMULA ONE has been an outstanding, if unusual, business success story. No enterprise is dependent on just one man, but it is not unreasonable to say that without Bernie Ecclestone the conditions that allowed the sport to grow so fast would not have been created. The Ecclestone revolution is not over, though. If he, and the new investors who have bought into his empire, do eventually take Formula One public with a stock market flotation, it is likely to change the very nature of the activity. Indeed, there must be a concern that in the drive to satisfy shareholders' desire for higher dividends each year through TV earnings and sponsorship, it will kill what remains of the sport. All that will be left is theatre, with everything else stage-managed to ensure the money keeps rolling in – just like all-in wrestling. Fans have already had a taste of this.

The opening race of the 1998 season, in Australia, was a contrived finish, with race leader David Coultard slowing to allow his McLaren team-mate, Mika Hakkinen, to win. And in the last race of the 1997 season, Williams' Jacques Villeneuve deliberately let the two McLaren drivers pass him (conversations detailing the collusion were secretly recorded and made public). The only beneficiaries of such incidents are the teams, their owners and the sponsors. The fans get short-changed and it is certainly bad PR for the sport. As former world champion Damon Hill said in a newspaper interview in 1998, drivers are 'caught in this bloody sponsorship and PR soufflé, and it's running everything'. Bernie Ecclestone and the companies that now control Formula One will certainly not want to kill the 'golden goose', though they cannot necessarily control what the teams do.

However, the threats to Formula One are not just coming from inside the empire, but also from outside. One such threat is the continuing expansion of America's CART Indy series as it continues to expand beyond its borders, building audiences and attracting sponsorship. Ecclestone needs to meet this challenge, which is why the return of Formula One to American soil in September 2000 (at the famous Indianapolis circuit) is so important. Although Formula One is broadcast in 202 countries, it cannot strictly be called a 'global' sport. There is no grand prix in Africa, though South African president Nelson Mandela met Ecclestone in the summer of 1998 to discuss holding a race, nor in the Middle East. And there are many other areas of the world where Formula One needs to build a following. Staging a race in America – the first since 1991 – goes a long way to establishing a truly global audience. In 1982, three Formula One races were held in America, plus another in Canada, but growing dissatisfaction amongst drivers and teams about the quality of the circuits caused the American races to be taken off the calendar. Watkins Glen, a road circuit in New York, staged Formula One between 1961 and 1980. Later, Long Beach played host with a circuit running along the harbour front and through Millionaires Row. Even with its plastic palm trees, however, Long Beach never came close to the atmosphere of Monaco. There followed some dismal races held in the car-park of Caesar's Palace Hotel, Las Vegas, and then in Detroit, Dallas and Phoenix. At Dallas, in 1984, the track actually crumbled in the heat.

Dislodging, or at least competing, with America's established formulae, Indy and Nascar stock cars (the latter being the most popular), is going to be a huge task for Ecclestone. US fans find their existing series accessible, and enjoy being able to mingle with drivers and teams. Formula One, on the other hand, still carries an elitist tag in America. But if Formula One can crack the US market the potential revenues could dwarf those from any other country. Without a large audience base, sponsors will show little interest. It was a disappointment for the Formula One establishment that after two years of negotiations Hollywood star Sylvester Stallone decided against making a film about the sport, preferring instead to base his movie around CART. The film would have been a showcase for Formula One and help educate the US public about the sport. But, in a reference to the 'fortress mentality' that for many people makes Formula One inaccessible, Stallone said that he found the sport lacked the personality and family feel of CART. Formula One's last race in America drew fewer spectators than an ostrich race being staged 10 miles away. No other country in the world has such a variety of motor racing, and Formula One will have to make a big impression to compete for audience attention with its thrill-a-minute, big-bang rivals. Soccer provides a salutary lesson of the difficulties. Despite soccer's World Cup being held in the US in 1994, the sport has still failed to ignite interest among much of the American public.

Owners of the Indianapolis circuit have spent an estimated $40 million preparing a 2.6-mile track for the American Grand Prix, and the organisers have insisted the race will be profitable in year one with more than 200,000 spectators, a tall order according to many observers. Certainly there can be no better place for the grand prix to be staged. Indianapolis is a racing town, and the Indy 500 is as special as the grand prix in Monaco. Few other US circuit owners were prepared to spend the money to modify their tracks, designed for the brute force of the engines used in the various American series. There was a proposal to construct a purpose-built circuit at Brandy Station, Virginia. But the chosen area just happened to be the site of the largest cavalry battle in US history, and after three years of legal wrangles, preservationists managed to get the plan overturned. The most intriguing prospect of recent years was a plan to stage a Formula One street race at Disney World, in Florida. Ecclestone held talks with Disney's motor sports division (the company already hosted Indy and Nascar events) but the talks were a non-starter. Disney's racing executive, Michael Waggoner, said it all fell apart because of money. 'Walt Disney wanted a large cut. Bernie wanted a large cut. You know how it is, we just could not agree on the figures.' Ecclestone had talked to casino millionaire Steve Wynn about building a circuit in Las Vegas, but they could not agree on the length of contract. A promoter called Ralph Sanchez, who runs the Homestead Circuit, near Miami, wanted to hold a Formula One race. Sanchez's argument was that the millions of European and South American tourists in Miami would guarantee a huge crowd, even if US interest was small. But it was Indianapolis that proved the most viable option. A new track more suitable to Formula One was built, though the racecars will still use part of the existing speedway track.

Another reason Formula One had to return to America was that it needed to fight CART in its own backyard. The CART series is slowly expanding out of its traditional heartlands, and has held races in Canada, Australia, Brazil and Japan. The FIA is so worried that it has rewritten its rulebook so that Formula One teams cannot compete in other single-seater events – that is, IndyCar races – without permission. If the CART series and audience interest continues to expand outside America, particularly in Europe and Asia, it will be a serious competitor to Formula One for sponsors, television time and spectators. CART is shown in around 188 countries, generating about 61 million viewers per race, according to figures from the organisers. The audience profile is much the same as for Formula One – predominantly males, under 40, with relatively high disposable incomes – and thus attractive to sponsors and advertisers. However, Andrew Craig, chief executive of CART, denies that he wants to turn his sport into a global brand like Formula One. Nevertheless, he is still looking at holding a race in Europe, with Germany tipped as the most likely first location. The series is screened live on the European satellite channel Eurosport, which gets about 600,000 viewers per race; other broadcasters in Europe, including Channel 5 in Britain, show highlights. The introduction of more overseas drivers to CART, following in the footsteps of Britain's Nigel Mansell and Mark Blundell, will also raise interest in Europe.

Andrew Craig believes there is room for both series to exist side by side. Yet, as the two have broadly similar standards and entertainment value, there will inevitably be a clash over which event is the best and which offers the most benefit to sponsors. (Not that this has not generated passionate debate already. But it will intensify, and become an important financial consideration.) Like Formula One, CART's need to expand is driven by its sponsors' desire to promote their global brands. A growth in the number of television channels worldwide should ensure that both series find an airing and that the public appetite for Formula One and other forms of racing is met. Ford, Honda and Mercedes supply both series, though that could change if global expansion continues to increase the costs of competing. Renault pulled out of Formula One in 1997 in order to fund an entry into CART to support a marketing push for its road cars in America. However, the French car manufacturer is expected to return to Formula One by 2002. Also, CART is in a better position to cope with tighter restrictions on tobacco sponsorship. Just five of the 28 cars racing in CART were sponsored by cigarette companies, whereas there were six tobacco companies sponsoring Formula One's 11 teams.

Ecclestone will also have to fight CART in Asia, though at the moment Formula One seems to be ahead of its US rival. Formula One is generally regarded as a purer form of racing than CART, with an emphasis on technology as much as entertainment. This has made Formula One very attractive to governments in emerging nations in Asia. These countries can use the sport as a symbol of cultural and economic advancement, as well as an aid to technology transfer for those companies that get involved. In Malaysia, as we have seen, the prime minister himself, Dr Mahathir Mohamad, was behind his country's plan to stage a leg of the Formula One series. Malaysia has built a 5.6-km racetrack, costing $60 million, and it is one of the finest circuits in the world. There is a lot of economic rivalry between Malaysia, Singapore, Indonesia and Thailand, all of which are anxious to raise their profile in the world. According to Dr Mahathir: 'Some people thought that Malaysia was a country in Africa, while others only knew that it was a country near the island of Singapore.' A showcase event like Formula One is seen as a way to change that perception. Even the tourist board admitted that more would probably be written about Malaysia during the three days of the country's first grand prix in 1999 by the 650 or so journalists likely to attend than in the whole of the rest of the year.

What dented Formula One's plans to tap new markets in the Far East was the economic crisis that destabilised Asia's 'tiger' economies in 1997. Although these economies are now picking up, governments are still thinking twice about the massive expense of preparing themselves to stage a Formula One race. Japan holds a warning for those who think Formula One's future lies in the Far East. In the late 1980s, on the back of Japan's property boom, wealthy individuals poured millions of dollars into the sport, setting up their own teams and sponsoring others. Japanese fans became some of the most passionate in the world, and drivers were treated like pop stars. Huge investments were made in circuits. Then property prices fell, the stock market crashed and sponsors pulled out. A Japanese Formula One team, Leyton House, folded soon after its boss was arrested for fraud. Other familiar Japanese teams, such as Footwork and Espo, also disappeared from the grid. The Autopolis, a massive new circuit, collapsed under the weight of bank debts. Japanese drivers lost their Formula One seats, and in 1992 Honda pulled out of the sport. The bubble had burst. Japan remains on the Formula One calendar, and there has been more interest from the country's sponsors in recent years as the economy climbed out of recession.

Cigarette company Mild Seven became a sponsor of Benetton; PIAA, an industrial group, backed the former Tyrrell team; and carmakers Honda and Toyota will soon be vying for supremacy with Mercedes and BMW.

Perhaps the lesson to learn from Japan, and from Malaysia and Korea, is that Formula One will go where the money is, following the ebb and flow of economic success and decline. The sport is flexible enough to move around the globe. This is to Formula One's benefit, though there are also inherent dangers. Formula One, like people, needs to keep roots somewhere. The core of the sport is located in Europe and, because of this, Formula One will continue to thrive in Europe regardless of the economic ups and downs on other continents. Ecclestone warned that the number of European grand prix will be cut if Formula One is banned from taking tobacco sponsorship. That old saying about 'cutting off one's nose to spite one's face' seems appropriate. Rip out the heart of Formula One and it will die. CART's Andrew Craig has clearly understood the importance of having roots. Despite his plans to expand overseas, Craig has stressed time and again that CART must never lose its US focus. If CART's overseas expansion were to implode, and the series needed to retrench, Craig wants it to have somewhere to retrench to.

The takeover of Formula One teams by corporate money and international investors has increased faster than most people could have anticipated. A benefit of this 'new money' is that the financing of teams becomes less of a struggle than it was for the owner-entrepreneurs. The downside, though, is that the characters who give the sport so much colour, men like Eddie Jordan, could be the last of a breed. American motor giant Ford, which had already bought the Cosworth racing engines company, bought Stewart Grand Prix and has renamed the team Jaguar in order to promote its luxury car brand. Warburg Pincus, an American investment group, has bought almost half of Jordan Grand Prix for £40 million. DaimlerChrysler, the US-German company that owns Mercedes, has bought 40 per cent of McLaren. British American Racing is owned, in large part, by tobacco company BAT. And Morgan Grenfell Private Equity, the London-based investment arm of Germany's Deutsche Bank, paid £77 million for a controlling stake in Arrows. This surge in interest from international motor manufacturers is arguably the biggest threat to Britain as the technological home of Formula One. If more major engine producers do all the technological work in-house, running their teams from their own R&D centres, it would be to the detriment of the pool of knowledge built up in Grand Prix Valley. It is quite possible, for instance, that Ford might choose to do more development work in America rather than at the facilities built up by Stewart Grand Prix, having a similar effect to a 'brain drain'.

The influx of corporate money would not be happening, of course, unless Formula One had the potential to offer a financial and marketing return. The monetary vaule of the sport has clearly soared in recent years. But this value has not risen as much as Ecclestone had hoped. The amount of money he anticipated raising through the flotation of Formula One Holdings was dramatically scaled back. And the planned stock market listing was eventually abandoned amid luke-warm interest from investors and doubts about the security of Formula One's television revenues because of the European Commission's investigation into whether the FIA is abusing its monopoly power. After three years this issue is still unresolved, and Ecclestone and the FIA have become, rightly, increasingly frustrated that the affair should have hung over Formula One's business interests for so long. There are signs that Ecclestone's grip on the sport may not last much longer, however. He and his family trusts have sold around 50 per cent of their financial interest in the sport, and Ecclestone's advancing age means that investors will want a more formalised management structure. The sale of half his stake, and a near £1-billion bond issue in 1999, means that despite the abandoned flotation Ecclestone has still been able to crystallise a fortune from the business he spent decades building. Around 50 per cent of Formula One is now owned by EM.TV, the German media group that owns the rights to the *Muppets* children's television show. EM.TV bought the stakes from Morgan Grenfell Private Equity and Californian investment group Hellman & Friedman for a total of $1.6 billion. Even if Ecclestone himself does not want to take a back seat, other powerbrokers within Formula One will have greater leverage to ease him aside. Yet, such is Ecclestone's importance for Formula One that, when he retires, McLaren's Ron Dennis predicts a short-term financial dip for the sport until investors and sponsors are comfortable with his successor (or successors).

One hundred years on from those rickety vehicles that raced across the French countryside, it is little short of astonishing that just 11 different race-cars and 22 drivers can now create such international interest. Whether it be governments wanting to use racing for marketing purposes, or 'anoraks' just fascinated by statistics and trivia, Formula One has the power to reach several strata of society and economy at the same time. Formula One has become a metaphor for globalisation, technology, modernity, commercial success and popular culture. This book has explored how and why Formula One became such a huge success. So, in a bid to claw back some balance, I will end on a note of caution. For, despite the remarkable achievements of Bernie Ecclestone and those around him, there is a lot wrong with Formula One. The power that the sport confers on those who control it is one cause for concern. This manifested itself in 1997, when Ecclestone and Max Mosley saw fit to challenge and threaten governments over the tobacco ban issue. Sometimes this power borders on arrogance, as when the FIA felt it could question the Italian judicial system's right to bring manslaughter charges against Frank Williams and five others over the death of Ayrton Senna. Also, Formula One is too secretive for its own good (it is not even known how prize money is distributed among the teams) and is, despite outside investors, rigidly controlled by a narrow group of people who are reluctant to let new entrants into the inner circle. There is still too much scepticism and suspicion among the financial community, something that will have to be overcome if Ecclestone and EM.TV are ever to resurrect flotation plans. Money is power in Formula One and so often that has overridden the interests of the fans and the entertainment. Perhaps the last word should go to Jackie Stewart, so often the conscience of Formula One. He summed up the concerns when he told his friend Murray Walker, the television commentator: 'This sport of ours has become a giant. Its future prosperity is in our hands. If we are anything less than totally responsible we could lose it. The bigger it becomes, the larger the target it is. We have to keep our own house in order.'

Index